New Age Spirituality

BY DUNCAN S. FERGUSON

Biblical Hermeneutics: An Introduction

New Age Spirituality

AN ASSESSMENT

Duncan S. Ferguson, *Editor*

WESTMINSTER/JOHN KNOX PRESS
LOUISVILLE, KENTUCKY

Unless otherwise noted, scripture quotations are from the New Revised Standard Version of the Bible, copyright © 1989 by the Division of Christian Education of the National Council of the Churches of Christ in the U.S.A., and are used by permission.

Scripture quotations marked JB are from *The Jerusalem Bible,* copyright © 1966, 1967, 1968 by Darton, Longman & Todd, Ltd., and Doubleday & Co., Inc. Used by permission of the publishers.

Scripture quotations marked KJV are from the King James Version of the Bible.

Book design by Publishers' WorkGroup

First edition

This book is printed on acid-free paper that meets the American National Standards Institute Z39.48 standard. ∞

Published by Westminster/John Knox Press
Louisville, Kentucky

PRINTED IN THE UNITED STATES OF AMERICA

9 8 7 6 5 4 3 2 1

Library of Congress Cataloging-in-Publication Data

New Age spirituality : an assessment / Duncan S. Ferguson, editor. —
1st ed.
       p.   cm.
     Includes bibliographical references and index.
     ISBN 0-664-25218-4 (pbk. : alk. paper)

     1. New Age movement.   2. Occultism—Religious aspects—
Christianity.   3. Spiritual life.   I. Ferguson, Duncan S. (Duncan Sheldon),
1937–
BP605.N48N49   1992
299'.93—dc20   92-19750

Contents

CONTENTS

Foreword

It was Plato who told us that Aphrodite, Greek goddess of love, had two manifestations. On the one hand there was the "common Aphrodite" who manifested herself in a bewildering variety of erotic forms; from her, we could say, come the realms of heedless sexual promiscuity and pornography. But there was also the heavenly Aphrodite, who was the goddess of all truly loving relationships; indeed, it was she who even led mortals to a relationship with God. Something like this could also be said of "New Age" thinking. On the one hand there is the common variety of so-called New Age phenomena; to this belong such things as the cruder forms of divination and a potpourri of occultists and users of mind-altering drugs out to sell their wares as "new" when, in fact, most of them are about as new as the Old Testament—in which we find many such phenomena described. But there is also the higher form of New Age thinking. This is manifested wherever people reach out for genuinely new ways of thinking about themselves, the world, and God. Some of our best and boldest minds today belong to this category of New Age thinkers and seekers, and they are sincere people, with bold minds and hearts. This is the true New Age, and its ranks include scientists, psychologists, and members of established religious faiths and traditions, including mainstream Christian denominations.

The book you are about to read, *New Age Spirituality: An Assessment,* is authored by persons of the genuine New Age. Most of them are experienced and sincere Christians. All of them are reputable people who present to us in the several writings imaginative and sound ways of rethinking and reexpressing old ideas. While the reader of this book will learn some things about the "common New Age" thought, which he or she will find educational, the heart of this book is its ability to lift our minds and imaginations to see the meaning of life, scripture, ourselves, and God in a fresh and new way. The writers are both bold and conservative. They are conservative because they conserve that which is valid in the old traditions and ways of looking at things, and bold because they reach out to find new ways to understand and express the old truths.

The reader of this volume who is open to new ways of thinking will come away not only with an appreciation of what the New Age involves, but also with insights and visions that will be challenging.

JOHN A. SANFORD

July 24, 1991

Introduction

The motivation for this series of essays on New Age spirituality grew out of the conviction that many Christians and others in our culture have been intrigued by the phenomenon we have come to know as the "New Age." Unsure of its validity, confused by its beliefs and practices, and curious about whether there may be something "in it" for them, people have asked questions, engaged in discussions, and bought books in order to learn more about New Age thought. But balance and perspective are not easy to achieve by random reading and conversations. It is my hope that *New Age Spirituality: An Assessment* will enable people to understand the many-sided character of the movement and to make a balanced assessment of the movement's value for them, our society, and the world.

The book is undergirded by several assumptions. The first is that New Age thought and practice is not a monolithic and ordered whole. Rather, the movement is as diverse and unordered as scattered stars. Our goal has been to look at the stars in the context of the night sky in which they appear.

The second assumption is that New Age thought and practice are not all good or all bad, regardless of how they may have been characterized by adherents and critics. Part of the problem in assessing the movement is definition. What does one assess? What is the New Age? Is it crystals or ecology, occultism or "new" physics, Wicca (witchcraft) or transpersonal psychology? One might well be critical of a certain practice or belief (for example, the use of psychedelic drugs), but very open to another practice or belief (such as environmental activism). The irony is that, on occasion, both have been attributed to the New Age movement. Our goal has been to provide a balanced assessment of the multifaceted movement.

A third assumption underlying this volume is that we live in a special time, one of unprecedented change, one filled with overwhelming problems, and one in which people long for a new and nurturing spirituality. It is a critical moment, a kairos, and it is out of this moment that the New Age movement has emerged. Our goal has been to provide ways of thinking about our time and of providing direction in the quest for a spirituality which is life-giving.

A final assumption is that we believe that God is speaking in this moment. The divine language may not be the language of our traditions and assumptions, but a new language altogether. May we have the ears to hear.

The book is divided into three major sections. The first provides the context of the New Age movement by examining its psychological, sociological, historical, and philosophical dimensions. The second section explores the content of New Age spirituality, seeing it as a quest for the divine, for authentic selfhood, and for planetary transformation. The final section is a critique of New Age spirituality, assessing its strengths and weaknesses and proposing that some of its themes may be useful in the formulation of a spirituality for a "New Era."

The opening section of the book, "Spirituality Across the Ages," begins with an essay by Dr. Andrew Canale, a Roman Catholic Christian, a therapist in Boston and author of *Masters of the Heart* (Paulist Press, 1978) and *Understanding the Human Jesus* (Paulist Press, 1985). Canale provides an analysis of the enormous pressures that our society and world place on all of us. These pressures make us desperate, and we long for a Center to give coherence to our lives. New Age spirituality, in its diverse forms, has provided ways for people to embark on a spiritual journey in order to find the divine. Canale contends that it is only in finding God that we find our way in a confusing and chaotic world.

Carol E. Becker, director of the Department of Communication for the Evangelical Lutheran Church in America, takes a more sociological perspective. She raises the poignant question of how in any age or culture we can hear God and, more particularly, how in our age and culture we can hear God. She describes the New Age movement as one option that has emerged in our culture that attempts to hear the divine voice, and one that has broad appeal, given the contours of our culture. Becker then offers a challenge to the mainline denominations on how they might communicate the Christian message more effectively and offer hope to a generation seeking a spirituality that deepens and gives meaning to life.

Well-known Episcopal clergyman, professor, and author Morton Kelsey moves to a more historical perspective as he traces the perennial quest for the spiritual life. He contends that Western materialistic culture has not provided a compelling spiritual vision. Many seekers have turned toward the East, to the great religions of Asia, to find a spiritual home, and New Agers have been among those turning East. He then makes a forceful case for ways in which the Christian faith can be reformulated, drawing on biblical foundations, in order to provide a spiritual vision for this age.

In the final chapter of Section One, Dr. Glenn A. Olds, educator, statesman, philosopher, and Methodist clergyman, probes the metaphysical underpinnings of our time and the New Age movement. He sees New Age thought as a natural outgrowth of our historical circumstances and philosophical assumptions. He then assesses the movement's enduring and constructive themes as well as its limits and liabilities.

Section Two, "New Age Spirituality: A Journey of Growth," is both a descriptive and an analytical treatment of the movement. David Spangler, author, teacher, and New Age spokesperson and critic, opens the section with a discussion of the New Age as a journey toward the divine. He points out the diverse and complex nature of New Age thought and carefully distinguishes between that which he judges to be of great value and that which is of lesser value.

The part of the New Age that is of great value is the emphasis on exploration and discovery, development and empowerment, service to our planet, and transformation and emergence. He then raises the questions of whether the New Age movement is a religion (not really) and whether it is an authentic path to the divine (yes, in many ways).

Carl Raschke, scholar, author, and professor at the University of Denver, discusses New Age spirituality as a journey toward self-discovery. New Agers, appreciating the rich variety and lack of orthodoxy in the movement, can select from a broad range of options in their journey of self-discovery. Interestingly, the journey of self-discovery borrows freely from the "grammar" of modern physics and speaks of vibrational energy as the source of power for self-awareness and self-actualization. Personal transformation and self-discovery are parts of a larger whole, linked to social and planetary transformation, and thus one's personal identity is founded on a cosmic transformative vision of life.

Vivienne Hull, cofounder of the Chinook Learning Center on Whidby Island near Seattle, continues the discussion of the New Age movement's planetary vision. Hull begins her chapter by recounting her experience in Northern Ireland as a child, the impact of the worldview-altering 1960s, and the discovery of a new and compelling spiritual vision, a vision that is the foundation of the work of the Chinook Learning Center. Rather than "New Age," which has too many questionable connotations, she prefers to speak of the transformational movement, one in which we have "discovered" our interdependent relationship with the environment. Hull argues for a new way of seeing and acting, one that might be described as eco-spirituality.

The final section provides an assessment of New Age spirituality and proposes directions for a spirituality that can speak to "our age." Dr. Lisa N. Woodside, vice president and dean for academic affairs at Holy Family College in Philadelphia, provides a positive assessment of New Age spirituality. Well aware of its limitations, she nevertheless describes the movement as making a contribution to personal, social, and planetary transformation.

Dr. Harmon Hartzell Bro, author, scholar, and codirector of

Introduction

the Pilgrim Institute (a center for the study and nurture of the spiritual life) in Centerville, Massachusetts, offers a more critical appraisal. He points to the excesses and extravagances of the New Age movement, questions its philosophical assumptions, and argues that the movement has genuine limitations, not the least of which is the way the movement handles evil.

In the final chapter, "Spirituality for a New Era," Matthew Fox, priest, noted author and articulate spokesman for creation-centered spirituality, raises and suggests answers to four crucial questions: What is the New Age? Why is there a New Age movement? What are the strengths and weaknesses of the phenomenon we know as the New Age? and, What are the elements of a spirituality for a New Era? Throughout his discussion of these questions, Matthew Fox speaks of the need for a paradigm shift, a new cosmology, a new Pentecost, which converts us to an organic and interconnected view of the universe and a responsiveness to the moving of God's Spirit.

As editor, I am especially grateful to the authors of the several essays in this volume. Each in his or her own way has been patient and gracious, provided valuable suggestions for the tone and structure of the book, and, most importantly, provided a thoughtful, heart-full, spiritual, and profound chapter. To each of them, I am very grateful. I am grateful also to the help and encouragement of the good people of Westminster/John Knox Press and especially to Alexa Smith, friend and editor. Drew Stevens prepared the manuscript with great care and provided helpful suggestions along the way. Dorothy and Brian, the loves of my life, were patient and supportive, as were my co-workers in the Committee on Higher Education of the Presbyterian Church (U.S.A.).

DUNCAN S. FERGUSON

New Age Spirituality

SPIRITUALITY ACROSS THE AGES

Across the ages, the human family has been engaged in a spiritual quest, a quest that has taken a variety of forms depending on the culture and the historical circumstances. Section One explores this theme and suggests that the particular circumstances of our time have contributed to the rise of New Age spirituality.

1

The Cry of the Desperate: Christianity's Offer of a New Age

ANDREW CANALE

For many people, organized religion has lost its healing power. It seems dead, drab, anachronistic, even embarrassing and unenlightened to them. Some people, confronted with this lack of healing power, seem to put themselves on "cruise control" and proceed through life as though everything is fine. In the process, they may become alcoholic, workaholic, addicted to sleeping medications or other chemicals, pursuing lives committed to deadening the pain of the meaninglessness at their center. But for many, the pain is there, never absent, like a sore tooth aching. If one touches a sore tooth, a jolt of pain fires through the body. When we have toothaches we seek out a dentist. But what if we have a soul ache? To whom do we turn? The abuse of alcohol or sleeping medications, or clinging to other people, is the "treatment" that many choose. But it is a treatment that ultimately fails because it covers the ache rather than curing it.

After a time, the soul ache can become so pronounced that a person can no longer ignore it. Present life strategies cease to be effective in covering the pain. What then? Some turn to their ministers to find solace and comfort. In doing so, some discover that their clergy, though often not admitting it, are in the same quandary as they are.

People are hungry for God. They are searching for God. Even when they don't know it (as those with addictions), their center and goal is God.[1] God is a mystery. God is the name we who aren't atheists give to the core meaning of life. God is the impulse toward growth and wholeness and compassion and love. People are hungry for an experience of deep meaning; they want there to *be* a meaning.

Andrew Weil in his book *The Natural Mind* has noted that it is a human tendency, part of our very being, to seek altered awareness.[2] When organized religion doesn't offer its members a deep experience of altered awareness, but rather only drab, dead repetitions, many people go elsewhere. Again, they may choose "materialistic" avenues such as drugs, alcohol, sex, and work in a desperate search for this altered awareness that will take them beyond their empty lives.

Others turn to New Age spirituality. What is the New Age? I posed the question to several people as I began thinking about this chapter. I heard all sorts of responses:

"It is a new kind of music, isn't it?"
"I think of the new physics. Quantum mechanics. Quarks."
"To me, it seems a boring, amorphous thing."
"It is Satan at work, trying to take people away from Christ."
"I never heard of it."
"It is the way I find my soul. It gives me life."

In the literature on New Age we find the same rich variation of response. New Age can include, but is not confined to, past life regression, channeling of spirits of the dead, crystals, theosophy, Eastern religions and yoga (both thousands of years old), the search for self, meditation, autogenic training, music, est, dream work. It refers to thinkers who speak specifically for the New Age, to philosophers who posit an unseen movement, a conspiracy, an emergence of new life and creativity in several areas of scientific and daily life. It is concerned for ecology, political justice, the end of hunger.[3] In fundamentalist tracts, it is seen as satanic and signals the end time; biblical Christians are told to recognize it as the Antichrist and to prepare for the end and the second coming of Christ.[4]

Clearly, the New Age means different things to different people. Throughout this book, New Age spirituality will be examined from several perspectives. In this chapter, I have in mind the large group of desperate people who are bereft of meaning systems and without a felt connection to core loving reality. As noted, many disillusioned searchers are looking beyond the church for an experience of God. Desperate people tend to be very vulnerable. There is an urgency in many of them to connect and belong, which often supersedes clear thinking. Their need for belonging can preempt their discernment about the goodness of that to which they choose to belong. I believe this is one of the key factors in the power exerted by cults, when desperation is met by the promise of belonging. The person has only to give up everything. Now, Jesus said much the same thing. We must lose our life in order to gain it (Luke 17:33). In itself, losing one's life can make sense. One cannot find new life or enter a new age until one has given up one's old life. But to what or whom do we give our lives?

I believe that there is a great, wild, transformative meaning at the core of life and that there are ways to gain access to this meaning. Anything less than profound connection to this meaning fails our desperate searcher. I propose it is to this wild, transformative meaning that we give our lives.

But such meaning isn't easily found. Witness the thousands of people who seek help from psychotherapists, spiritual directors, and the New Age movement. Without proper guidance, these desperate ones can be seriously damaged in their search. For there is evil in life, a destructive reality that separates people from God and from one another. Fundamentalists make much the same claim. I part with the fundamentalists on the issue of evil when they negate people and movements (such as the New Age movement) on the basis of one-sided literalist biblical interpretation rather than by applying the biblical ethic of love. It has been my sad experience that fundamentalists sometimes become what they abhor: a closed group, denying freedom and growth to their constituents, cultish, and unable to meet their fellow human beings in love because they instead "satanize" them. I know people who years later feel the dreadful negative effects of their encounter with fundamentalism of

5

this kind and struggle to see that their real selves are loved by God. There is a passion for God in fundamentalism that is admirable, but only when it isn't exclusionary.

It is not easy for most of us to find our way in life. There are evil forces in the world. Witness war, poverty, hunger, torture. But we must not damn the desperate. Rather, we must open our arms to them and help them find their own way. We must show them, or help them see, that the God whom we claim to be the center of life is at the center of *each* life, residing often in the cry of desperation itself.

The New Age movement is here understood to be a variety of responses to our culture's materialism and shallow spirituality.[5] At its best, it demonstrates the human longing for belonging, meaning, and love. At its worst, it preys on desperate people, robbing them of their financial resources and, more importantly, of their power of choice. I do not believe in a God who wants goose-stepping automatons parroting the life of Jesus or anyone else. The God in whom I believe cries in each soul for that person to become his or her real self, and longs for the particular mystery embodied in that life to unfold. When churches, or philosophic principles, or governments, or parents, or New Age thinkers and gurus deny others their mysterious unfolding, they are working against God. I believe that God wants, even more than the desperate searchers themselves, for them to find their way. God may be the very cause of their desperation, that toward which they desperately want to move while they have no clue how to do so.

David Spangler's vision of the New Age is one that cares for the earth and all the earth's creatures (see chapter 5). He suggests that it is possible to have inclusive visions that value all people and strive to bring them to community and hope. His is a "high road" view of the New Age, a longing for a compassionate world in which hunger and poverty are alleviated, creativity is invited, deep change allowed to unfold, and exclusivity rejected. None of these values is inconsistent with Christianity. In fact, Christianity at its best lives by the same principles. Viewed in this light, Christianity and the New Age movement need not compete. Rather, they need to cooperate with each other for the sake of the desperate ones.

Spangler notes that psychic phenomena are a common occurrence in the New Age movement, but that they are not central to the coming of the New Age. When psychic events are seen as the primary proof of the validity of a guru or group, we are in dangerous territory. Likewise, when psychic phenomena are cited as proof positive of the presence of the demonic, as is often done in fundamentalism, an equally dangerous closed-mindedness ensues.

Psychic events happen in people's lives. They are reported in the New Testament in various places. For example, when the angel Gabriel appears to Mary, when Joseph is told in a dream to flee to Egypt, and when Saul is knocked to the ground on the road to Damascus and hears Jesus crying out to him, Christians believe that God is acting in a powerful way and to significant ends. One would expect modern Christians not to deny God the same power to break into our own lives.[6] Tragically, this is what many of us do. We ignore our dreams. We ignore the strange opportunities that life presents us to show compassion to our fellow beings. Could it be that the desperate ones are angels (*angelos* in Greek means messenger) sent by God to awaken us to love and to show compassion more deeply? Could it be that we are the bringers of the New Age for God, that through our compassionate love of the desperate ones, the lost, the suffering, the strange, the dying, even our enemies, we are provided the opportunity to bring God's New Age that Jesus called the kingdom of heaven?

I believe that Christianity has a profound message that can reach the hearts of desperate people and usher in a New Age. But this can be so only if we open ourselves to the wildness and desperateness of Christianity itself. Christianity pictures God coming into the world as a human being to show us that there lies at the depth of life a wild, loving God who will do anything to bring us home, to give us a sense of meaning, to break through to us in overwhelming love. If this is so, then Christians have a mission to the desperate and to all those seeking a New Age in which they are included. How are we to bring this message of inclusivity to our desperate compatriots? Not by ranting and raving. Not by "demonizing" them. Not by mocking their search. The way to reach them is by entering their world and helping them to open to the God who resides in their hearts.

Meeting the Desperate
in Their Own Land

In my work as a psychologist, I have the opportunity to share with consciously desperate people every day. Many people disclose in therapy that they are at their core frightened that they don't belong, that there is no community that will receive and love them as they really are. As they open up in therapy and discover that they aren't rejected, they often become eager to try to find this experience of belonging in a wider context. Many have been so injured by organized religion that they go everywhere else to seek belonging. The judgmental attitude evidenced in many religious institutions has demonstrated to them that they are not wanted there. The Christian's task, as I see it, is rather to seek out the desperate, to feed the hungry, to visit the imprisoned, to heal the sick. Jesus is asking Christians to enter into the world of the desperate and the disfranchised, to go to the core of their hurt, because there we will both find God.

But we don't often do this, for the simple and profound reason that we fear desperation ourselves, because most of us are desperate too, except that we have been able to hide from our desperation through our diversions and possessions. We don't have to stand in line hoping for our day's gruel or flee an armed enemy or watch our loved ones die of illness and starvation. And yet, many of us are inwardly starving. We have made refugees of parts of ourselves. Our desperation is unwelcome, our sexuality demonic, our anger and sadness taboo. To look deeply into the eyes of the desperate is to see ourselves. I have had several conversations with a Haitian friend who is adamant that his people are not helped by handouts from gracious or guilty people from outside Haiti. Rather, they need people responding to the poverty of Haiti to do so from their own sense of desperation and need, from their own poverty of spirit, to join with them to begin to create a better world for both parties.

When we acknowledge our own desperation, we can meet other desperate people where they are. We can move into their metaphors of meaning, step into their world, and share the unfolding of their lives. In doing this, we will sometimes be exposed to values and beliefs different from our own. It helps no one, particularly the desperate, to have his or her beliefs mocked, beliefs that may be clung to as a last resort. One wouldn't insist that a man let go of a piece of driftwood that is keeping him afloat in the middle of the ocean. Some Christians might counter that we offer a ship of safety; the man must let go of the driftwood if he is to climb into our boat. But to this man, this "Christian boat" may look more like the pirate ship that sank his own little boat in the first place. To carry the image one step farther, many have been at sea in the middle of Christianity unable to find their way to life. They often begin to explore New Age practices hoping there to find a friendly ship.

I once worked with a woman who searched deeply for meaning in Jungian psychology, feminism, astrology, and the New Age movement. Like many women, she felt outcast in her social and religious life. Her patriarchal upbringing brought clearly to her the message that she was a second-class citizen. Her lot was to marry a man of her faith and to serve him; only thus would she be loved and have value. She tried desperately to succeed at this, but had the misfortune to marry a man whose values fully agreed with the dominant patriarchal values. He too saw her as a second-class citizen. She was dying in the marriage, unable to make connection with him or with her core self. Only after the marriage dissolved and she embarked on her own journey did she begin to become real. Jungian psychology provided her a way to explore the inner depths of herself and opened her to feminism. Feminism taught her that she was not a lesser person but a woman of great value, who was enraged at the demeaning treatment she had received throughout her life. She came to experience God as a great grandmother as well as a great father. Astrology pictured for her that the universe is orderly and interested in her welfare. She realized that she had always felt, as a woman, unworthy of the universe's care.

She began to attend New Age conferences with great excite-

9

ment and became more and more convinced of her own value. One such New Age event is of particular interest to our present discussion. She attended a workshop, during a time of great turmoil, at which she had an experience of two past lives that deepened her understanding of why she suffered so much from abandonment and an inability to relate to men in her present life. She reported that she experienced in one past life the moment that her husband and two children were stolen from her and never returned. She then experienced another past life, which ended violently with her heart being cut out of her body. She returned to the present full of grief but with an abiding sense that she had discovered the cause of her present life's misery in her past lives. When she related this to me, she conveyed her utter amazement and her certainty that she had experienced the truth of her past. Furthermore, it showed her the task of her present life. She began to focus intensely on her lifelong issues of abandonment.

Her experience presented me with an intriguing problem. While I believed fully and affirmed the reality of her experience, I personally didn't believe in past lives. Her profound breakthrough challenged me and my beliefs.

I want to turn now to my journal writing of the morning after our session. The initial writing of that morning (not included) records several personal concerns expressed in dialogue with Christ. Then the dialogue turned to my encounter with this woman.

ME: My meeting with R.S. yesterday. Her powerful experience of reincarnation, past lives, where she discovered that her heart was cut out. What about reincarnation?
CHRIST: Two things in the mystery. Love is central. And you are you.
ME: The second means?
CHRIST: You have you-ness. When your you-ness touches another's, you move with that one toward we-ness. This authentic you-ness and we-ness *is*. Rebirths are toward you-ness.
ME: Then there are rebirths, past lives?
CHRIST: It doesn't matter; whether there are or aren't, you are you. If you have lived many lives toward this, you are here. If your

creation started in 1949, you are here. You are asking your question. You want to know if God's genuineness calls you, Andy, to be. Yes. God calls *you* to be. God loves you, your particularity. Reincarnation does the work of eternity on earth. One positive thing about it. If people believed deeply that they could come back to a burned-out world, or to poverty, they might in their selfish fear work for justice. I told you in my words about doing for the least. Doing that is doing for me. The work of reincarnation can be done in a life. Find love. Live your life in God and your acts will bring you to God.

Let's notice several things. This woman's powerful experience entered my own questioning prayer life. Christ received the question and responded, neither affirming nor negating the fact of reincarnation. Christ's response assured me that I personally matter to God no matter what the ultimate truth that lies hidden in the mystery. Further, I was strengthened in my resolve to accept her experience at face value. Finally, her goal was not to become a past-lives *aficionada,* but to find the meaning of her life. I could not help her without stepping into her world. And I could not truly step into her world if I didn't explore my own beliefs about past lives. Christ through my imagination helped me be open to her and affirm her while affirming the depth of my own value.

Christianity in a Time of Stress

As I write, the daily newspapers are full of articles about poverty, hunger, murder, strife in South Africa, Kurdish refugees, the hundreds of oil wells burning in Kuwait, unemployment, economic disaster, murders in our cities, drugs, nuclear waste. We live in a desperate time. Materialism has failed to provide us with a sense of comfort or an ability to control the problems of our world. Within people, the same situation exists. There is meaninglessness, anxiety, despair, depression, hopelessness, loneliness, hunger for love.

The distress that individuals feel parallels the distress of the world. Has Christianity anything to offer us in this distress? For me, the answer is a resounding yes, *if* Christianity goes into the world and brings Christ to the desperate. I believe that the goal for the Christian isn't to bring people to Christ so much as it is to bring Christ to people. "When did we feed you, clothe you, visit you in prison?" "When you did this for one of the least of these." (See Matt. 25:34–46.) There is plenty of opportunity to bring Christ to people. As we know, drug abuse, workaholism, and other dysfunctional patterns are ruining lives. People are seeking out New Age groups, expanding their consciousness, using crystals, and communicating with the dead, as well as seeking to combat hunger, poverty, war, and the environmental crisis. Most Christians will agree with some of these approaches and find others frightening, dangerous, and weird.

The world is itself frightening, dangerous, and weird. To paraphrase scientist J. B. S. Haldane, the universe is not only weirder than we imagine, it is weirder than we *can* imagine. We need to acknowledge this and not try to hide in a bland, resolved Christianity, saying, "God will take care of it all." In our fear of the New Age, many of us point to psychic phenomena, the encounters with the dead, the use of crystals. "These things are weird," we say. "They make no sense." Of course they are, for reality itself is weird.

Have we the courage to examine how weird Christianity is? Resurrection strikes me as a much weirder event than reincarnation. Reincarnation, as you know, is the belief that all of us return to earth again and again in our karmic movement toward nirvana, wholeness, God. Our acts in one life affect how we will return, and in what form, in the next. There is a kind of cosmic logic here, a determinism that reaches beyond the individual life and unfolds over many lives, ultimately bringing each person to fulfillment.

Resurrection, on the other hand, jars the cycle of life and death. It breaks the old pattern into pieces. Reality has changed, Christ is risen. The person who you are is offered eternal life.

Reincarnation teaches there is an order in the universe. As we realize the unfolding of our many lives, we can find peace, accept our present condition, and move toward cosmic fulfillment. Or we can choose to work harder in our present incarnation to find enlightenment, as the Buddha teaches, and thus end the cycle of death and rebirth.

Resurrection ends the cycle of death and rebirth in a different way. It explodes into history with Jesus. Christianity proclaims that an altogether weird event occurred after Jesus died, and that this event changes reality or, if you prefer, discloses to us that core reality is different than we thought. It ushers in a New Age.

God is acting in a new way in the resurrection, inviting us more deeply into life. Resurrection suggests that the pivot point in life is the human soul. The soul that catches the fire of resurrection is changed, opened to God's love, freed from chronic desperation, and desires to share this good news with others. It seems to be the very nature of resurrection to want to share itself, to spill itself out, to come to others freely, to be an outpouring of God's self-giving love and life. The evidence throughout the Acts of the Apostles supports this. Peter and the other disciples move from place to place bringing the good news, even though ultimately it costs most of them their lives.

This is problematic stuff for desperate people. "I can have this life but it's going to kill me? What is resurrection, anyway? Did it really happen? What has it to do with me?" These are important questions. If the pivot point in life is the human soul, then resurrection needs to happen in the desperate person's own soul, not just be reported and believed because someone else says to. Many times I have heard people cry out that they find themselves outside the fold. The promise of resurrection, not fulfilled in themselves, makes them even more desperate. Add to this the worldview of materialism, prevalent in our age, which proclaims that the only real events are those that we can measure with our senses and replicate in laboratories, thus making resurrection and all other nonsensory, nonreplicable events appear to be mere nonsense. But this materialistic assumption doesn't end desperation, because materialism itself fosters desperation. What it offers does not soothe, heal, or transform.

We need to meet the desperate where they are, suffering under a materialistic perspective that makes them feel hopeless, helpless, and purposeless. The Christian mythos, as here understood, challenges this materialistic view. Simply stated, Christianity shouts that there is new and great life in each person's soul. Desperate people want new life, desperately. But many of them can't believe in it. Christianity has been ruined for them by being presented as a rule of law handed down by a judgmental God who is keeping track of their every little thought, word, and deed. For others, Christianity has failed in times of crisis by offering empty platitudes but no real spiritual sustenance. It is not surprising that many have turned against Christianity. This is a tragedy, for Christianity should be proclaiming that a wild God of love is running toward us, longing to bring us home, desperate to be with us. This movement of God can give meaning to people's desperation. They are desperate for a good reason. They want God.

It is not an easy thing to bring God's life to desperate people already wounded by their religious upbringing. The way to start with most people is to listen. They just aren't open to being "converted." People need to tell their desperate stories. They need others to step into their stories with them, to share their pain. At the core, desperate people are profoundly isolated. Materialism serves this isolation, as we have just noted, by philosophically denying the possibility that inner spiritual events are real. Thus the only inner events that succeed in being heard, real cries of anguish, are seen as evidence that something is very wrong in the person. Something *is* wrong. Human beings aren't meant to be isolated. We are social creatures, who come into our real being by sharing with others. Without communication, we are less than we can be. Compassionate listening to another's story invites that person into human relationship. So many of us have never had our stories fully accepted and appreciated, and consequently feel like the people cast into the outer darkness who are weeping and gnashing their teeth.[7]

We need to join sufferers in this outer darkness rather than relegating them to hell. Jesus models this in his own life as he dines with tax collectors, prostitutes, and other outcasts. God, he proclaims, is like the prodigal's father who lifts his skirts and runs toward the returning child (Luke 15:11–32). Desperate people need time to be with others; they don't need fixing. I remember working with a woman whose life had fallen apart in every way. She cried out her need for God, but said she had no idea how to pray.

"What would you say to God if you could?" I asked her.

Immediately, these words burst from her: "Goddammit, God, you've got to help me!"

"That is your prayer, then. Pray it."

I feel comfortable with this kind of unorthodox praying. It is real. It came from the woman's heart. She could cry it out with the passion of the psalmist. And she felt heard in praying it. The secret of prayer, as Jesus suggests, is to go to your private place and God will be there, and God will give you your reward (Matt. 6:18). This is precisely what she did.

God wants us to be real in prayer. If we are in despair, we should pray our despair. If we are sad, we should pray our sadness; if ecstatic, share our ecstasy with God; if angry at God, be angry. This was brought home to me several years ago, during one of my own yelling sessions with God. After I had forcefully expressed my angry feelings about my predicament at that time and sat waiting for a response, I heard in my imagination the following words: "Finally, Andy, you have come into your anger. I have been here all along, waiting for you." The effect of these words was to let me know that my anger was not only accepted but "God-occupied." By opening to my anger, I found a deeper connection to God and to myself.

The Christian story states that outcasts are in, that the last shall be first, that the desperate publican gets in, but the self-satisfied Pharisee doesn't (yet). In a profound sense, desperation is *potentially* good news. It opens us to our absolute need for God who, Christianity seeks to assure us, has a deep love and need for us.

That said, how do we meet this need? So far, we have named compassionate listening to the person's story in order to bring that story to resurrection. How do we get to resurrection? Desperate ears hear the painful words "You have to die. You have to pick up your cross and follow." This hurts. We want something more like Shadrach, Meshach, and Abednego's rescue in the fiery furnace (Dan. 3:26–28). Douglas Dawe in his book *Jesus: The Death and Resurrection of God*[8] describes Shadrach and his friends as apocalyptic heroes whom God rescued at the last moment. This was the apocalyptic formula of the time. The hero was put to the test, was threatened with death, and at the last moment rescued by God.

Jesus wasn't rescued at the last moment. He didn't come down from his cross as his taunters demanded (Mark 15:32). He died. God did not protect him. Dawe argues that the death of Jesus breaks the apocalyptic hero pattern. His death brings with it the death of God the protector. His disciples fled not so much from cowardice as because their expectations of his apocalyptic heroism had been dashed. They had lost God. Perhaps Judas thought he was playing his part when he turned Jesus over to the authorities, for this brought about the apocalyptic moment. But when he kissed Jesus in the Garden, he saw that Jesus would die. His despair came in the discovery that Jesus was not going to follow the pattern. He hadn't brought Jesus to his heroic moment; he had betrayed him unto death.

So death is the way. Letting go of all security. Giving oneself to God, who is not going to protect you from death. The game isn't protection but rather, as Dawe suggests, transformation. Jesus broke through God the protector to an even deeper experience of God as transformer. It is this God, who doesn't rescue, who brings resurrection, who, to quote Dawe, "did not fill the disciples with comfort and peace, but . . . with terror and awe in the face of the breaking in of a Beyond that they had thought empty." The disciples, like ourselves, were cast beyond their prior beliefs into desperation. It was there, at the center of desperation, that resurrection could happen, could emerge as "a ground for human hope."[9]

The ground of hope, then, is to die and find God the transformer. We are to be transformed. "Into what?" the desperate one asks. "What, who shall I become? Will it be any better? Or will I only be desperate in another key?" The answer Christianity gives, I think, is this: "You will be transformed into a lover. It will be better for you, though you will still have moments of desperation. But the shape of your desperation will change. You will experience something of the reign of God and will desperately long for more. You will wish for the healing of your enemy. You will want the reign of God to flower into being."

We arrive here at a fundamental issue. If God is all-loving and wishes wholeness and full life for each of us, why are there starvation, violence, poverty, illness, and the host of other problems in the world? Walter Wink suggests that these ills are due to other forces occupying the world with us, biblically named the principalities and powers, that interfere with God's purpose.[10] Wink describes these "Powers" as great sociospiritual forces that operate in outer reality. He names corporations, nation-states, economic systems, and religious hierarchies as examples. The powers have both inner and outer manifestations. Corporations and churches have inner spirits that dictate what can happen in their sphere of influence. When powers go against the will of God, they successfully block (for a time) God's intentions. Prayer provides the way to open to God so that God can act. Wink cites the book of Daniel as the place where the role of the powers in blocking answers to prayer was clearly identified for the first time. Cyrus has just freed the Israelites and promised to rebuild their Temple, but the Israelites are not rushing to return home. Daniel is overcome with anguish and fasts for twenty-one days, all the while praying fervently to God. At last, an angel arrives and explains to Daniel that God has heard his prayer from the start but that it has taken this long for the angel to get beyond the "prince of Persia" (see Daniel 10).

This story marks the dawning of awareness that we are not alone with God, that there are forces that actively block the coming of God's reign. It is these powers that Paul refers to when he writes, "For I am persuaded, that neither death, nor life, nor angels, nor principalities, nor powers, nor things present, nor things to come, nor height, nor depth, nor any other creature, shall be able to separate us from the love of God . . . in Christ Jesus our Lord" (Rom. 8:38–39, KJV). Death, life, angels, principalities, powers, the present, and the past all exist; but none of it, according to Paul, can separate us from God if we are in Christ, if we follow him to the death.

This is an awesome and audacious promise to make to desperate people. It acknowledges the reality of other forces but says, God hears you! You can't be separated from God!

Not surprisingly, such good news will be challenged by some desperate searchers. "If this is so, why do the powers hold sway? Why doesn't God put the powers to rout?" Christianity offers the mythological answer that war occurred in heaven and several of his angels fell with Lucifer (Rev. 12:7–9). We argue that these angels have been trying to force their will on the world ever since, and with some success. Madeleine L'Engle in her novel *A Wind in the Door* portrays evil as the Echthroi, beings whose purpose is to bring people and creation to nothing, to "*x*" them from existence, causing a rip in the fabric of the universe.

Myth and story seek to portray the awareness that something is wrong in our world, that negative forces are bent on destruction, and that there is something we can do about it. Many New Age thinkers avoid the problem of evil. They propose variations on the theme that the universe is one and whole. Our wholeness, they say, can be found by entering into this cosmic oneness. Christianity will have nothing of this. Rather, we live in a universe that is groaning and in travail (Rom. 8:22–23). There are malignant forces that would lead us away from life. We need discernment to guide us toward that which is life-giving and away from that which brings death, including those powers that serve their own selfish goals rather than serving God.[11]

Jesus taught that when we cry out to God for our every need, God will hear us and respond to our prayer by contending with those powers (for example, corporations, churches, nation-states, our inner negativities) that oppose God. In the civil rights movement, in Gandhi's struggle to free India from Great Britain, in many similar struggles today, people are praying to God to open the powers to justice and placing their own bodies in harm's way to act for justice. They are praying and acting in love. This is precisely what Jesus did. He prayed with his disciples and alone. He acted. He opened his arms to outcasts, touched the unclean, and healed the sick, who most people believed were being directly punished by God. He told people to love. "Love your neighbor as you love yourself." "Love your enemy." With the Samaritan story (Luke 10:25–37), he brought these two commands together. The apparent enemy, the Samaritan, is the one who aided the injured traveler. This little tale radically challenged the people and the authorities. The reign of God, he proclaimed, is one that embraces the desperate and brings them back into community.

But the community didn't want the outcasts back. For his efforts, Jesus was destroyed. He took a direct hit from the powers and the evil acting through them. God didn't protect him from the powers, but let him drink the dregs of his suffering. According to the Gospels, never once did Jesus rail against his persecutors. He loved them, asked for forgiveness for them, invited a thief into Paradise, and cried out his own forsakenness to God. In this cry, we hear naked humanity, destroyed by the powers, utterly alone, but still screaming to God, who didn't protect him.

Resurrection. The word jars here. Hellish death, then resurrection. Jesus opened a way for God to act by utterly submitting to the powers rather than responding to them in kind. God then acted in a shocking way—resurrection. Even the powers that destroyed him, even utter bereftness of God, didn't separate Jesus from love. Dare we see that Jesus freed God to explode into life in this dramatic way? Dare we see that the desperation in the cries in our own souls is in fact God's groaning seeking words and action? Can we desperate people believe that God is the source of our desperation? that God is longing to come in love for all of us, and each of us? that our desperation is God's doorway, and the more we open the door, the more access we give to God to come among us?

Christianity states that this is so and promises resurrection and eternal life with God to the desperate. If we can open our eyes to one another and see that the other is Christ (Matt. 25: 34–45), if we can bear the force of the powers without acting destructively, our desperation will open into deepening relationship with God and other human beings. We will long to feed the hungry and visit the sick. We will long to embrace our enemy in love. It is time to hear the cry of the desperate in the world and in our own souls, and to realize that this cry is the voice of God. As we do so, God's New Age begins once again.

2

In Any Age: Can We Hear God?

This is the New Age.

Close your eyes and you will see clearly.
Cease to listen and you will hear truth.
Be silent and your heart will sing.
Seek no contact and you will find union.
Be still and you will move on the tide of the spirit.

These words are not from the Bible. They are from a shampoo brochure, which encourages us to "walk the path of purity with Aveda."

This is the New Age. *Open Exchange,* a Bay-area publication, lists therapies, classes, and spiritual practices as a kind of New Age newsletter. *Common Ground* lists a cafeteria of over a thousand options for personal transformation and growth. A brain gym can put you back in the flow. The Army recruits with the slogan "Be All That You Can Be." In therapy, adults are learning how to play in the sand. Sensitivity seminars promise to teach men how to cry. Massage has nonsexual significance.

This is the New Age. Witchcraft and mythology are in vogue again. But witches no longer emerge out of *Macbeth* or *Snow White and the Seven Dwarfs* as the embodiment of "pure evil." They now also represent the dark and mysterious power of the feminine in both men and women, and many who feel this power are proud to call themselves witches. Mythology is different too. As feminists look boldly for female images of divinity, which some claim are not encompassed in the Judeo-Christian tradition, stories of the ancient gods and goddesses dimly remembered from high school Latin or English class suddenly take on new meaning. The goddesses take center stage, as archetypes of the feminine attributes in us.

This is the New Age. Crystals and meditation can enhance your understanding of the present and future. Psychic referral hot lines are available if you need one. In New York City, you can call a 900 number to play Black Jack, get your soap opera update, hear your horoscope, arrange a date, or give your confession. In any city in the country you can buy New Age books or listen to New Age radio stations. In her hit show *The Search for Signs of Intelligent Life in the Universe,* Lily Tomlin parodies the New Age couple, Lyn and Bob. Lyn in remembering their first date:

> We smoked some paraquat-free Panama Red and then we made love. Afterwards, we talked into the night. Bob poured out all his feelings about things that concerned him: megavitamin therapy, solar energy, the ecosystem and ending world hunger through tofu consciousness. We made love again. And then stopped and had a Trail Mix snack. We talked till dawn, exchanging Patti Hearst theories, and then we fell asleep. By morning we were in love. Bob is a dream come true . . . a New Age Ward Cleaver.[1]

Even Winnie the Pooh knows about the New Age, and teaches it to children (and adults) in *The Tao of Pooh.* ("While Eeyore frets . . . and Piglet hesitates . . . and Rabbit calculates . . . and Owl pontificates, Pooh just is."[2])

This is the New Age. Astrology figures into presidential politics. Health food stores, holistic health practitioners, and yoga instructors are increasingly popular, as are acupuncture and vitamin therapy. People are discovering themselves, self-actualizing, realizing their full potentials, becoming aware of their inner voices, transforming their lives. Something is up. People are getting "into themselves" in a spiritual way. The phenomenon of the New Age is real. Or is it?

Equipped with the reporter's questions—Who? What? Where?

When? Why? and How?—I as a communicator and all of us who are Christian should be skeptical of our capacity to lump all these things together and call them New Age. That in itself is a story. It makes great copy. We all like catch phrases. And so "the New Age" has become one of the hottest stories in the religious press. But is it the real story?

Our Perspective on the New Age

Behind the phenomenon of New Age is a phenomenology—a way in which we organize our sensations of our world. What makes us put so many different things into one category called "New Age"? What is the phenomenology underneath the New Age concept? How do we organize our thoughts about the phenomena in contemporary religion, especially now, especially as Christians?

Because we are human, we emphasize the common themes in those different from us. Often those common themes carry negative connotations. The human mind is equipped to stereotype. To put human activities as diverse as the classical therapeutic process and psychic reading and witchcraft together in the same category illustrates, first of all, our capacity to overgeneralize. Our willingness to settle for one category to describe many diverse processes reveals our inherent tendency to think in "them and us" terms.

Second, the phenomenology underneath the concept of the New Age illustrates our human capacity to put ourselves in the center of the universe and others on the fringe. It's easy for us to take the high ground in the center of the religious world. We're mainline! It's very easy to presuppose Christianity as a geo-psychic center and to lump everything on the fringes into one category, until that category is no longer useful. We are not only egocentric, we are geocentric and Christocentric. But the sun does not revolve around the earth. So we may well ask: When does the mainline Christian perspective on the religious experience become less than useful?

Third, the phenomenology we use to discern the New Age reveals our dependence on past patterns, concepts, and categories. We use the past to order the way we see the present. Sometimes that's good. It can be to our benefit to see some things in light of the past. Perhaps there are Gnostic parallels between the twentieth century and the first. Maybe there are pagan similarities with the Hebrew scriptures. But maybe the past does not contain the present. Perhaps new wine requires new skins. Indeed, artificial comparisons of the superficial coincidences between past and present, between New Age and the Gnosticism of the first century, or between New Age and the Hebrew scriptures are based on our own retrogressive preoccupations, and they can be dangerously misleading. They distract us from the true dialectic challenge of the present.

I am reminded of *The General,* a novel about a bright young officer who, by a series of accidents, becomes a general and is hailed as someone new and different who might break the stalemate of World War I. He was so good at working the system, fighting in the trenches, duking it out, that he has missed an essential point. World War I could not be won in the trenches. It took a new idea—tank warfare. And someone else thought of it.[3]

So it is for us, the mainline Christian faith groups. Rubricating what we consider "the fringe," using our past to interpret and address strange or difficult new ideas, isn't going to help us with anything but our own misunderstanding. Acupuncture and yoga, for example, are more different than Lutheran and Church of God. Some Christians have compared New Age thought to Gnostic heresies of the past. It is true; some New Age thinking is Gnostic in that it speaks of a "way" or "special insight." But Gnosticism implies a spiritual reality that is superior to the physical. Is this a fair characterization of New Age thought? In some ways, New Age thinking is frankly more physically centered than contemporary Christianity. In fact, women theologians are suggesting that Christianity itself is somewhat hostile to the human body, and may, in its own way, be the basic Gnostic expression of our culture and time.[4]

These theologians call us to confront the goddess. In reforming images of the goddess, they strike at the estrangement of our culture, which, they claim, has been heightened by patriarchal religions, including Christianity. The goddess is not a person or an idol, then, but a representation of immanence. She is a symbolic recognition of the value of physical power that comes from within us rather than the power we wield over others. The image of the goddess is meaningful because it calls to memory the ancient myths of the goddess as birth giver, mother, weaver, earth, flame, web, wind, and ocean. These are images of connectedness, sustenance, healing, and creating rather than "dominion over." They are earthy, physical. And, indeed, the goddess does represent feminine power, the power of the dark womb, the physical in us. It is a power Christianity has not embraced.[5]

But the intent here is not to argue the fine points of Gnosticism in either New Age or Christian thought, but to realize that the present has a distinct possibility of being different from the past. And past responses may no longer be appropriate. Though past phenomenologies may give us insight, they can also imprison or cause us to misunderstand. So the first task of the communicator is to challenge conceptualizations with healthy skepticism.

The Real New Age Story

Yet, there is something going on. Is it New Age or is it something else? That's the reporter's question. And the reporter in me keeps asking the question even if the answers become more difficult, even when they begin to point into the heart of those interviewed, into the framework of our own mainline consciousness.

Although it is a more difficult story to hear, and harder to write about, the real story behind the New Age is the story of three critical cultural trends of the late twentieth century: the failure of secularism to convey hope, the reversal of a decline in religious consciousness, and the enduring human yearning for spiritual meaning.

German philosopher and sociologist Jurgen Habermas traces the collapse of classical religious consciousness in contemporary Western culture.[6] In a secularized world it is no longer necessary or even desirable to be religious. Philosophers and sociologists since Karl Marx have predicted that secular philosophical systems would fill the void in meaning that religion had previously given people's lives. But secular philosophy has also failed. Why? Secular thinking faced not only the fixations of a technocratic consciousness but also, at the same time, the collapse of religious consciousness. Since the secular interpretation of the world depends precisely on coexistence with a widely influential religion of the masses, its ability to provide "substitute meaning" is an illusion. Only religion can speak to people en masse of hope, because it alone speaks in symbols, signs, images, rhythms, and icons to which people can relate emotionally as well as intellectually.

Even after assimilating utopian impulses from the Judeo-Christian tradition, secularism cannot bring us, as the Cookie Monster says, "everlasting joy and happiness." It has not been capable of infusing life with meaning because, in the secular worldview, death renders all of life meaningless. "Life's a bitch," as the bumper sticker says, "and then you die." People not only don't want to believe this, they cannot. There is too much loneliness, brokenness, fear, isolation, failure, accidental dismemberment, sudden loss, sorrow, dread, stupidity, and irony to life. In the face of pain, ultimate nothingness is deeply troubling. But that's the gospel of secularism. It doesn't give life meaning in the same way that the religious hope of salvation has. In the industrially advanced societies of which our culture is paramount, we observe for the first time as a mass phenomenon a shocking reality: people do not expect salvation. They do not hope for redemption. And yet, even though ours is no longer a religious culture, we know intuitively that salvation is necessary.

This loss of hope, resulting in an automated sense of despair and shallow pleasure, has been devastating. We live in meaningless times. We certainly have had our warnings. Bertrand Russell was one of the first voices, in the 1920s:

> Nothing in America is so painful to the traveler as the lack of joy. Pleasure is frantic and bacchanalian, a matter of momentary oblivion, not of delighted self expression. Men whose grandfathers danced to the music of the pipe in Balkan or Polish villages sit throughout the day glued to their desks, amid typewriters and telephones, serious, important, and worthless. Escaping in the evening to drink and a new kind of noise, they imagine that they are finding happiness, whereas they are

finding only a frenzied and incomplete oblivion of the hopeless routine of money that breeds money.[7]

Could it be that with the death of Christianity as a meaning system, and the ultimate emptiness of American secular culture, the deepest human yearnings of this nation are now being drawn to a variety of new and old religious expressions? Is that the New Age story?

Russell's observation is dramatically updated and made less sexist by Rabbi Harold Kushner, who points to the failure of contemporary life to generate joy.[8] We seem to be content with the absence of pain. We are preoccupied with a therapeutic model that focuses on the personal past but does little to articulate a future. And, preoccupied with the individual and her happiness, we too often preclude the ultimate sources of joy inherent in being connected with causes, ideas, and values that transcend the self.

Here, if we are willing, we can meet the goddess again. This time, she looms as an image of what we have lost—our grounding, our connectedness. She is Gaia, the earth mother. She represents for us our intuition that we are connected to the earth and everything in it. In Greek mythology, Gaia is the first mother, the mother before all time. In her contemporary re-formation, she is "the living presence of earth."[9] Neither secular philosophies nor Christianity has done justice to Gaia and what she represents.

The image of Gaia raises a question: Could it be that in a world based on individualized, secularized, hedonistic, materialistic satisfactions, millions of people are now unhappy and are looking for something more? Is it possible that they are not finding it in the sermons they hear on Sunday morning, but instead in New Age formulations?

In tracing the growth of secular individualism in American culture, Robert Bellah says that we have lost that sense of cohesiveness that binds people together.[10] We live parallel lives alone. Our religion is ourselves. He echoes what my own parents said on their return from a year in Africa more than twenty years ago: the most shocking thing about American society, once you've been away from it, is to see how completely every value is sacrificed to individualism. There is no collective good left for us. Strangely, the loss of the collective good has left us with private unhappiness. As John Donne wrote in 1611:

> Tis all in pieces, all coherence gone
> All just supply, and all relation:
> Prince, Subject, Father, Sonne, are things forgot
> For every man alone thinkes he hath got
> To be a Phoenix, and that then can bee
> None of that kinde, of which he is, but hee.[11]

But are our souls big enough to contain our own divinity? Are we corporately and spiritually bankrupt? Are millions of people asking: Is that all there is? asking for a meaning for their pain? direction for their destiny? or even for a destiny to cherish? Are millions now seeking what Joseph Campbell calls the soul's release from its exile in a world of organized inadequacies?[12] Are people moving back into the religious?

Habermas sees a renewed interest in various religious efforts as a reaction to the despair, emptiness, loneliness, and meaninglessness of contemporary life:

> In reaction to the mass loss of the religious certainty of salvation, a new Hellenism is taking shape, that is, a regression below the level of identity reached in communication with the one God of the monotheistic high religions. Many small subcultural ersatz religions are forming in marginal groups that are extraordinarily differentiated geographically, socially, and with respect to content. These ersatz religions range from transcendental meditation to new communal rituals and half-scientific training programs to collective self-help organizations (often with goals that are only apparently pragmatic) to small activist groups trying to transform the world under the sign of political theology, anarchism, or sexual politics. Perhaps all these subcultures are based on a similar motivational structure. From the perspective of the theological tradition, these new interpretations of the world and of human existence present themselves as a new paganism which finds expression in a new pluralism of idol worship and local mythologies.[13]

Walter Capps also speaks of the quest for transcendence.[14] Some thirty years ago the death of God was announced, and the prediction was that we would become increasingly secular. Instead there has been a resurgence of religious commitment and a host of religious phenomena: the rise of neo-Pentecostalism, evangelicalism, the quest for spirituality, renewed interest in Roman Catholic retreat centers, prayer, liturgy, cults, and the boom of the electronic churches.

Communicating Hope

The reporter in me suggests that whatever is going on with the New Age has to do with this deep human yearning to be religious: a yearning that is not met by the formulations of a secular worldview or by current mainline organized religion.

Further, it is not in our best interests to understand this problem in retrospect, that is, using the past to interpret the present. That would be like standing on the shore talking about the good old days, and missing the boat to the future. Habermas suggests that such retrospectively oriented comparisons are dangerous. They do not help us address the conflicts inherent within the New Age itself. A good example of this is the New Age emphasis, on the one hand, on personal motivation and private life and, on the other, on a new political reality or utopia based on new ideologies. Both alternatives have inherent difficulties. But it is clear that we must view these ideas out of our own understanding of community and koinonia, rather than Gnosticism or paganism. That is, we must ask ourselves, as Christians, how we can be a community rather than occupying ourselves with criticism of the New Age movement for its Gnostic or pagan tendencies.

Another example is the New Age emphasis, on the one hand, on the very old and, on the other, on the very new, which plays into American schizophrenia regarding time. Again, we must put aside our own orientation toward the past and consider these ideas equipped with our now deep understanding of the Christian perspective on time and hope, expressed in biblical eschatology.

The reporter in me says that the real story regarding New Age is not how we explain these new phenomena using known categories, but how we renew the faith in a meaningless, empty, and unhappy time. The task before us today is not neoorthodox. It is neoexistential.

Part of that existential call is a call to communicate the hope that we know—actually to re-form culture with religion. The task is to communicate a meaningful hope for a people who have lost their way. That, after all, is what the New Age movements are doing, and what the Christian traditions must reclaim. In reclaiming this ability, we mainline churches will also be reformed.

Breaking out of the mainline box. First, it is time for a new religious consciousness for Christians. The New Age movement calls us to break out of our mainline boxes. We can no longer preoccupy ourselves with classical understandings and debates. Our current physical condition on the globe and the ache in people's hearts for a physical faith require us to consider new understandings of incarnation. Any physical discipline can teach us that there is more to a life of faith than knowing how to *think* about God the right way. Physical discipline can help us experience faith in our bodies. Only then can we truly know what grace is, and love, and hope. Seldom do our mainline traditions offer us ways to experience religion in this way, the very way in which Hammer calls young people to experience their faith, dancing and singing to exhaustion, when he performs his hit song "Pray."[15] Yet the Christian tradition of the Middle Ages understood the dynamic relationship between faith and the physical self, in ways that we seem to have forgotten. Meister Eckehart, Hildegard of Bingen, Mechtild of Magdeburg, all Christian mystics of the Middle Ages, describe the divinity as rooted in the physical, as "mysterious, changeless, and the source of all birth and rebirth."[16] Somehow we need to discover our bodies: our personal and our corporate bodies. And that rediscovery of the physical possibilities for faith must extend into an intuition regarding the planet and the body of Christ.

Here, finally, if we have the courage, we as Christians can come to terms with the goddess. We have seen the goddess as an image of feminine power, the power that heals the duality of spirit and matter. In this aspect the goddess heals our estrangement. And it is only a deepening of our understanding of the goddess image to see her as Gaia, the earth mother. Gaia helps us see ourselves as part of nature, and therefore to see God in the physical aspect of all things. The Christian doctrine of creation on the other hand, currently suffers heavy criticism for allegedly contributing to the exploitation of nature. If we have dominion over nature, does not nature exist to serve us? Not if we are able to see the immanence of God in nature.[17] In so doing, we incorporate the attributes of the goddess's immanence and a motherly ability to heal our estrangement from God. We therefore reclaim, as Christians, the feminine aspects of God and bind ourselves to all creation.

As Christians we must also start to answer the New Age question: Does anyone love me? There is probably no more profound affirmation to this desperate question than the classical concept of God's enduring grace. But we turn grace into such a complicated concept that, for most people in our culture, it remains the best-kept secret of the faith. The doctrine of grace needs to be communicated in a fresh way for a generation aching to hear the words "I love you." Our failure to say that clearly to a culture in desperate need of Martin Luther's insight is a disgrace to our heritage from the Protestant Reformation of the sixteenth century.

We can also create meaningful hope by redefining the way we teach. When I was a girl I memorized over and over again from the catechism: "What does this mean?" Well, What does it all mean? is a basic question behind New Age perspectives. Christians need to reshape the question we all learned. We need to ask that question about things other than the Ten Commandments and the creeds of the church. What does this mean? And this? And this? And this? We need to shape an expanded catechism for a meaningless time.

A radical catechism, a new sense of love, Christians in touch with the physical dimensions of faith—all are necessary in order that we might communicate a meaningful hope for our culture and our age.

Making sense in our time. Widespread interest in New Age should tell us that we are not speaking to the hearts in our audience. And so my second observation is that all of us must face human despair and meaninglessness with words and signs that make sense for our time. This is especially true for preaching, a critically important aspect of the Christian response. The proclaimed word can make a difference. It is communication. David G. Buttrick raises important questions and challenges for preaching to an audience searching for meaning, and living in a media age.[18] He asks: What is your intention when you preach? When you stand in the pulpit, what is your audience awareness? Within the first two minutes, have you convinced the man in the back pew that this whole thing matters to him? It's a sexist French phrase, but "style is the man himself." What's your style? Are you dull? When people look at you preaching, what do they see? And are you always able to point beyond yourself to the meanings and loves that address the private pains that have entered the hearts of your people? People need to hear meaningful love every Sunday.

A mass faith system. Third, let's commit ourselves to a mass, rather than elite, faith system. Broad public knowledge about New Age is due in large part to its successful use of mass media. Observing this should readily teach us that we can no longer afford to ignore mass media. In a country where one fourth of the people cannot read, and another fourth do not, it is arrogant and foolish to assume that what we say in print will be communicated. We are people of the Word. But we live in an age when that word must not only be made flesh, it must be made visual so that it may dwell among us. Mainline churches need to be represented on television because that's where the people are. "For most people in the United States today, the primary source of news, information, entertainment is television. . . . By the time most of our children have completed high school, they will have spent more time with television than with their studies or with their exposure to any religious teaching."[19] Television is the primary "place" people go to get answers to their values questions! It is time, then, that the mainline religions demonstrate that religious television is not necessarily bad religion.

A corollary to this point is that we must undertake to demonstrate our lives of faith visually in congregations. As individuals, we are no longer known by our past, by our parents and who they were, because we no longer live in the established community where our extended family has lived for years, perhaps even generations. We are no longer people of the "village." Instead, we live in the "camp" communities where people are transient, newcomers are the norm, and our families are not present. We are known to one another only by our stories. And the pervasiveness of television causes us to expect to learn those stories visually through video, art, experience, symbol—but not primarily through print, which has been the principal medium of sharing since the Reformation.[20]

Technology and intimacy. Fourth, we need to deal with the dialectic between technology and intimacy. In many ways technology can pull us apart and make us less personal and even lonelier. A computer does not love us. And technology may make our lives so complex that it is hard to sort out what it does all mean. A computer does not give meaning. It only rearranges data. Still, technology can rearrange the way in which people are related to the facts of life and to each other so that we see new visions and create new relationships. Christians need to use technology, for the express purpose of making the world a more intimate and loving and meaningful place. We need to network and connect. We need constantly to emphasize access for those least likely to have it.

The power of communication. Fifth, we need to reexamine the power of communication. Thirty years ago, Hannah Arendt redefined power as communication.[21] For Arendt, power is not the forcing of one's own will on another. Power is instead the capacity to agree without coercion on a joint community action. Such power is based on clear communication. And clear communication results in action. What usually passes for power, forcing one's will, Arendt calls not power but violence. Language, speech, art, and visuals enclose the power to shape community action. In the past thirty years it has become increasingly clear that what is new about our age and time is how we communicate. And we sense at some level that communication is the power to effect change. Christians need now to reflect on how to become again the powerful communicators we were four centuries ago. The widely held idea that mainline Christian churches are "in decline" and that the New Age movement has captured the imagination of a broad audience should tell us this, above all. How can we use communication to address twentieth-century issues? We must see this as a power issue. If we communicate the faith, if we work toward uncoerced community decision that calls for joint actions, we begin to address the challenges of the New Age dynamic.

Public vs. private. Sixth, the New Age challenge calls us to address the public versus the private in our culture. What is corporate responsibility? Robert Bellah points to an individualism that is so dominant that it now threatens to destroy the fabric of our culture.[22] No wonder everyone is running around so unhappily, searching for this and that. It's hard work for every person independent of every other person and completely on her own to find her own meaning system, her individual place in the universe, her own values, and her own happiness. Yet that is what we have come to: self-help through our independent miseries. Let's get it together. In our creed we call ourselves a communion of saints. Empty, lonely, insignificant? Try community. Not the latest self-help group, but the oldest and newest and broadest community around. Do we need to reshape our churches? How often are we truly welcoming of the stranger, supportive of those going through change in their lives? The single mother who attends church with her children and is greeted by the question "Is your husband parking the car?" has reason to ask us if we understand what being a community means. It means that our old way of doing things, our comfort with ourselves, must change.

Community is also basic to good communication. Community and communication come from the same word. And the best communication of the gospel requires community. In the old East Germany, radical secularism reinforced by a hostile government resulted in a decline in biblical and theological awareness in young people. The situation is similar here, but less pronounced. At first the East German church responded to the crisis in biblical and catechetical literacy with a back-to-the-basics classroom attitude and approach. Although exposure to the tradition increased, young people still did not retain and use what they learned. Only after retreat models were used, to establish the church as a place where young people could find community together, did the subject matter. Communication of the faith requires us to be a community of faith. Unless we are vital communities, whatever else we stand for will not matter on a grand and tragic scale.

The need for depth. Finally, our sense of Christian spirituality, our art, and our symbols need to be opened to a new depth—communicated in a more profound nonlinear way so that the individual and the group or tribe are reunited in a journey of faith. The phenomena usually grouped together as New Age exhibit a richness of symbol and graphic interest and attention to symbolic meanings. Although the Christian tradition is more powerful and rich and complex in its symbolic and artistic history than any New Age faith, it often seems sterile and verbal and literal and wooden in comparison. What a tragedy! We need to touch again our spiritual depths, the power of our myths, and the richness of our symbols, and speak with them in a visual age. We need to see how our own spiritual depths and complex symbols relate to complex late-twentieth-century yearnings.

We need to reform our identity. We need to preach with power. We need to become visual. We need to stand together in community. We need to hear again the rich spirituality of our faith. We need these things now because we, like the early Christians, live in a New Age—an age when people are hungry for faith.

Jesus understood this. And so in the evening on a Sunday after his death, when the disciples were gathered and the doors were shut, the Gospel of John tells us that Jesus came into the room, stood with them, and said, "Peace be with you." Without saying more, he showed them his scars. The assembly rejoiced that the crucified Lord was resurrected. Nothing else happened. But the good teacher Jesus knew to repeat his lesson. So he said again, "Peace be with you." Then he added as a further explanation to a group that was gathered in fear, concerned with its own preservation, "As the Father has sent me, even so I send you."

The world outside may indeed be full of strange new ideas, but we are sent into it, to discover the promises being fulfilled despite the meaninglessness of our times. This is what the church can and must do. The New Age is outside our doors. Why not address the real New Age challenge, and make it possible for people to be Christian again?

3

The Former Age and the New Age: The Perennial Quest for the Spiritual Life

MORTON KELSEY

The New Age movement, diverse as it is, is largely a reaction to the dominant, rational materialistic worldview of Western culture. The thought and practice of Western Christianity have been accommodated to this materialistic point of view, and have little place for religious experiences as a way of deepening the spiritual life and giving evidence of our natural human contact with the spiritual dimension of reality. Conventional Christianity that relies on authority and reason, rather than on human experience, has become unpalatable to many modern Western religious seekers. In its most vital days the Christian community laid great emphasis on the human experience of the risen Christ and on the gifts of the Spirit, observable evidences of the spiritual dimensions' influences on our ordinary human lives.

If the traditional churches are to reach modern men and women who are no longer impressed by authority and reason alone, they need to consider more seriously the many ways in which human beings experience the divine, and then provide both a theology and a practice that facilitate religious experience.[1] Modern Christianity needs to reexamine its early and enduring traditions concerning prayer, revelation, spiritual healing, dreams, discernment of spirits, the gifts of wisdom and knowledge, the gifts of proclamation, and the experiences human beings have of eternal life. Unable to find direction in just these areas, the New Agers have looked to Eastern religions or to any other source that offers them experience of the spiritual dimension without seriously considering reality, the worldview underlying these practices.

Let us begin our attempt to understand the New Age and its relationships to traditional Christianity by examining three different ways in which human beings have viewed the world and the place of the spiritual dimension within it. We will then offer some suggestions as to how the Christian community can give people of our present age what they are seeking within the time-tested framework of its profoundly transforming religious tradition. We shall look first of all at Western materialism, then to one sophisticated strand of Eastern religion in which ultimate reality is perceived as essentially mind-soul and physical reality as a confusing illusion, and then we shall move on to the religious point of view that both the physical and spiritual worlds are real and ultimately significant. Human beings are more consistent than we ordinarily realize. What we view as important, significant, and real usually determines what we perceive and how we live our lives. What we do is better evidence of what we truly believe than what we profess with our lips.

Western Materialism

If we travel to a safe distance from Western Europe and those countries that inherit its culture, we shall find little understanding of the idea that matter alone is real. The people in China, Central Asia, rural Africa, or South America perceive the spiritual world to be as real as (or more real than) the physical world. The purpose of religion from this point of view is to help us deal with this nonphysical or spiritual reality, which can have a tremendous influence on our lives in this world, and which determines the nature of our continued existence after the body has died. We find very few places or times in history where the view is held that the tangible, earthly side of existence alone is real.

In China a small number of pure materialists emerged over the centuries, but were never taken seriously by the general public. In the Greco-Roman world, the rational materialism of Aristotle and other thinkers never took hold. However, in the seventh century Aristotle's thought became the philosophical framework for much of Islamic thought and then was passed on to Europe by Thomas Aquinas as the new and permanent view of the natural world. In order to fit this view into Christianity, he added another dimension to the ordinary, natural world: the supernatural. However, human beings had no *natural* contact with this dimension.

As Western thinkers became more secular, they began to doubt the existence of the supernatural dimension proclaimed by the church and turned their entire attention to the physical world. Thomas Hobbes was one of the first thinkers to provide an entirely materialistic view of reality. Then came the development of nineteenth-century science and its tremendous discoveries. The majority of these scientists believed that matter consisted of ninety-some elements: little hard, round balls that bounced against each other in a random way, according to Isaac Newton, to produce all the multiplicity of things we find within the world. At one point life developed spontaneously and by chance, and then through the survival of the fittest emerged into the higher animals and finally evolved into rational human beings. What we are and what we do were viewed as simply the result of blind forces, and understanding them was merely a mechanical problem "depending entirely on the magnitude and direction of producing causes."[2] Both behaviorist and biomedical treatment of psychological problems operate on these assumptions. Skinner called the human personality the ghost in the box, and biomedical practice often tries to handle all emotional problems by drugs that alter the chemical imbalance or physical structure of the brain. I have treated the development of the materialistic worldview at greater length in my book *Encounter with God*.

Let us diagram this point of view, the idea that human beings are nothing but the mechanical result of physical particles, whether they are atoms or quarks.

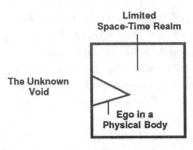

FIGURE 3.1

Within this point of view, all talk of the human spirit lasting beyond death or of a spiritual dimension of reality is pure nonsense. The Jeffersonian New Testament eliminates all the healings, spiritual entities, prayer, God, and the ideas of incarnation and resurrection, retaining only the moral teachings of Jesus. From within this worldview, Thomas Jefferson has the proper understanding of the New Testament. But, as I have demonstrated in *Encounter with God,* some 49 percent of the New Testament texts assume a spiritual reality, or "stupid superstition." Two schools of thought, however, both very influential in modern theological circles, consider that these passages have no significance today: The dispensationalist treatment of the New Testament text states that these supernatural occurrences occurred through God's waiving natural law in order to get the church established, and then were withdrawn. The rational materialists hold that these strange things never happened in the first place. When I was ten years old I read the Acts of the Apostles. It was as exciting as *The Wizard of Oz.* I knew that my father viewed the Bible as only a guide to morality. So I asked my mother, who had been reared in the dispensationalist tradition, why Christians didn't do what the apostles did. I received the answer, "God let those things happen just to get the church started and then took away those gifts." I put the book down and didn't look at it again until I went to see if I could find meaning in seminary for the morass of agnostic materialism in which I had been raised and trained.

Western culture gave birth to the first predominantly materialistic society in which inorganic matter was seen as the final and only reality. The wars and conquests of this society have not been totally benign; Western society has spawned two of the most devastating human conflicts that the world has known. The Nazi ideology that sprang out of it would have delighted the Marquis de Sade. A growing counterculture has come to doubt the basic materialism of Western thought. In addition to this disillusionment, increasing contacts have been made with Eastern religions that offer a totally different view of reality and practices that give access to experiences other than those of the five senses.

The best of modern science has rejected the view of nineteenth-century science and confesses that it knows very little about the ultimate nature of matter, and what it does know is painfully paradoxi-cal. Einstein showed that Newton's laws apply only to a small segment of reality and not to the very large or very small. Heisenberg, one of the greatest physicists of all time, has shown that by observing matter we change it and will never know exactly what it is. He writes in *Physics and Philosophy* that science has become so skeptical it has even become skeptical of its own skepticism. He also states that the highly defined works of physics have all changed their meanings in our times and that the natural words like soul, spirit, and God may have closer connection with reality than the words of physics. Gödel has demonstrated that even mathematics is not certain and computers can spit out entirely irrelevant answers. Human logic always needs the confirmation of experience before we can be sure of its conclusions.

The New Biology, by Agros and Stanciu, shows that Darwin's premise about the struggle for survival of the fittest is only one side of the story, and that purpose may well be built into the DNA. In the field of medicine we find the statement that faith may be as specific a remedy for some diseases as penicillin is for some pneumonias. Few students of psychology are entering graduate programs for advanced degrees in behaviorist psychology. Transpersonal psychol-ogy seems more relevant to them. Andrew Greeley has given data in *The Sociology of the Paranormal: A Reconnaissance* that 39 percent of his carefully selected random sample reported that they had had overwhelming religious experiences, and a larger number reported experiences of extrasensory perception. In a post-test recheck he discovered that half of those who had had these religious experiences were so intimidated by their materialistic culture that they had never told anyone of their experience before being asked the question by those doing the survey. The last person to whom they would tell such experiences would be a professional religious person, because they didn't believe in such things anymore.

The materialistic view of reality is no longer the most modern to a sophisticated Western understanding of reality. In addressing the American Psychological Association in 1955, Robert Oppenheimer pleaded with the largely behavioristic audience not to base their psychology on a nineteenth-century view of physics which modern physics had abandoned. The full evidence suggests that the ultimate nature of matter is a mystery and cannot be explained from the old mechanistic, materialistic view. *That view can only be held by faith;* the shoe is on the other foot. And yet few theologians in our day know that science has changed its point of view, and most modern academic theology is still written from within the rational materialistic worldview and so has little place for facilitating religious *experience*.

From the materialistic stance, the spiritual quest is at best a dead-end street and at worst illusion and self-deception. The result is that few mainline churches offer prayer groups in which people can meet to discuss their spiritual experience and pray together; have ongoing classes in how we can pray and meditate, and how we can care for one another; make available regular healing services, or are open to the full range of the gifts of the Spirit. And yet all these practices were part of the life of the vital early Christian community and have continued without interruption within the Eastern Orthodox tradition right down to the present time. Seeking the direct experience of the spiritual domain and not finding it in the traditional churches, many people are turning to New Age and Eastern religious groups for spiritual guidance. One cannot understand New Age religion without an understanding of Eastern religion.

The Religions of India

Few Westerners have much knowledge of the depth and wisdom of the religions of India. We cannot understand the universal, perennial, spiritual quest unless we survey the great religions that sprang from the culture of that great subcontinent. These religions start with premises quite different from the Western religions to which we are accustomed. They begin with ideas diametrically opposed to the materialism of the West. However, the religious leaders of India have been pondering the nature of the spiritual world and the meaning of life for four thousand years. They have probed this dimension of reality with the same intensity that Western scientists in the last two centuries have delved into the nature of the material world. Dating back two thousand years before the time of Christ, the Vedas and Upanishads have recorded the spiritual aspirations of the people and offered instructions on the journey to spiritual fulfillment.

Out of this tradition has developed a culture in which the most honored people and the highest caste are the Brahmans, the religious seers, who came closest to understanding reality. This society has probably lasted longer without significant change than any other human society. The religion of Hinduism has a limitless number of gods and goddesses and will welcome the gods of other religions into its pantheon; Jesus and Allah are both welcomed and embraced. Gandhi, probably the best-known religious figure of our century, is the product of this tradition. Hare Krishna and transcendental meditation are both missions of this tradition to the West, although somewhat superficial examples of the real depth of Hindu religious practice. Surveys show that over 10 percent of the American public have had contact with TM. Hinduism spread through Southeast Asia and is still firmly entrenched in Bali, where I experienced its vitality a few years ago.

What are the basic ideas of this religion that directly or indirectly (through Buddhism) has touched the lives of half the world's population? First of all is the belief that beneath our ordinary personalities lies our true being, atman, and that this is identical with Brahma (God, the divine, the ultimately holy). The full meaning of life is discovered as people experience this identity and are freed from the chain of reincarnations that are inevitable until we come to this knowledge and experience. The second basic premise follows from the first. Since the goal of our lives is the recognition of one's timeless reality, history and the individual life in this material world have little ultimate significance. Ordinary experience is part of the web of maya (illusion) that keeps us from realizing our true identity. Accounts of human lives, biography or autobiography, are irrelevant. (It must be noted that one of the paths to enlightenment, the pathway of love or bhakti-yoga, sees love and caring for other human beings as the best way of coming to enlightenment, a good example of the inclusive framework of Hinduism.)

The third core idea is the teaching that four different disciplines (yogas) lead to true self-realization. The first is rigorous intellectual understanding (jnana-yoga), through which one comes to know that only atman is real and is identical with Brahma. The second is the way of love. Indeed many Hindus see Jesus as a particularly luminous expression of bhakti-yoga. From this point of view, God is not so much to be merged with as adored. And we grow and develop as we love all those creatures who carry atman within them, no matter how depraved they seem. Karma-yoga is the third discipline that leads to the goal of life, the use of work as a discipline of growth. People do not have to leave the world; they can live within it and become more and more detached until they reach fulfillment. Raja-yoga offers the fourth and the best-known discipline for coming to enlightenment. This discipline consists in the deliberate seeking of experiences of one's oneness with Brahma. Students on this path learn first of all to control the body and then the mind and spirit. This arduous pathway leads to the experience of samadhi, where subject and object merge. This way is eloquently described in the Hindu scripture Bhagavad Gita. It is little wonder that Westerners fleeing from the stifling materialism of the West and looking for experience are drawn to this discipline. These practices require constant effort and the help of one who has already mastered them (a guru). They also require the adoption and understanding of the Hindu view of reality.[3]

Buddha was born around 560 B.C. in northern India. At that time Hinduism had lost its soul. Religious leaders had abandoned their responsibilities, and elaborate ceremonials had taken the place of transforming worship. Buddha saw the suffering of humankind and offered a religious method for transcending the agony of existence. Buddha was raised in a protected environment, the son of a king. When he came to know the reality of the world outside the palace—a world of poverty, misery, sickness, infirmity, and death—he determined to find a way to relieve the suffering of humankind. After years of searching, he came to enlightenment sitting under a bo tree. His very title, Buddha, means the one who is awake. He immediately set out to share with human beings of every caste and description the secret of enlightenment that he had discovered, a secret that could bring people to the final reality that transcends our suffering and gives timeless bliss! Until he died in his eighties, Buddha traveled over most of India, sharing his good news. Along with Jesus the Christ, Buddha is the most widely known religious leader in our world.

Siddhartha Gautama, the Buddha, was brought up within the traditions of Hinduism and studied and became very skilled in raja-yoga. His essential outlook on life and reality was that of Hinduism, but Buddha was a reformer and taught that the endless speculation about the nature of reality and involved ceremonial ritual were keeping human beings from the core problem of life, overcoming human suffering. The way he offered was a purified and simplified Hinduism similar to the reformed version of Protestant Christianity.

This path was a discipline by which humans first of all see that reality in its essence is good and that our misunderstanding of it is what causes the disaster of human existence. One well-known Buddhist text begins with these words: "All we are is the result of what we have thought."[4]

The goal of this practice is achieving or coming into nirvana. Characteristically, Buddha never described the nature of this goal. He avoided all religious speculation. Whatever else can be said about this state of being, in it all suffering is extinguished. Some interpreters describe it as a state of bliss similar to atman's realizing identity with Brahma. In nirvana people are relieved of the burden of endless reincarnation, although Buddha never spoke with certainty about reincarnation. At this point the person who is truly enlightened (awake) can step over into nirvana and disappear from this vale of suffering, or this person can forgo that bliss and return to teach and guide people toward their awakening. Buddha taught the path to nirvana and yet lived the way of the bodhisattvas, those who returned with mercy and compassion to help eliminate human misery.

The psychiatrist C. G. Jung wrote that religious experience is a necessary aspect of the mature life. He was much impressed with the religions of Asia, but he warned Westerners that they could achieve the results promised by these religions only as they steeped themselves deeply in the basic worldview of the East and followed their vigorous practices. Those who try to get a quick fix through Eastern religions and do not understand the training and disciplines required in them can run into dangerous psychological difficulty. Some adherents of the New Age movement take on Eastern thoughts without Eastern discipline. Jung believed that Western women and men do better to seek religious experience within the Western worldview that we are about to present. However, the East offers an attractive and consistent religious way.

The Eastern religious view that has made the greatest impact on the West and the New Age movement is its most distinctive view. In this view God is seen as the only true reality and everything is, in the last analysis, in perfect harmony, all life ruled by the perfect justice of the law of karma. Evil and suffering are the result of misunderstanding the ultimate nature of ourselves and reality or the inevitable consequence of our self-centered desire, which throws us off balance. Evil has no objective spiritual reality in itself. This view can be diagramed in the following way:

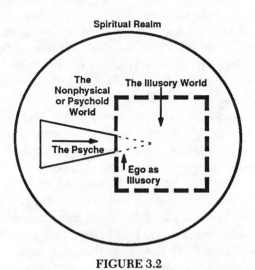

FIGURE 3.2

44

How important it is to remember that the religious seeking of India contains many different points of view! The view that we have diagramed is just one strand of the metaphysical and religious thought and practice of India. The classical Hindu pantheism and belief that human experience is illusion has, however, arisen spontaneously in the West in Mary Baker Eddy's *Science and Health,* and more recently in *The Course in Miracles.* This view underlies much of New Age practice and theory.

Another View of Reality and the New Age

There is still another way of looking at basic reality. Judaism, Christianity, and Islam spring out of this other worldview. In it, both the physical world and the spiritual world are real and both are created by the Divine, who cares about what goes on in human lives and in history. The Holy manifests itself in both a real spiritual and a real material dimension of reality. Let us diagram this point of view that brings together the two previous diagrams:

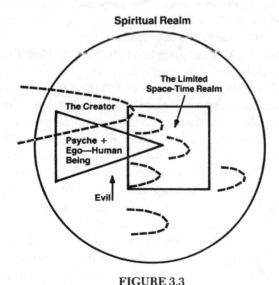

FIGURE 3.3

Judaism

Judaism has few followers compared to the other great religions of humankind, but its history stretches back nearly four thousand years and its traditions have been continuous. In addition, Christianity has emerged from the bosom of Judaism and cannot be understood without reference to its Jewish origins. The basic early traditions of Jewish scripture were incorporated into Christianity as the Old Testament, and Christians have often referred to themselves as the New Israel. Islam, also, has been deeply influenced by Judaism, and the Islamic scriptures, the Koran, retell much Hebrew history. The prophet Muhammad also saw his people as descendants of the Jewish patriarch Abraham.

What is the genius of Judaism? The Hebrews saw themselves as a people who had been called by God to be the chosen people. God created both the heavens (having both a spiritual and physical connotation) and the earth and saw that they were *good*. This God called Abraham to become the father of a new people who were to be a holy people and live out a new way of relating to the Divine. Their God was holy and could not be pictured in any way; Yahweh cared for the people as a mother for her children. Yahweh saved them in their escape from Egypt by intervening and rolling back the waters of the Red Sea. God then gave them their law; and, in spite of their faithlessness, God led them into Palestine, the Holy Land, the promised land that was to be their home.

Yahweh raised up leaders for them, but the people did not show the compassion to one another that God showed to them. God then raised up prophets who foretold disaster as well as the message of God's righteousness and love. These prophets speaking and writing in the eighth century B.C. were the first known religious leaders to bind together inextricably the holy and the moral, ultimate power and loving-kindness. The prophets saw the dissolution of the Jewish kingdom as the result of the people's disobedience. However, Yahweh did not forsake his people even then, but brought them back from exile in Babylon and reestablished their political autonomy, until their land was conquered and destroyed by the Romans and the Jewish people were dispersed throughout the Roman world.

Yet they maintained their identity until they returned to Palestine after World War II to establish the modern Jewish state. For eighteen hundred years, in the face of persecution and the holocaust (in which a third of the number perished), the Jewish nation maintained its identity without a homeland.

Judaism is a religion of a book, the Bible. It was not followed literally, but interpreted and reinterpreted through the centuries. Two other great bodies of religious literature grew up during this time—the Talmud, with comments on and interpretations of the Torah, or law, and the Midrashim, which gave explanations of all aspects of life by the revered leaders of Judaism. Once I was lecturing on the subject of healing and said that Judaism laid no emphasis on healing. A rabbi present spoke out: "You are right that the Old Testament has little place for healing, but remember that only Christian fundamentalists take that book literally. Jews interpret it through the Talmud and the Midrashim." Rabbi Bruce Adams, writing on the subject of sexual orientation, stated this same attitude toward scripture as well as I have seen it expressed: "When we study Scripture, we believe that more important than what the Bible says literally, is what it stands for in principle, based on a deeper understanding of the totality of revelation."[5] Judaism has continued to grow and adapt to a changing world.

Judaism stands for monotheism, the equality of human beings, open inquiry, compassion, the meaningfulness of history, and God's continuing revelation and action within the historical context. Prayer, continuance of historical rituals, and a sense of being a chosen people have enabled the Jews to remain faithful to the God who has brought them through trials and persecutions. Three of the best-known names in our time, Marx, Freud, and Einstein, bear witness to the vitality of the Jewish people. One Jewish scholar, Pinchas Lapide, writes in *The Resurrection of Jesus: A Jewish Perspective* that of course Jesus was raised from the dead, because you cannot account for the Christian church without that event. He then states that he sees Christianity as the Jewish mission to the Gentiles.

Christianity

Christianity picks up and heightens God's interest and involvement in human history. A group of broken and disillusioned disciples reeling from the impact of the brutal crucifixion of their leader were suddenly transformed. These Galilean hillbillies, as Pinchas Lapide calls them, were transformed by the resurrection and healing presence of their risen master. The experience of the risen Jesus meant to them that evil and death had been defeated. There was nothing left to fear, and with a joy that was almost unknown in the ancient world they went out to spread the good news that God had entered the world, had put off the majesty of the Divine, and had taken the status of a slave, being born as a human being. Jesus then humbled himself, obediently accepting even death, death on a cross! Because of this, God glorified him in the resurrection so that all would know that Jesus is the visible human expression of God and that evil and death were conquered (Phil. 2:6–8). Only after this experience did the disciples realize the true nature of the One whom they had been following.

The infinitely loving Holy One had entered history to seek out all human beings and draw them into the kingdom of heaven. Jesus began his ministry proclaiming: "The kingdom of God is at hand." The resurrection was the confirmation of that message. Jesus spoke of God as Abba, a word meaning *daddy* or *papa,* a familiarity unthinkable to Jewish leaders at that time. In his teaching on prayer, he taught that this loving God could be addressed as a child speaks to a loving father. Jesus told the story of a son who left home and squandered his share of the family property only to be received back into the father's embrace and showered with gifts and a feast. Jesus was stating that God was like that father. In the resurrection Jesus lived that story. The crucifixion-resurrection affirmed that evil was indeed real, and at the same time that evil was not an essential part of reality: it had no place in eternal life.

One scholar has estimated that three-fifths of the Roman world into which Jesus was born were slaves or had no real freedom. To people in this condition, the idea that the ultimate nature of reality could be a God like the one Jesus described and exemplified was unbelievably good news. The message spread like wildfire. Those attracted to the new religion had to spend an arduous training period of three years to be admitted into full Christian fellowship and be allowed to share in the sacrament of Eucharist (thanksgiving), in which they touched and were fed with the very life of the risen Christ. The Roman emperors tried to stamp out the Christian fellowship because the first allegiance of this people was to their God and not to the Empire. They continued faithful to their fellowship and daily worship at Eucharists in hidden places, in spite of the consequences. If a Christian man was found at such services, he might be tortured and slain in the arena, his wife and children could be sold into slavery, and his property confiscated and given to the informer who reported his religious practice. Still, in less than three hundred years, this religion had attracted nearly half the population of the Empire, and then became the established religion of the Greco-Roman world.

Part of the sense of joy that filled the Christian fellowship came from the individual Christians' being filled with the Holy Spirit and becoming instruments of empowered love. They expressed it in these words: "Jesus became what we are in order that we might become what he is." They believed that they really met Abba and the risen Jesus in their prayer and Eucharist. These experiences were so real to them that they did not distinguish clearly between those revelations received through tradition and those they experienced in the Spirit. Both were recorded in scripture, and this ambiguity causes problems for biblical critics who view only the historical statements as valuable. The early Christians also believed that God spoke in dreams and visions that came spontaneously and unsought. All the major leaders of the vital early church believed that God was constantly reaching out to human beings to give direction and love. One early Christian leader wrote that God only spoke in visions to those who were too stubborn to listen to their dreams.[6]

Nearly as many verses of the four Gospels are devoted to Jesus' healing ministry as to his teaching. In the Acts of the Apostles, we find the disciples healing the same sicknesses of the mind, soul, and body whose healings are attributed to Jesus. Their master commissioned them to preach, teach, and heal, and they did so. Paul wrote in his epistle to the Romans that he preached the gospel by words and deeds, with signs and wonders, by the power of God's Spirit (Rom. 15:18–19). In *Psychology, Medicine and Christian Healing* I have described how central this ministry was to the life of the growing church. Nearly all the leaders of the church through the first five centuries of the church's life spoke of this ministry and of their involvement in it. In the Eastern Orthodox Church this tradition and practice has never ceased. In its most vital periods, the Christian church has been a healing community. This healing aspect of religion has been another interest of the New Age movement.

Jesus believed that human beings are in touch not only with a physical reality, but with a spiritual one as well, and the creative and destructive spirits are found in both. Human beings need to learn how to invoke the angelic and avoid the demonic, and this requires the gift of discernment. Christians through the power of the Holy Spirit can have gifts of knowing and understanding of both physical and spiritual dimensions of reality that far surpass the knowledge provided by the five senses. And then there are gifts of ecstatic speech and of prophecy, through which the Spirit speaks to Christians and through them to those around them.

The pagans watched the Christians and said in amazement: "Look how they love one another." The Christian community lived the kind of love that Jesus revealed as the essential nature of God. All were welcomed, slave and free, rich and poor, the sick and the broken. The first free hospitals for the care of the sick were founded. This spirit of care and concern for others met the needs of the isolated and oppressed people of that world. The Christian community expressed the love for which human beings were hungering then as they are now.

As the crowds came to watch the Christians die in the arenas throughout the Empire, they could hardly believe their eyes. The Christians were so certain about life after death, of their entrance into eternal life and the kingdom of heaven, that they not only died bravely, they died with joy. They had already tasted something of the kingdom of heaven for which they prayed in the words Jesus had given them. They had a God who had died on a cross and was resurrected, a God who would bring them through death to an infinitely better life than one could find in this mortal, earthly world. The blood of the martyrs was indeed the seed of the church.

Unfortunately, the Christian community did not retain this vitality. Once it became the state religion, it became involved with affairs of the Empire and in hairsplitting theological discussions. Then with the mass baptisms of pagan barbarians following the conversion of their kings, Christianity in the West became more of an identity than a transforming experience. The vital experience of the loving God and the hope, love, joy, and healing power that characterized the ordinary early Christian occasionally appeared in individuals who were called saints. But Christianity in the West entered a dark era.

Islam

In the seventh century of the Christian era, a new major religion emerged among the Semitic people of desert Arabia. A great religious leader was inspired by the spirit of Allah, the only God. The words that came to him in a trance were written down and are the religious core of what became a new religion of a book, the Koran. It is difficult to explain how an unlettered person with no literary background could have produced a work of such majesty and poetic beauty. Among Muslims the book may not be used in translation, as it loses its almost mystical power.

Although the followers of the many gods of Mecca sought desperately to disparage and destroy Muhammad and his teaching, this new leader finally gained the allegiance of his countrymen and became the religious and secular leader of the Arab people. United by incredible religious fervor, these people conquered much of the world and established an Arab empire that stretched from China to Western Africa and Spain. A brilliant and sophisticated civilization developed, equal to any in the tenth and eleventh centuries A.D.

This religion is known by its adherents as Islam. The word from which this name is taken is the *salām,* which means both peace and surrender. The goal of the followers of this religion is to develop "the perfect peace that comes when our lives are surrendered to God."

The basic theological views about God, human beings, creation, and judgment are very similar to those of Judaism and Christianity.

The Muslim, the follower of Islam, is follower of the straight path, not the devious one. Islam is a masterpiece of simplicity and clarity. The Five Pillars of Islam sketch clearly the nature of this faith. The first pillar is the creed of Islam: There is no God but Allah and Muhammad is his prophet. This faith, like Judaism, stresses strict monotheism. Because Muhammad's sayings in the Koran are seen as the final and total revelation of God, nothing may be added to or subtracted from this book. The second pillar is the necessity of constancy in prayer, in which the faithful turn five times a day toward Mecca, bowing to the ground and praying in praise and supplication to Allah. This practice keeps God constantly before the attention of the Muslim. The third pillar is that of giving 2.5 percent of one's income *and property* for the poor and disadvantaged each year. The fourth pillar is the observance of fasting during the month of Ramadan, to give thanks for two of the most important events in the life of the prophet. The last pillar is the requirement that all able-bodied Muslims who are financially able make a pilgrimage to Mecca once in their lifetime.

In addition to these basic laws, Muhammad provided rules and regulations to cover every detail of life. Although his standards are different from those of Western culture, the prophet brought a new level of religion and civilization to the people of Arabia and the Muslim world. For those who wish a clear and simple religious faith in which few questions remain about the details of life and belief, Islam offers a clear way. There are many in our present age who are seeking just this kind of religion. We see it in the rise of Christian fundamentalism. Islam may be the fastest-growing religion at the end of the twentieth century just because it offers complete authority and consistency. We find liberal, mystical, and literal interpretations of Islamic faith, just as we do in Judaism and Christianity.

The New Age

As we survey the overall religious climate of the West in the latter part of the twentieth century, two developments are striking.

The first is the growing number of people who are seeking religious security and certainty in the literalism of fundamentalism. From its beginning in the middle of the nineteenth century, this movement has been an attempt to find a secure religious framework in the midst of the growing agnostic rational materialism of Western culture, which has no place for any significant religion. By strict and literal interpretation of a book that gives final knowledge of religious reality and life, people can hang on to their religious belief. The early Pentecostal movement emerged from this background, but stressed, in addition, the experience of the Holy Spirit. Most Pentecostal churches withdrew from secular society and demanded that their members withdraw from contacts with the movies, plays, and other expressions of materialistic culture. This attitude is similar to Islam's emphasis on the book and not unlike the fundamentalist movement throughout Islam.

In more recent years, the so-called New Age movement has arisen as another reaction to the agnostic materialism of society which has filtered into church life and theology. Most of the major denominations have had little place for religious experience or the *experience* of a spiritual dimension of reality. Dr. C. Peter Wagner, professor of missions at Fuller Theological Seminary, has pointed out that most Christian missions have failed because the missionaries have been more intent on Westernizing third-world people than in Christianizing them. Early Christianity was a religion of experience as well as of creed. Men and women need to be empowered by the Spirit if they are to live the radical Christian ethic of prayer and love.

The interest of the New Age movement has not been for security, but for experience of the nonphysical dimension of reality. It is not so much new (except that it is new for Western culture), but is rather an eclectic group of practices from different ancient world religions, particularly those of India. We find a keen interest in prayer and meditation as a way to religious experience and knowledge, in dreams as another avenue revealing the spiritual dimension, in channeling (being instruments of the spirit world, speaking through human beings), in afterlife (often understood as reincarnation), in metaphysical speculation, healing by religious or psychic means, in extrasensory perception, in the ability of mind to create reality, and an almost total avoidance of the problem of evil.

Prayer and meditation have been an essential part of nearly all the great religious traditions. However, in recent years these practices have not been an integral part of Christian teaching, except in the monastic tradition. Even after seminary training, I had no knowledge of these practices. I learned the practice of using Christian images in meditation only as I came to study the theory and methods of C. G. Jung. I realized later that imageless meditation has been a strand of Christian tradition and is now well presented in the writing of Basil Pennington and others. I am married to one for whom this imageless (apophatic) method is very meaningful. Similar practices of prayer are found in Buddhism and Hinduism. Even though several sociological surveys have revealed that Christians desire instruction in prayer more than any other teachings, few mainline churches provide ongoing classes in prayer or prayer groups in which people can talk about their prayer life and pray together. These methods of prayer were used in the early Christian churches, kept alive in monasticism, and renewed during the Reformation. The dream as the natural altered state of consciousness has been valued in all religious traditions that value images. I have shown in my book *God, Dreams and Revelation* that throughout the history of the churches, dreams have been considered one way by which God communicates with human beings and that we would do well to take them very seriously. A recent book by Joel Covitz, *Visions of the Night,* reveals the continuing development of the same tradition within Judaism.

Channeling is really a form of extrasensory perception, in which an open individual becomes a channel through which a spiritual entity speaks from beyond the borders of the individual psyche. This practice was well known in the church, the prophets being those who spoke God's message and words. Tongue speaking was seen as a language of the Spirit that was unintelligible to the speaker. These states have much in common with dreaming. The dreamer becomes a stage upon which something other than the conscious ego stages a drama. The important question in channeling is what spirit is speaking in these experiences. Since few of those who use New Age methods believe in the reality of evil, little attempt is made to discern whether the reality contacted is creative or destructive. Although most major religions teach that contact with a spiritual world is possible, they are very cautious in evaluating these experiences. The problem of evil is avoided in most New Age groups. In *The Christian and the Supernatural,* I have shown that all of us have some capacity for extrasensory perception. ESP is not evil in itself, but like any gift or capacity this one can be used for good or evil. In my experience, church choirs have been more a source of divisiveness than tongue-speaking groups. We don't abolish them for this reason.

Buddha noted that human beings were universally faced with several problems that caused great sufferings—sickness and old age, poverty, and death. The major religions offer ways of dealing with these human concerns. Sickness can be psychological or physical. However, nothing can cause despair and physical disease more than fear and hopelessness. Old age often brings infirmity and crippling. Death casts us into the unknown. Buddha offered detachment as a solution to human misery. Hindu and Chinese religions offer a psychoreligious theory and practice of healing. Christianity, as we have seen, was viewed in the Greco-Roman world as basically a religion of healing. Christianity sees the healer as an instrument of the creative divine Spirit. In this view, the healer's capacity to heal depends more on that individual's closeness to God than in specific knowledge of the body or its spiritual-psychological nature. The New Age is much involved with the practice of psychospiritual healing. However, the Christian tradition of healing is so little practiced within the churches that most followers of the New Age movement have turned to Chinese or Hindu practices to find methods of healing. And yet seemingly impossible cures have taken place in Lourdes and elsewhere by Christian healers.

From the point of view of materialism, mind equals brain. When the brain ceases to function at death, the personality is simply snuffed out. It is difficult for most people to face extinction, particularly if life has been traumatic and tragic. Sir James Frazer, the great anthropologist, in his monumental study of immortality notes the universal conviction of all "savage" people that continuance of life beyond death is no more doubted than their present existence. In a recent book edited by Gary Moore, *What Survives? Contemporary Explorations of Life After Death,*[7] the subject of life after death is examined in depth. However, in this "New Consciousness Reader" no mention is made of the vivid Christian belief in our vision of the kingdom of heaven. And yet this conviction was visible in a fearlessness of Christians in the face of torture and death that stunned the ancient Western world.

Most people in the New Age turn to the East for their views of human survival after death. In spite of the fact that in these religions reincarnation is something to escape in order to find bliss or nirvana, reincarnation is seen by many New Agers as a satisfactory means of survival. Little or no attention is paid to the Judaic, Christian, or Muslim belief in a spiritual dimension of reality into which human beings can pass at death. How few sermons are heard, and how few classes are presented, on the Christian vision of the nature of the kingdom of heaven that we taste in this life and will know more fully after death! John Sanford has recently published a definitive book entitled *Soul Journey: A Jungian Analyst Looks at Reincarnation,* showing that there is no evidence for early Christian belief in reincarnation.[8]

Christianity has made caring for all human beings more central to its practice than has any other world religion. Jesus says that we become his followers only as we love one another as he has loved us. Paul writes that without genuine caring and love, all our spiritual efforts are in vain. True love that Christians showed for one another was the only other feature of their lives that impressed pagans as much as their fearlessness before agony and death.

Concluding Suggestions

How can the Christian community meet the religious needs of modern men and women pointed up by the New Age—needs that are not now being met by most Christian churches? We conclude with several suggestions that can meet these religious needs.

First of all, the Christian community needs to present in sermon and through adult education the *fact* of the resurrection of

Jesus and the effect that it had on his followers. Something happened that transformed these human beings and still has the same power of transformation in the lives of people today.

In order for people to believe in the teachings and the resurrection of Jesus, people of the West must be offered an alternative worldview to the prevailing materialism of our times. They also need to see that a worldview exists that provides for both the spiritual and the physical reality created by God; Eastern idealism is not the only alternative.

People do not learn to deal with the infinitely profound depth of God and the spiritual world all by themselves. We don't put students in a classroom and tell them to come up with differential and integral calculus. They need to be taught. Each church needs to provide classes in forms of prayer. This is only possible if seminaries are training pastors in prayer, contemplation and meditation, and group process.

In addition, each Christian fellowship needs to provide prayer groups led by informed Christians in which people can share their spiritual lives and religious experiences and pray together. These informal prayer groups will give life and body to formal preaching and sacramental services of the church.

Phillips Brooks is reported to have said, "Be kind, for everyone is bearing a heavy burden." Hurting people need the healing mercy and love of God in their spiritual, psychological, and physical pain. Classes need to be provided that show the reality of the church as a healing, listening, and loving community. It is not easy for us to love one another. Regular healing services give evidence that we care about all kinds of human suffering and reach out to human need. Reaching out to the poor and broken is another evidence of love in action. When people meet to learn how to listen and to love, they will find that they need the gifts of the Spirit if they are to make progress toward that goal. We cannot love those we have not learned to listen to.[9]

Jesus presents a magnificent view of the kingdom of heaven in the Beatitudes. The beggars in spirit, the mourning, the humble, the seeking, the single-minded, the merciful, the peacemakers, and the persecuted will all find a place in the kingdom. There they will find new life, be comforted, made inheritors of earth, have their deepest seeking satisfied, receive mercy, see God, and as children of God carry on heavenly work and play heavenly games. This is the goal that Jesus sets before us, and it needs to be preached and taught and lived again and again. How few sermons or classes deal with the kingdom of heaven, here and in eternity!

One of the problems of the church is that little *experiential* learning is provided for adults who can then pass this knowledge on to their families and those around them. The church has nothing to fear from the New Age when it preaches, teaches, and heals, when it brings the good news of Christianity by example and with power to seeking, hurting, hungry human beings.[10] Adult Christians need to continue to learn and grow if they are to bring the good news of transformation and eternal life into our broken world. The New Age practices point up areas of human need with which Christianity can deal with greater depth and wisdom than any other group. The practice of vital apostolic Christianity can meet all our needs as it did those of the chaotic Greek and Roman world. We need to get back to our powerful Christian roots and deal with all aspects of our confused human lives.

4

The New Age:
Historical and
Metaphysical Foundations

GLENN A. OLDS

Leibniz once wisely said, "We are usually right in what we affirm and wrong in what we deny." The modern era, conditioned by Cartesian doubt, *dubito ergo sum,* easily rationalized *cogito ergo sum* into a "scientific" method become messiah, and it could be characterized by a negative universal, negating anything not conforming to the method. Nothing that cannot be observed, confirmed by controlled experiment, or proved by formal logic can be known or—taken ultimately seriously or ironically and finally—be real. This reductionistic perspective, initially a tentative method dealing with the external world and sustained by a flowering empirical and mathematical model, seemed so successful in its easy extension to the personal and theological that it was almost as innocent and unsuspecting as it was consequential.

As the British historian F. Edward Hulme observed, epochs in human history may be characterized not by what they look *at* but rather by what they look *through* in viewing everything else. This modern philosophic and cultural mind-set, like old-fashioned blinders for horses to prevent them from seeing anything but the road before them, gave a penetrating view of a special slice of reality, but, alas, blinded and sterilized, seeing almost nothing else. In spite of poetic, romantic, existential, and theological protest along the way, the slow conspiracy of this sweeping denial of the importance and validity of anything beyond its captive methodology has essentially shaped our modern era, with enormous consequences for the search for meaning and spirituality.

The inhibiting seeds of skepticism, so innocently sown, like ancient acid have eaten away the foundations of faith and called into question the classical assumption of the West; for example:

— The superanimality of the human (more human than animal)
— The subordination of nature (nature depends on more than itself for its meaning and cosmic status)
— The objectivity of value (our judgments of value tell us something about what is ultimately real)

Sustained as the enduring legacy of the Greek, Roman, and biblical cultures of the West, synthesized by Aquinas, and providing a dependable base for the cultural evolution of the West, these assumptions were only slowly eroded and then inverted in modern times. The frequently unvoiced credo of our modern methodology reverses this classical perspective. Its reductionist logic issues in the paradoxical affirmations of our time, perverting the perspective of faith; for example:

— The animality of humans (that humans are only animals and are to be read backward and downward, and not forward and upward)
— The priority of nature (affirms the primacy of the objective natural world over all subjective domain, and rejects its subordination to any larger order of meaning or design)
— The subjectivity of value (reducing all objective value, claims of value, the good, or God, to relative transient and subjective grounds)

This stubbornly subtle and increasingly self-conscious outlook only slowly and successfully eroded, challenged, and eventually substituted for the spiritual ground and outlook of the West its views of God, the good, and the self. Signs could be seen in the beginning and continuously in early scientific challenge of Christian cosmology and orthodoxy, authenticating the inwardly subjective in the rise and role of secular psychology, in varieties of existential systems, popularization of Eastern spiritual traditions, and, most recently, in the crumbling of the outer forms of Christian orthodoxy in authority and practice.[1]

This challenged and changing climate has created a spiritual vacuum within which new (and not-so-new) spiritual forces have begun to appear. It is an inevitable consequence of challenge to the basic assumption of the age, its secular orthodoxy, limited methodology, and implications for knowledge and faith.

The excitement and yeasty ferment of this time and condition are what the New Age spirituality and movements are all about. They appear within traditional Christian theology and practice, between Christian perspectives and other authentic religious traditions East and West, and within secular orthodoxy, making room for neglected aspects of the self, value, and the Divine. And, more recently, synergistic, synchronic, and integrative holistic efforts to embrace and transcend both classical and contemporary scientific views reach toward a fresh third-millennium perspective adequate to the growing knowledge of the *intimate, ultimate,* and *inclusive* dimensions of our human and cosmic venture.

Failure to understand the bankruptcy of modern secular assumptions, the context and significance of this restless and resilient feature of our modern times, has tempted every religious tradition to reassert its authority and orthodoxy, and sometimes almost fiercely, resistively, defensively, and exclusively. This ferment, frequently fed by fear and fanaticism, collides daily, if gallantly, with perennially renewing strands of not-so-orthodox Christian traditions and newly emerging perspectives. They appear in shifts in scientific orthodoxy, occult and metaphysical traditions gaining new vitality, Westernized accommodations of Eastern tradition, new legitimacy for myth and metaphor, depth and transpersonal psychology, and an emerging "Aquarian conspiracy," to use Marilyn Ferguson's trenchant phrase from her pacesetting book to describe this network of *new forms of spirituality* (my terms and emphases).[2]

Clues to the source and vitality of these movements can be seen against the background I can only sketch in this brief chapter. More formidable and comprehensive studies abound[3] on this emerging crisis of culture, suggested by my little volume *The Christian Corrective* as early as 1951.[4] Centers of interest and influence that shape the New Age spirituality are, sequentially:

— Innovations of the Spirit within: orthodox traditions and epochs
— Esoteric traditions, paralleling and interacting with religious tradition
— Eastern traditions in resurgent relevance to the West
— Modification of the scientific methodology through myth, metaphor, and transpersonal psychology
— New and challenging paradigms provided by the existential, feminist, ecological consciousness, and liberation theology movements

The Roots and Fruits of the New Movements

Innovations of the Spirit

Innovations of the Spirit are on solid ground in every religious tradition. Though Jesus himself stood squarely in this tradition ("I came not to destroy the law, but to fulfill it," Matt. 5:17), he both challenged and changed its course. His admonition "You can't put new wine in old wineskins" (Matt. 9:17) should be the classical alert to this possibility. Its lively wisdom within and beyond the religious community in every generation is part of the unfolding of faith from the early fathers and mothers through Francis of Assisi, Teresa of Ávila, Peter Abelard, John Hus, Martin Luther, George Fox, John Wesley, Jonathan Edwards, and Mary Baker Eddy, to our own time with Ivan Illich, Thomas Merton, Huston Smith, Dorothy Day, and others.

Small wonder in this age of shifting foundations and fluid faith that this chorus of voices in the name of the Divine Spirit should be at work on the boundaries of mainline orthodoxy (an interesting metaphor for fixed tracks, secure roadbed, and no chance of leaving the road except by accident or retirement).

It would exceed the scope of this short assignment to characterize this independent group from charisma to cosmic consciousness. Their themes generally center on the primacy of personal experience, self-authenticating revelation, spiritual power or powers claimed or exhibited, and some form or other of explicit freedom from the "bondage" of the traditional orthodoxy from which it springs.

At their best, these leaders tend to challenge, cleanse, catalyze, and renew old and tired frames of reference. At their worst, they become excessive, exclusive, self-serving, and often self-destructive.[5]

More substantive is the Eastern Orthodox tradition of the immanence of God, present in all things, investing the secular with sacred overtones, and bridging to the contemporary, secular orthodoxy of ecological wholeness. This tradition expands beyond the theological nakedness of most of modern Protestant thought, which rarely developed a substantial theology of nature. Rather, in its accent on individual salvation and compartmentalizing of faith and science, Protestantism has provided few bridges to the new preoccupation with nature (caring vs. technical and manipulative relationships to the physical world).

This recent concern, reported in the Global Forum's two recent meetings in Oxford (1987) and Moscow (1990), is bringing religious, political, and scientific leaders together around the themes of creation and environmental issues. These themes are only now asserting themselves within the traditional churches.[6]

Esoteric Traditions

Anyone familiar with Manly Hall's classic work[7] will understand the pervasive, often subtle or silent, influence that esoteric traditions from before the Essenes and onward have exercised on our faith.[8] Special studies of our U.S. founding fathers, the symbolism of our Great Seal, the imprint of our money, even parts of the design of our government and policy reflect these traditions.[9]

Fascination with the metaphysical has attracted such diverse thinkers as Immanuel Kant and Benjamin Franklin, William James and Ralph Waldo Emerson, Albert Schweitzer and C. D. Broad, and Henri Bergson. Though rarely explicit, their thoughts seldom have been addressed by traditional Christian leadership. They have provided a source of challenge and interest increasingly evident in New Age dialogue and encounter.[10] The metaphysical is especially apparent in the fields of healing and health, therapies of all kinds,[11] cases of multiple personality and schizophrenia, charismatic "gifts" of tongues and prophecy meditation, "channeling," high and low prayer, personal empowerment, and a range of anomalies of consciousness such as ESP; remote viewing; self, time, and space transcending; "out-of-body" experience; and the rest.[12] Increasing numbers of "the faithful" have strayed from the mainline churches to inquire into, if not personally invest in, these esoteric paths and claims, which often run parallel to traditional faiths.

Eastern Traditions

Even as Eastern Orthodoxy (Greek, especially, and Russian) speaks a welcome word to the secular environmentalist and the ecological component of the New Age spirituality seekers, so the pantheistic perspective of Eastern religious traditions that finds the Divine all and in all has had an infectious resurgence in the West in our time.[13]

It is hard to know how influential these traditions were in feeding the rebellion on the campuses in the 1960s, '70s, and '80s. Students could readily perceive the bankruptcy of scientific reductionism in dealing with basic human and social problems. Further, there was a perception that the traditional forms of Christian orthodoxy were shopworn, exclusive, or just plain irrelevant. The young people were encouraged by new understandings of the interdependence of all events and human conditions and theories. And here was the opportunity for authentic experiential entrance into the world of *intimacy, ultimacy,* and *identity* through discipline and practice that the Eastern traditions at their best offer.

All undoubtedly played their part in the mushrooming of Eastern ashrams all across America, midwifed by gurus and by fresh, provocative practitioners of natural health, disciplined sharing, and the intentionally simplistic life-style.[14] In spite of contemporary excesses such as the corrupting Cadillacs,[15] brainwashing tactics of powerful leaders, deceptive financing, and self-serving exploitation attributed to the movement, thousands of our young, and some of our old, were finding meaning in these groups that was not present, at least not for them, in conventional religious institutions and traditions.

The Eastern traditional emphasis on the immediacy of the Divine was in contrast to the philosophical and religious dualism that had haunted the West since Descartes. The deistic strain and new orthodoxy's emphasis on the transcendence of God invited, through its exclusivity, this form of New Age spirituality. New Age spirituality's emphasis on personal discipline, direct illumination, enhanced sensitivity, and widened awareness was a welcoming vestibule for many waiting in the cold outside an abstracted Sunday religiosity. Additionally, its quasi-pantheistic sense of the Divine in and through all creation, and particularly in nature and all forms of human life, echoed the emerging environmental and ecological concerns of the more scientific-minded.

The compassion of Buddhism and pacifism in the face of an unpopular Vietnam War among many of the young and leaders of an emerging popular culture seemed a welcome alternative to the perception of a morally hypocritical and unauthentic Christendom.

Part of the scientific heritage that declared the primacy and independence of nature, and the unsubstantial reality of the subjective self, was to sunder this living and sustaining relationship to nature captured by Eastern thought. Despite efforts, first by John Dewey and his followers and subsequently by Whitehead and his students, to heal this "bifurcation" between nature and human nature for a more organic view of human, natural, and cosmic "connection," the implicit dualism persisted.

The power of technology accentuated the alienation of the human from nature as measurer and master, as opposed to partner or, in the Eastern tradition, potential affinity in creation. Small wonder these movements flowered in the fallow soil of Christian caring, reconciling love, and the sense of stewardship for the earth. Efforts at communities of commitment and sharing, with intentional simplicity of life and integration of meditation and work, sprang naturally from this perceived missing component of practice in much of conventional religiosity.

In historical reflection, it is not surprising that it was the American philosopher John Dewey, with his rejection of dualism and transcendence and emphasis on the experiential whole for learning and life, who exercised the first enduring "Western" influence on modern Chinese thought.[16] Nor is it surprising that Whitehead's rejection of the dualism of the West made surprising common cause with forms of Eastern thought and reconstruction of the spiritual dynamic in the newer naturalism.[17] This implicit effort to shift the philosophic tradition toward a more comprehensive wholeness in outlook and practice anticipated the more recent critics and rejections of the earlier narrower views with which we began the chapter.

Modifying the Scientific Traditions

Those familiar with Dewey and pragmatic, naturalistic, and Whiteheadian emphasis on "experience," process, and emergence could not be unmindful of the depths of stirring against the reductionistic, dualistic, and abstractly rational perspectives of the modern scientific tradition. After all, Darwin had disclosed our bodily and organic link to nature and earlier forms of life. Freud had revealed dimensions of the self deeper than conscious rational thought; and Jung had mirrored its shadowy side and features of the archetypal heritage in search of a soul. Einstein clarified the "bankruptcy" of the scientific preoccupation with isolated "atoms" and "simple location," and advanced his watershed view of relativity: that there are no isolated events but rather interconnected space-time events amid the interrelatedness of all aspects of reality.

Such generic thinking, however marginal to the focus of faith, was bound, ultimately, to sift down into all ways of viewing ourselves and our world, requiring us to rethink our common assumptions.

The popular paradigm, or fundamental way of viewing the world, had to shift! Much of the supportive substructure of the New Age was provided by Marilyn Ferguson, Fritjof Capra, Ken Wilbur, Rupert Sheldrake, Willis Harman, and Paul Davies.[18] These authors, in their own way, pushed back the narrow horizons, pointing to events and behavior from the microcosm to the macrocosm, inviting a more open, instructive, and integrated view.[19]

The narrower, rigid, mathematical/empirical/experimental model of the "hard sciences" would give way to complementary modes of learning/knowing, and embrace other "languages," myth, and metaphor for expression.[20] Evidential realities were permitted back into a richer landscape of reality, and dimensions of human experience were legitimized. With earlier inhibitions relaxed, a fresh new openness and expectation entered with New Age thinking. Abuses always accompany the new and swiftly shaped faddism, escapes into fantasy, nihilistic narcissism, and the cult of the occult. But these were aberrations. The channel of the mainstream was changing. Only now are we beginning to see the outline of that new and larger "paradigm."

The Emerging Paradigm

Building on the insinuations of new insight from within the sciences, the New Age "movement" has been carried forward by a wider wisdom about nature and human nature, advanced by environmental and ecological interests, and with constructive contributions from feminist, liberationist, and consciousness studies. The counterculture of the 1960s was an instinctive reaction to the "scorched earth" image of Vietnam,[21] heightened awareness of the population explosion's impact on fragile life-support systems,[22] increased visibility given the human exploitation and open desecration of nature for narrow profitability or human short-range gain, and nuclear threat to all forms of life.[23]

As the scientific view of the "otherness" of nature gave way to more integrative notions, it was predictable that our views of nature would be increasingly humanized and spiritualized. The first global conference on the world's environment in Stockholm in 1972 reinforced this perception of "Only One Earth."[24] It gave scientific, moral, and religious grounding to the striking imprint on the world's collective experience of seeing the Earth for the first time, through the eyes of the astronauts, from beyond itself in earthscapes from the moon. It would be hard to exaggerate the psychic impact of that loosening of the mind from old and archaic images of the Earth, our home: solitary splendor, unique and fragile presence in the vast sea of space and galaxies of stars, immense durability and dependability. This invited reconsideration of our estimation of ourselves, our violent and manipulative cultures, and the shocking neglect of any "caring" concern for this our human home.

It is natural that the holistic, synoptic, nurturing features of the feminine in human thought and life should connect with the ecological movement, emerging in part from the muscle-bound manipulations of the masculine in Western culture. In Rachel Carson's *Silent Spring*, they came together early and powerfully to inform a nation and a world. Barbara Ward and Rene Dubos's *Only One Earth*, a decade later, reinforced this connection. Margaret Mead's eloquent voice and systematic study from the Museum of Natural History moved it forward. And, still a decade later, it was brought together in Linda Olds's books and writing, *Fully Human* and "A New Ecological Ethic."[25]

Scant attention has been paid to the deeper masculine metaphor of power, control, and mastery at work in the emotionally sterilized "scientific" method. Metaphysics increasingly exposed this method as too narrow and inefficient to carry the full weight of truth about our world and ourselves. Like a fresh spring from the high mountains, a torrent of literature and leadership on this theme began to emerge from many quarters. Even in the hallowed halls of theology, the queen of the sciences, the female metaphor found its place.

Conventional churches, Protestant and Catholic, would have to attend to this new metaphor, even in the language of literature and prayer, as well as in theology and practice.[26] The predominant paternal and masculine reference to God, and even the assumption of our relation to nature ("dominion") was to undergo searching review.

Slowly, this "conspiracy" of consciousness made its way into a widened mainstream spirituality, which first acknowledged and then incorporated environmental awareness and human wholeness. The human potential movements, concern for total "fitness,"[27] ecological sensitivity, and even "cosmic convergence" are alive and well in our time and confirm "passage" into a New Age.

Paradoxically, it has been the inability of the masculine model, with its penchant for violence and control, or the scientific model of technology and power to heal the broken self, nature, or world that has prompted, if not inspired, these movements. They search for more comprehensive and effective models for understanding nature, human nature, and community with which to usher in the New Age. They provide the opportunity as well as the necessity for the enduring and constructive themes of the New Age spirituality.

Enduring and Constructive Themes

Since other chapters of this volume will be devoted to critical evaluation, these suggestions can be offered only as samples for assessment. There are at least a dozen features deserving of mention.

1. The New Age closes the parentheses opened by Descartes, launching the modern world with its own *cogito ergo sum*. It affirms the intrinsic integrity and inviolate authenticity of the *self's awareness of itself*. It anchors all features of consciousness—whether thought, doubt, pain, or volition—in this central affirmation of being. However narcissistic this may become if consciousness stays inward-looking only and captive of its own self-consciousness, rightly grasped its claims to selfhood, truth, and reality are *prima facie* evident. At its best, the New Age pushes beyond this subjective "starting point" to meet, relate, and transform all relationships that encounter this threshold of consciousness.

2. The New Age affirms the primacy of *personal choice* and *responsibility* as uniquely human and deeper than gender, status, security, or external authority. This radical uniqueness of every person, often exasperating to establishments and communities of every kind, ensures the movement's irrepressible angularity and

fresh new forms. Susceptibility to the cults of individuality does not mask this intent, but only its susceptibility to perversion.

3. The movement affirms, as a counterpart to the above, the intrinsic and personal *access to the Divine*. Though at times blurring any sense of distinction between the Divine and the self, New Age thinkers expose and criticize the excessive transcendence, inaccessibility, and guilt-inspiring "otherness" of God. The affirmation is not just immanence or identity with the Divine, but in the larger setting of knowledge and certitude, the scientific tradition–engendered accent on open *access*.

4. The New Age draws much of its energy from emphasis on *synergy*. It is an interesting counterpoint of individuality to affirm that "the whole is more than the sum of its parts." This holistic, encompassing intent, reflected in the ecological and feminine correctives, runs through both its ideology and practice.

5. The fullest *potential* of the human is central to the movement's influence.[28] This view is not shallow optimism, but "potentiality" in its rich Aristotelian sense as *fullness of being*, which embraces the *shadow* as well as the substance of the self. This affirmation has pressed psychology, education, sport, medicine, and even politics beyond conventional boundaries.

6. *Elevation of feeling and affect* to a proper mode of relating and perceiving is intrinsic to much of the New Age literature. *Compassion* is more than blind passion or unbridled emotion. It is a mode of comprehending and relating to all others, reciprocally acknowledging integrity, presence, and value. It is a way of being, knowing, and acting simultaneously and comprehensively.

7. The New Age confirms access and individuality with *affinity for immediacy*. It is skeptical of all forms of mediation, whether messiah, priest, politician, or any arbitrary authority. Though vulnerable to all forms of authority, this penchant for the consciousness of *now* in the full immediacy of the present and presence is unmistakable in its literature.

8. The New Age sometimes appears to float on the *power of positive thinking*. There are echoes and overtones here of Christian Science,[29] principles of health through affirmation of the mind, and the optimism of faith. But, even beyond these distinctive thinkers

and practitioners, there is an amazing residual energy in principles and practices operative in many pulpits in America.

9. The movement has done much to develop a *theology of ecology,* in the care and tending of a small planet. This reverential regard gives a quasi-mystical cast to both its writing[30] and practice. It has affinity with the spiritual intent of all religious traditions in its regard for creation as mirroring (theism) or identifying with (pantheism) the Divine. Often, even in rejecting any form of religiosity, the sense of the sacred in the mundane echoes in practitioner and prophet alike.

10. The New Age has recaptured the insight of *innocence.* The childlike qualities of wonder, trust, spontaneity, and play characterize many of its "disciplines," or "games," and encounters.

11. At times, to borrow a phrase from John MacMurray, the New Age has struggled to put *another "o" in God's name.* It has been specific in its quest to rescue *value, meaning, and goodness* in nature and human nature.[31]

12. The New Age works at restoring *balance* into the human equation. However, the movement itself, in the interest of correction, sometimes goes too far, unbalancing a critical tension essential to hold together elements of bodily or mental health, community, or global society. Basically, the New Age drives toward balance.

Whatever else may be said, these are strong strands in any new cloth our age may weave into a garment to clothe the twenty-first century. But wherein have these strengths been compromised and gone astray? The wisdom of Leibniz with which we began helps us here.

Limits and Liabilities

Here too, while it may not be cheaper, it is perhaps clearer to characterize shortcomings of the movement by the dozen.

1. Though knowing may be anchored by self-consciousness, *objective reality* is not always or necessarily constituted by it. The perils of this perspective, given classic form in criticism of Berkeley's *esse est percipi* (to be is to be perceived), intrude in a

wide range of New Age perspectives. In reaching for full correction to the scientific neutralization, or even nullifying the role of mind in objective reality, the movement frequently overreacts to make mind the sole constituent of reality. The end of this route, like the symbol of the snake swallowing itself, is to swallow up reality in a self-conscious ingestion of all reality reduced to its self-authenticating encounter. The *mode* of the *beyond* is not necessarily the same as *within!*

2. The second liability flows from the first, a *mistaken reductionism to solipsistic subjectivity.* Much criticism has been directed to the New Age's self-serving, self-seeking, and selectively narcissistic roots here. It should not be called "me-too-ism," but rather "to-me-ism." It mistakes the window for the world, and perverts what we look *through* to what we look *at.*

3. Ironically, the early sense of the New Age that the secular had been stripped of anything sacred turns into the *rejection of anything transcendental* that might give it meaning. In saving the near and immediate from oblivion and loss of value, it commits the fallacy of inversion, claiming that only the immanent has meaning. Losing any cosmic sources or vindication of value or calling as a higher and other referent for consciousness, the movement surrenders any objective source of authentication for its own claims to truth.

4. The movement enshrines *simplicity,* to the denial of *complexity.* Oliver Wendell Holmes was fond of saying that he wouldn't give a fig for simplicity this side of complexity, but he would give his life for it on the other. There are too many obdurate realities in the human and cosmic situation to be easily reduced to any simplistic view. We are still struggling, a century after Einstein, to finish a unified theory of nature, alone, much less human nature, or the Divine as well. It would be ironic if in the protest of one form of reductionism, we should be trapped in another.

5. *Potentiality is not actuality.* Though all becoming is impregnated with being actual, that does not imply a straight line toward actuality. Indeed, being human may be in part the art of negotiating limits.

6. Feelings may attest to the presence of value, but *they need not authenticate or clarify it.* The New Age is easily confused by this.

Feeling may be blind, as is often the case in rage, shame, pity, or love. They also may be mistaken, as in fear, blind trust, or passion for power. Some of the tragedies committed in the name of New Age religion lurk here.

7. The *fullness of immediacy* in New Age thought and practice *is too narrow and shallow* a "now." Though immediacy escapes the simonized sterility of secondhand symbols, which in much education and common life passes muster for "experience," it cannot escape the impoverishment bought at surrender of memory, reflection, or anticipation. Indeed, one mark of self-consciousness and thought is that they provide that element of distance essential for rational judgment and perspective. Mediation of terms, events, or persons is essential to a more comprehensive life.

8. *Symbols as conduits of thought must not be confused with constituent reality.* This old rational trap is revisited in much antirationalism of the New Age. Saying it is so does not make it so. And symbolic solutions at the level of rhetoric are not to be mistaken for real solutions at the level of reality. This is why much of New Age thinking is considered fuzzy, impractical, or irrelevant. Buzz words do not a building make!

9. Much of the movement is vulnerable to an enduring dilemma of all pantheism. If God is all and in all, *how can meaningful distinctions be made* within or between elements of reality or preferences, for choice or action? Even fragile forms or pacifism, vegetarianism, and voluntary simplicity founder over the *reductio ad absurdum.* Why should *any* form of life be given up for any other? And why, if all mirror the Divine, should one value, perspective, or person be used to arbitrate the truth of any other? Even reduction to silence, which the ancient sophists thought was the only position one could take in such an argument, is in itself an affirmation, albeit nonverbal!

10. Closely akin to the above, the New Age illustrates the *peril of integration by reduction.* Paradoxically, in the interest of becoming more holistic and inclusive, the movement frequently becomes narrowing and exclusive. Exclusivity, peril of all movements, is

self-contradictory when applied to "integrative" views. And a well-rounded perspective with a *short radius* gives us a narrow and limiting whole—almost a hole!

11. A searching Christian critique of the New Age is that it has *no clear theory of sin or evil,* and overlooks the human propensity to perversion. As a corrective to a fatalistic materialism, it goes too far in neglect of limitation, power, alienation, and violence. It has not adequately found or stated any new form of power that authenticates its optimistic assumptions about nature or human nature, which are "seldom ever mild." And, finally,

12. As the New Age matures, as all movements tend to do, it is inclined to *make a new orthodoxy out of its revolt against the old orthodoxies.* Hitler, in *Mein Kampf,* put this perilous tendency graphically when he said, "The weaknesses of democracies are their temptation to imitate our methods to fight us." And the weakness of the New Age is to make this assumption "old hat," and convert creativity into a new conventionality. One often sees this trend as a movement beginning outside the church and opposed to the church, then turning into a new church or churches with their own tenacious orthodoxy.

What may be said, finally, of this exciting epoch of transition? As the old ideas grind down, and new and fresh insights crowd to take their place, what may be learned from the spirituality of the New Age? This challenge to change should not be strange to the Christian tradition in any of its forms. After all, the Christian community's earliest and ablest missionary, Paul, in an age of dramatic transition, was an educated Jew, using another and then more universal language, Greek, under the protection of Roman citizenship and the Pax Romana, to bring the message and work of Jesus to an indifferent, if not antagonistic, world. He sought then, as thoughtful faithful now must do, not to put new wine in old wineskins, or to prejudge, and thereby preclude a fresh witness of the Spirit to a tried and tormented world. He sought a fresh vessel. The lessons are several:

1. Never seek to imprison a living God in any dead word, symbol, tradition, or orthodoxy.

2. Be prepared to acknowledge that surprise is the counterpart of God's amazing grace, which is too abundant and unfathomable to be captured finally or fully by any age or system.

3. In the light of the potentiality of our human nature and its becoming, be prepared to follow spontaneously where the Spirit may lead without *limiting* the process, but aware of its—and our—limits.

4. Objectivity in knowledge or reality does not mean finality, but only dependability; relativity does not mean subjectivity, but interconnectedness.

5. The discipline, public verifiability, and universality of intent in the sciences is an important instrument of knowledge, including theological. New and richer methods of knowing must be forged with comparable dependability to accommodate a wider and richer access to reality than we are now prepared to accept.

6. Organized religion and traditional faith need perpetual challenge and change to remain fresh and resilient. Personal renewal is at the root of that change, which it should reflect and accommodate.

7. The global village, now our real and only home, requires that our faith must reflect this new awareness of cultural and cosmic diversity, minimizing violence and maximizing community. Each distinctive difference in perception, conception, or encounter with our multifaceted world must be dealt with as and for what it claims to be, or is! Ours is to acknowledge and accommodate, not to ignore or assimilate.

8. In pursuing the above task/opportunity, expect new forms of synergy, integration, and energy renewal. The third millennium needs to come in with its own claim to spirituality and power of a New Age. And, finally,

9. Common needs and tasks are about to challenge and harness together the best of the New Age and all our religious traditions. Problems of human hopelessness, alienation, and impotence; threats to human life and the environment; rationalizing and restraining overpopulation; wiser use of natural, scientific, and technical resources; integrating the secular and sacred, scientific and religious, personal and global values—*all* await our endeavor.

If this New Age was heralded as a conspiracy, let us mature it with openness, season it with enlightened partnership, and correct it with a wider, better grasp of what it is to be divinely human, or if one prefers, humanly divine! This is the root and the fruit of the matter. This is a metaphysical and historical footnote to our amazing time of transition. It could be, as Kierkegaard reminded us, the way God puts on the garment of time to move slowly through the earth!

SECTION TWO

NEW AGE SPIRITUALITY: A JOURNEY OF GROWTH

The New Age movement has many dimensions. In fact, dedicated adherents and informed observers do not always agree on what constitutes the movement. Section Two acknowledges the diversity in the movement and explores its many themes by describing it as a journey toward the divine, toward self-discovery, and toward planetary evolution.

5

The New Age: The Movement Toward the Divine

DAVID SPANGLER

Is the New Age a new religion? Does it possess a new spirituality capable of leading an individual toward the divine?

Other authors in this book have written essays exploring the history of the New Age movement (the idea of an emerging New Age can be found in almost every culture, extending back for thousands of years), some of its current manifestations, and a critique of both its strengths and its weaknesses. For me to explore these topics in this essay risks both being repetitive and diverting us from the central theme suggested in the preceding questions. If readers are interested in my own thoughts on these matters, I refer them to the reading list for this chapter.

Interestingly, I have never been asked whether or not the New Age is a religion by anyone who is actually involved in it. During the past thirty years of my own association with the New Age movement, I have never met anyone engaged in any kind of New Age activity who has thought of herself or himself as having joined a new religion. This question, when it arises, always has come from someone who is looking from the outside at the bewildering and diverse array of groups, activities, beliefs, practices, ideas, and attitudes that are lumped together under the heading of "New Age" and who is understandably seeking some familiar label with which to categorize it all. Sometimes that question of whether or not the New Age is a religion masks a deeper and more urgent question: Is the New Age a threat to me and my beliefs? Is it a competitor?

My response to this question has always been that the New Age is not a new religion. One does not become a "New Ager" in the same sense that one becomes a Christian, a Muslim, or a Buddhist. The New Age does not have a single, cohesive doctrine to which everyone ascribes; it does not have a central spiritual founder like a Jesus, a Buddha, or a Muhammad. It does not have a unified set of spiritual practices or a common pattern or focus of worship. It does not have a well-defined spiritual path toward the sacred. There are some groups who identify themselves as being New Age who do have a centralized doctrine, an orthodoxy of worship and practice, and have been founded by individuals whom they revere as being spiritual masters. These groups are the exception, though, rather than the rule. The New Age movement as a whole does not have these characteristics.

Here is a metaphor that sums up my perspective. Christianity is like a great cathedral rising around a central spiritual and architectural theme. While it encompasses numerous denominations and sects within its boundaries, not all of whom agree or get along with one another, the architecture of Christian spirituality is unified in the Person of Jesus Christ, his incarnation, and his redemptive mission.

By contrast, the New Age is more like a flea market or a county fair, a collection of differently colored and designed booths spread around a meadow, with the edges of the fair dissolving into the forested wilderness beyond. Where the cathedral may be a place of worship, the fair is a place of play and discovery. It is filled with a vitality, a wildness, a tumult of different voices and things to see and do. There are jesters and tricksters, magicians and shamans, healers and mystics, and the inevitable hucksters eager for a quick sale before packing up and moving on. One can be overwhelmed by the diversity in the fair, but also one can find new connections between old patterns and gain unexpected insights and revelations.

If I go to the New Age fair, I discover that it is made up of a bewildering variety of tents. A friend of mine in Britain, Dr. William

Bloom, recently coedited a book called *The Seeker's Guide: A New Age Resource Book*. It is designed, as its title suggests, to give an interested seeker an overview of all the activities, philosophies, teachings, and ideas that at one time or another have been lumped under the term "New Age." Here is a partial listing of the table of contents:[1]

Goddess Spirituality	The Sacred Planet
The Gaia Hypothesis	New Biology
New Physics	Chaos Theory
Systems Theory	Altered States of Consciousness
ESP	Near Death Experiences
Meditation	Reincarnation
Neopaganism and Wicca	Women's and Men's Mysteries
Celtic and Mystical Christianity	Jewish Kabbalah
Martial Arts	Shamanism
Native American Spirituality	Psychic Development
Channeling	Astrology
I Ching	Sacred Dance
Humanistic Psychology	Transpersonal Psychology
Diet and Nutrition	Homeopathy and Naturopathy
Herbalism	Chiropractic
Acupuncture	Yoga
Intentional Community	Holistic Business
Holistic Education	Ecofeminism
Green Values	Sustainability
Alternative Energy Sources	Deep Ecology

Obviously, this is a highly diverse list (and, as I mentioned, it is only a partial one). It should be apparent that many of the topics listed have existed long before the modern New Age movement, and many of them would not name themselves as being New Age. What links them together is that each of them offers a challenge or an alternative to the dominant materialistic, patriarchal paradigm of contemporary Western industrialized culture. They each offer an image or process of transformation either for an individual or for the culture as a whole.

Each of these topics represents a tent in the fair. To pick out one or two tents, such as the channelers or the psychic power enthusiasts, and say that they represent the whole fair is to miss the large picture and invite misunderstanding. Using such criteria is like defining and critiquing Christianity as a whole based solely on the teachings of the ultraconservative Kingdom theologians or of one of the televangelists such as Jimmy Swaggart or Brother Robert Tilton in Dallas. Because of this, many critiques of the New Age in the media or in the writings of fundamentalists, while occasionally penetrating and accurate with respect to a single phenomenon, are often grossly misrepresentative of the New Age as a whole.

Looking at the tents in the New Age fair, we may draw certain conclusions. First, much of what we call New Age really represents what historian of science Thomas Kuhn first called a "paradigm shift." This simply means a change in how we view and understand the world. It is a change in the foundational story from which we derive the goals and values that guide our culture. Much of this change is in how we scientifically understand the nature of reality (a shift, for example, from the Newtonian clockwork, mechanistic universe to one that is, in the words of a British physicist, more like a "great thought"). Much of it is in how we define ourselves in relationship to the earth; it is painfully obvious by now that our culture has failed to understand, appreciate, or honor the ecological interconnectedness of life on our planet, with results that are potentially catastrophic. Other paradigmatic changes are social, political, and economic in nature, such as the feminist critique of the patriarchal nature of many of our institutions.

Though many individuals in the New Age movement may look on these various paradigmatic changes as proof that we are entering a New Age (and they are certainly evidence that our culture is undergoing transformation, which is, after all, the essence of the New Age idea), none of these changes is the product of the New Age movement itself. The new frontiers and discoveries in science, the increase in ecological awareness with the resulting worldwide Green movement, and the feminist or women's liberation move-ment would be happening whether or not there were such a thing as the New Age. It is safe to say, though, that the result of these paradigmatic transformations will be to create a new culture very different from the one we have known.

Another conclusion we can draw from looking at the list of "New Age" topics is that many of them belong to the area of personal development, psychology, medicine and healing, and psychotherapy. They represent ideas, practices, disciplines, and procedures for an inner journey into the depths and recesses of our human consciousness. They are paths and techniques for discovering latent human potentials and for uncovering many of the mysteries of the psyche.

Because in the past spirituality and religion have been primary avenues for making the inner journey, it is understandable that someone could see in the various psychotechnologies and therapies, which include transpersonal psychology and investigations into altered states of consciousness (or what anthropologist Michael Harner, a leading investigator of the worldwide shamanistic tradition, calls states of Non-Ordinary Reality), what appears to be a religious undertaking. I shall have more to say on this in a moment, but the fact that many aspects of the New Age movement, including those such as psychic exploration, channeling, and past life regressions which the media love to focus on, are concerned with an inner journey into the psyche does not mean they are concerned with a spiritual journey, much less one leading to a deeper experience of the divine.

As above, though, the point needs to be made that while many of these investigations and therapies are without question transformational in their intent and effects, they are not necessarily products of a New Age movement. They have for the most part evolved quite independently out of medical and scientific research into the interaction of brain, mind, and body and out of the growing field of alternative healing methods based on ancient disciplines such as acupuncture and herbalism. While the New Age movement embraces many of these psychologies, therapies, and theories—either for commercial reasons or as proof that our culture really is transforming—they would have come into being anyway without the existence of the New Age idea.

As for New Age spirituality, here too the notion of a New Age movement can be misleading. Much of what constitutes spirituality within that movement is really the investigation and practice of alternative or ancient religious traditions such as Buddhism, Zen, Taoism, Hinduism, Sufism (the mystical side of Islam), and the like. The rise of neopaganism, Wicca, and shamanism and the growing interest in native American spirituality are largely due to the desire for a religious sensibility that honors the sacredness of the earth and of nature, that includes and honors the feminine as a coequal aspect of the image of the sacred along with the male (actually transcending gender images of divinity), and that is ecologically sound, and in which, further, the experience of the sacred is not necessarily mediated through a professional priesthood or clergy. Recently, the recovery of the ecologically concerned, creation-centered, and feminist sides of Christianity in the form of both the mystical tradition and the Celtic Christianity of Ireland and Britain during the first millennium after Christ has allowed many Christians who do not wish to leave their tradition to follow some alternative spirituality an opportunity to discover and practice their faith in a more holistic manner.

Clearly Buddhism, Sufism, Taoism, shamanism, native American spirituality, and Celtic Christianity are not products of a New Age movement; they do not constitute a "New Age spirituality" different from anything that has gone before. They do constitute traditional spiritual paths. It is quite erroneous and misleading to say that someone who chooses one of these paths as his or her primary route into the divine is following a "New Age religion" or worse, the "religion of the New Age."

So, if we take away paradigm shifts due to scientific, technological, and social changes, new psychologies and psychotherapies, as well as older, nonallopathic healing methodologies such as herbalism, and the practice of Oriental, shamanistic, or mystical religious traditions—none of which originate with or are totally defined by the idea of a New Age—what do we have left? What is authentically and uniquely "New Age" within which we might find some new and revolutionary path into the sacred?

The idea of a New Age, as I mentioned, is an ancient one. It can be found in every culture in one form or another, leading me to think of it as a planetary myth or as an archetypal image within the collective human psyche. It is an idea that has certainly appeared from time to time in the history of Western civilization, usually in a Christian context as the appearance of the millennium, but also in Jewish tradition as the expected messianic age. In fact, there is currently an international movement within a faction of Orthodox Judaism proclaiming that the messianic age is about to begin, a movement based on the perception that the Hasidic Rabbi Menachem Schneerson, head of the Chabad movement, is the long-awaited messiah.

The current New Age did not just spring into being during the '50s and '60s. It has roots in a variety of philosophical, social, and religious movements of the past century, including the American Transcendentalists and the Romantics. Even in the eighteenth century, the English poet William Blake spoke of the immanent coming of a new age. He in turn was influenced by a prophecy by Emanuel Swedenborg, the Swedish theologian and mystic, that the New Age would dawn in 1757, beginning with a transformation of consciousness.

The contemporary New Age began as a prophetic movement based on an astrological interpretation of history that every two thousand years or so humanity moves into a new age in which civilization is predominantly influenced by the qualities of the particular astrological sign that rules that age.

So, for the past two thousand years we have been under the sign of Pisces, and now we are entering the Age of Aquarius. The movement was also fueled by psychically received prophecies of the coming end of civilization and, after a time of trial and tribulation, the beginning of a time of great abundance and peace. Paranoia about nuclear warfare all through the 1950s and '60s certainly created a climate in which such prophecies could flourish.

So the New Age is first a prophetic idea, and as such it presented a critique of modern Western industrial civilization as being too materialistic, too destructive of the earth, and too callous toward the needs of human community and social justice to survive. It was in this form that I first heard of the New Age in the late '50s.

However, as a prophecy the New Age was something to believe

85

in but not something that offered a means of creative participation. That is, the Age of Aquarius would come whatever I or anyone else did or did not do. Western civilization was doomed for its sins, and while a better world was coming, it would do so thanks to divine intervention (or, in some prophecies, extraterrestrial intervention— UFO's have always been part of the New Age subculture). One did not create a New Age; one waited for its predestined arrival. Certainly, there was no spiritual practice involved, other than believing in the prophecies and doing whatever one needed to do to be a good and virtuous person so that one's "vibrations" would be attuned to the new world and not to the old one. If this sounds familiar, it is because this prophetic aspect of the New Age rests squarely in the tradition of American millenarianism, substituting the Aquarian Age for the kingdom of God and sometimes extraterrestrials for angels, which simply served to give the prophecies a secular and technological flavor appealing to the gadget-oriented American consciousness. Given the history of apocalyptic movement throughout the life of the United States, the New Age idea is really as American as apple pie and baseball.

It is my opinion that if the New Age had remained simply a prophetic idea emerging from the fringes of society, it would probably have remained a marginal subculture and might well have disappeared altogether by the dawn of the 1990s. The fact is that there is very little creative energy around waiting passively for something to happen, especially when time after time the prophetic events have not occurred when they were supposed to.

Instead, the New Age idea found a more energetic lease on life by piggybacking on a number of other events that took place in the '60s and '70s: the civil rights movement, the drug culture, the hippie counterculture and the search for social alternatives, the antiwar movement, the rise of humanistic and transpersonal psychologies, the popularization of Buddhism—especially the Zen and Tibetan varieties—and the new revelations and developments in science (such as the "new" physics), to name a few. Most of the people instrumental in bringing these new patterns and changes to the fore had never heard of the New Age and never thought of themselves as part of a New Age movement. However, as a transformational search to discover cultural alternatives took off in the United States, particularly in California, the image of the "dawning of the Age of Aquarius," as the musical *Hair* put it, became a symbol for the whole enterprise. Suddenly, the New Age was loosed from its rather narrow moorings in the psychic and UFO subculture of the United States and became an image for a wide-ranging array of exploratory efforts that both critiqued what was not working in the mainstream culture and looked for positive alternatives.

Actually, as one who lived through that change and in some ways contributed to the liberation of the New Age idea from its prophetic context, I look upon that change as inevitable, for two reasons. One lies in the nature of the twentieth century itself and the other lies in the deeper power of the New Age idea as a metaphor rather than as a prophecy.

The twentieth century has been a time of scientific, technological, social, political, and economic upheaval. Our generation and our parents' generation have seen a time of rapid change which is becoming ever more rapid. A friend of mine who died recently was born into a world in which the common mode of transportation was a horse and buggy. She lived to see the advent of radio, television, automobiles, airplanes, computers, space travel, and antibiotics. The Soviet Union came into being, developed into a nuclear super-power, then disintegrated and disappeared all within the lifetime of my parents. Transformation is not just an idea but a contemporary reality. To ask if there is any validity to the idea of a New Age is to miss the whole point of modern planetary experience. Compared to the world of my parents, we are living in a New Age right now. Even compared to the political and economic world of just three years ago, before the fall of the Berlin Wall, we are living in a New Age.

In short, the idea of an emerging New Age strikes a resonance in the collective psyche that goes beyond simple prophecy and becomes a description of the transformative times in which we are living. We are confronting (or are confronted by) the idea of an emergent future whose nature may be beyond our ability to imagine, at least using concepts familiar to generations of the past. It is no wonder, then, that an idea like that of the New Age should have emerged or become popular. Though it can attract fanciful attitudes and activities, there is nothing fanciful about the reality of entering a New Age itself. As futurist Kirkpatrick Sale said over a decade ago in his book *Human Scale,* it is clear that future observers of our time will mark the emergence of new age thought somewhere in our generation. The concern is what kind of new age it will be.[2]

The other reason the idea of a New Age grew beyond its prophetic beginnings is that it is a metaphor for the transformative energy and spirit of life itself. It is not an event but a state of mind attuned to possibility and potential, echoing the perspective of George Bernard Shaw when he said that others looked at what is and asked "Why?" while he looked at what might be and asked, "Why not?" In the Bible, God says, "I make all things new." It is this spirit of renewal and creativity, of revelation and emergence, that resonates within the idea of the New Age. Dutch futurist Fred Pollack wrote that without an image of the future as something that challenges a culture to grow and transform, a culture will die, and he stressed that a true image of the future is not the same as an image of progress, which is really an image of the past extrapolated into the future as more and better of what we already are familiar with. He was concerned that Western society had lost its image of the future, had, in fact, in its fear and despair over the potential of nuclear holocaust, lost a sense that there would even be a future.

The New Age is an image of the future. Its power lies in the fact that it is an image of transformation and potential. The New Age is a metaphor for creative possibility inherent in the moment it allows us to tell ourselves that "the past was terrible and the present is frightening and challenging, but a better future is possible. We can transform ourselves and our society through a combination of human imagination and effort and divine grace."

As a simple prophecy, the New Age idea becomes trapped in history as an event and subject to expectation. As a metaphor or myth, it paradoxically stands outside history as an image of the creative force within life, within ourselves, within the earth, within the cosmos, and within the sacred that can "make all things new."

When the media refer to the "New Age religion," there usually are certain ideas or practices that are held up as examples of what "members" of this "religion" believe and do. These include channeling or going to channels, talking with one's High Self (which is a personalized image of one's soul or of one's divine self), searching for information about past lives, and using crystals as a focus for psychic or spiritual energies.

These practices sound exotic, silly, and strange. However, we do well to leaven our consideration of them with a degree of humility and perspective. One person's religious practices may seem like basest superstition to someone else, and Christians have an unfortunate historical tendency toward religious imperialism, considering the spiritual traditions of other people as second-rate and quaint at best and demonic at worst. Contrary to the narrow perspective of fundamentalists of any religious persuasion (including New Age fundamentalists), God is larger than any particular path or belief, and to be present in a person's life apparently requires little more than the sincere openness and intent of a human heart to encompass a compassionate reality larger than self-interest and petty exclusiveness. We can never predict just what experience will suddenly, magically connect a person with the numinous, with the deep, loving mystery and presence at the heart of life. So it would be arrogant to say that searching for information about a previous life, communicating with nonphysical beings as or through a channel, or concentrating on a crystal to focus one's spiritual energies might not be just the experience, just the opening to the possibility of a reality wider than the material world, that transforms a person's life and leads to a further, deeper, and broader relationship with the sacred.

On the other hand, I feel we would be mistaken to see these as New Age spiritual practices or to use them to define the New Age as a religion. Like other practices and activities mentioned above, none of them originates with the New Age movement and they are confined to what I have experienced as a fairly small segment of that movement anyway. In his excellent study on channeling, *With the Tongues of Men and Angels,* Arthur Hastings points out the universality of channeling in all human cultures and the antiquity of this phenomenon. Likewise, probably more people on earth have believed in or currently believe in reincarnation and the power of past lives to affect current reality than do not, and only the tiniest fraction of those people, mostly living in Asia, have ever heard of the New Age movement. The use of crystals is no different from the use of any kind of talisman; the attribution to physical objects of spiritual and psychic energies and potentials, or imbuing them with such, is as ancient as humanity and as widespread. Given the right attitude, the use of a crystal as a focal point for devotion and concentration can be every bit as powerful and inspiring as the equivalent use of a rosary or some other object holy to a particular tradition. Seeking to attune to one's High Self is no different in theory from attuning to one's soul; it is simply another way of acknowledging that within each of us is a noble and spiritual aspect that can be a source of wisdom and love in our lives.

Not one of these practices is truly New Age in the sense of arising uniquely from the idea of an emerging New Age, whether seen as a prophecy or as a metaphor. All were being practiced before the New Age idea appeared on the contemporary scene, and all will probably continue to be practiced long after that idea has vanished.

Also, although these practices appear to be spiritual, in many cases they are more appropriately seen as psychological. The concept of the High Self, for example, is a category of the psyche within the teachings of psychosynthesis, one of the modern schools of psychotherapy; it is that part of us which can synthesize all other aspects of the psyche into an inner wholeness. Likewise, the search for past lives is often conducted as a form of therapy rather than as a religious exercise. As for channeling, much of it is being conducted, I have observed, as an examination of contact not with exterior beings but with unknown parts of the psyche, and the messages that come through are generally therapeutic and inspirational in nature—much like a good pep talk exhorting people to be loving and assuring them that they are loved in return (which is not a bad message when you think about it)—rather than mystical or theological. Arthur Hastings makes a similar observation in his book: "Contemporary channeled messages . . . are not equivalent to the literature of mysticism which focuses on salvation in Christ, union with God, or merging with the absolute. Contemporary messages tend to be in the intermediate realm of human striving to manifest qualities of love, charity, spontaneity, wisdom, truth, spiritual purposes, and values. Few of the channeled beings show familiarity with the mystical traditions or mystical experiences, at least as they have been described by mystics and practitioners. The presentation of most current channels is a popular and inspirational one."[3] This does not imply that the messages are worthless or coming from demonic sources, only that they are not addressing traditional spiritual issues. They are not offering spirituality as much as they are offering psychology, which, given the status of psychology in our society as being nearly a religion in itself, seems oddly appropriate! (For an interesting discussion on how psychology often supplants spirituality in our culture, I refer the reader to the November 1991 issue of *Sojourners,* a journal of "faith, politics, and culture," and to the cover essay by Richard Rohr, O.F.M., titled "When Psychology Meets Spirituality, Why Does Psychology Always Win?")

Of course, it is necessary to critique these various psychic and psychological practices when they become cloaked in a mantle of New Age spirituality and perceived as spiritual disciplines in their own right. There is a lot of distortion and silliness involved, resulting from a lamentable lack of discernment and good judgment, and if these practices are confused with the elements of a genuine mystical or spiritual tradition, the effect is like confusing costume jewelry with real gemstones, or the copy of a print with an original work of art: we diminish our ability to discern quality and craftsmanship when we encounter it. More seriously, we can diminish our willingness and ability to participate in the work of a real discipline—to sit every day in silence or in prayer, for example—once the excitement, the romance, and the glamour of our initial encounter have worn off. What is called New Age spirituality is often more like entertainment than spirituality. It excites the personality, whereas a true spiritual discipline seeks to quiet the personality so that it can be integrated into a larger, transpersonal reality.

One of the primary criticisms directed against the New Age is that it is self-involved and narcissistic. Its emphasis is on self-discovery, self-development, growth, therapy, and "creating one's own reality." I feel this is a valid criticism, though at times it is misleading, as it focuses on that aspect of the New Age which emerges from and reflects psychological roots while ignoring other aspects, such as the whole area of new paradigm investigations, ecological concerns, and so forth.

Because much of the modern New Age movement grows out of humanistic psychology and the human potential movement of the '60s and '70s, it does reflect an overbalanced emphasis on issues of the self and on interior realities as contrasted with concerns for social justice and planetary well-being, though as we enter the '90s, this is changing rapidly as the New Age movement takes on a more ecological awareness. In several New Age books and teachings one can find the self and inner consciousness being elevated as the central reality, which, of course, is a perspective not new with the New Age. There has always been a religious and philosophical tendency within Western culture to move away from the world, away from nature, away from embodiment and toward inner states, inner realms, salvation, and heaven. With the advent of psychology, this tendency has been given new directions and tools and a new impetus.

If the self is elevated within the New Age movement, this only reflects this cultural tendency. Politically and economically, our culture has practically created a cult out of valuing the self-sufficient, isolated, individual self to the continued detriment of real community. This leads to the fragmenting idea that all value lies in the unique self apart from any connections to the land, to nature, to other humans, to community. Nor have the churches been immune to this "individualization" of reality. A friend of mine who is a Hispanic theologian teaching at a local Jesuit college is continually shocked at the self-absorbed attitudes and values of her white, Anglo, middle-class students for the priesthood; their concerns are with *personal* salvation, a *personal* relationship to Jesus or to God, and *personal* holiness or spirituality, rather than with community spirituality, community salvation, or the community's relationship to the sacred.

So, if aspects of the New Age movement seem narcissistic, they are, but this situation is really only the logical extension of America's preoccupation with and love affair for the power and glory of the personal self, a preoccupation more than heightened by psychology and the emphasis on therapy, healing the wounds from one's personal past, individuation, and becoming whole *in oneself* rather than in relation to the larger world.

It is not surprising that this quest for the idealized self becomes confused with spirituality and the movement toward the divine. Both seem to be inward movements away from the world, and God is often confused with being a *state of consciousness* rather than the ground of being, the very root from which the structure and phenomena of consciousness arise. Since states of consciousness are that with which psychology deals, then at some level of logic, it can be assumed that God as a state of consciousness can be reached through psychological means.

Some of this confusion results from the undiscerning borrowing of concepts from various religious and philosophical traditions, notably those of the East. So, when a yogi, for example, speaks of attaining God-consciousness, we assume he is meaning the attainment of some lofty and cosmic psychological state, such as a clear and penetrating perception and understanding of God as a phenomenal object, or an understanding and perception of the world from God's point of view, where God is seen as an outside observer. What this borrowing fails to take into account is that for us a state of consciousness is a *phenomenon,* much as we often popularly view God, except in the mystical traditions, as a phenomenon or an object—a super object, to be sure, but an object nonetheless, something that can be imaged and described—while in the Eastern traditions God is beyond all phenomena: the No-Thing or nothingness about which nothing can be said. In this context, to attain God-consciousness in a mystical sense is to disappear as a phenomenal, isolated, individuated self separate from all the rest of creation, whereas in the West we would tend to see this state as a universal self, the ultimate individuation, the cosmos as person and the person as cosmos. There is a supposition, sometimes explicitly stated but most of the time operating as an unconscious background noise to our spiritual journey, that some transcendental psychology, filled with techniques and processes, can lead us to such a cosmic state. In effect, psychology becomes a form of modern Gnosticism. In the mystical tradition, however, it is made very clear that to blend with God is to go beyond image, beyond description, beyond phenomena, and beyond psychology and anything it can offer.

Many of the modern churches blend psychology with spirituality in a manner that further confuses the issue. As a consequence, even in mainstream culture, spirituality is often seen as a kind of psychological process or as something that should defer to psychotherapeutic processes. So it should be no wonder that the New Age movement reflects and at times amplifies this confusion. Psychology has many wonderful tools and insights to offer, and it can be an important adjunct to a disciplined spirituality, but it is not, at least in its current manifestations, a spiritual discipline in itself.

In the New Age movement, the psychologizing of spirituality leads to two general phenomena, both of which interfere with the movement toward the divine. The first is to turn one's attention away from the world and into the never-ending realms of the psyche. I have seen numerous promising spiritual projects and groups come to naught because the people involved lost their creative energy to endless rounds of processing their emotional and mental "stuff."

I grew up in Morocco and then later lived in Phoenix, Arizona. In both places we had dust storms, and even when the winds weren't blowing the desert into our homes, there was still dust in the air that just seemed to be forever settling out. No matter how often or how hard you dusted and cleaned, there was always new dust to take care of. Trying to clean the psyche of all its perceived blemishes seems to me like that. It is an endless process. Trying to become wound-free, I forget that my psyche is open to the wounds of the world, the pain within our collective unconscious. Healing our inner being is important, but if that is made the object of our spiritual journey, we may well find ourselves on an endless quest—I become perpetually self-absorbed to the detriment of my connections with the larger society and world of which I am a part.

The other extreme is to locate divinity within the self, so that if I go deeply enough or high enough within myself, I will find God. The ultimate expression of this can be found in those New Agers (fortunately a minority, in my experience) who simply claim to be

God. In this perspective, we each create our own reality, since that ultimate creative power that we call God is the essential nature of the psyche.

This is an attractive idea, and one that finds a certain resonance, unfortunately, in the American predilection for the self-sufficient individual, the one who makes his own way, takes care of herself in all circumstances, exhibits no weakness (and often little compassion), and expects others to do the same. It is Horatio Alger turned into a spiritual as well as an economic myth. "If everyone creates a personal reality," this myth seems to say, "then I don't have to bother with the poor, the disadvantaged, the oppressed; after all, they are creating that reality for themselves and if they don't like it, then they can change it. And if they don't change it, why, it must be because they don't choose to."

Needless to say, this is a prescription for selfishness and a withdrawal from the world. It ignores social injustice and closes itself to the real pain of others and to the ways in which we are all responsible for creating the conditions that contribute to that pain. However, though it finds a certain comic and tragic expression in the New Age movement, this kind of self-referencing, self-evaluating attitude is not a New Age idea. While certain New Age teachings may have wrapped it up in a spiritual glitter ("I can find my divinity, but if you can't find yours, that's your problem! Perhaps a few more lives will straighten you out; but in the meantime, don't get in the way of my utopia!"), we find the underlying attitude rampant in modern economics, politics, and religion: "I'm all right, Jack, and if you're not, then it's your own fault. If you can't make a decent life for yourself, perhaps you're just too lazy!"

Furthermore, there is in our culture an unconscious assumption of divinity, the shadow of which can be seen clearly in the ecological crisis facing us. There is no question that scientifically and technologically we have taken godlike powers to ourselves, and in our cavalier and utilitarian attitude toward the earth and other species have often given a religious imprimatur by assuming we are God's favored creation on the earth, and that all the riches and resources of the earth were basically created for us to use at our whim and pleasure. We definitely assume a godlike position of deciding issues of life and death, existence or nonexistence, for millions of other life-forms. One need only remember Reagan's Secretary of the Interior James Watt saying in effect that we need not be concerned with conservation or ecology, since Jesus was returning soon and the world would be destroyed anyway! More recently, Senator Slade Gorton of Washington State announced that logging jobs should have preference over the lives of endangered species such as the spotted owl, as if a U.S. senator should decide whether or not the spotted owl has a place in God's plan and creation and therefore whether it should live or become extinct.

In my own experience, I have been criticized by Christian fundamentalists for promoting an ecological ethic, since dealing with the world in any way is trafficking with "Satan's realm," while the whole ecological movement is a "satanic plot" to prevent good Christians from enjoying the fruits of the earth and from being free to mold the world to fit a humanly conceived notion of an earthly paradise. The fact is, as has been demonstrated again and again, we do not know enough about the nature of the interconnections and interdependencies of life and the mystery of God's creation to be able to mold it to our needs and desires without risking seriously unbalancing the well-being of the world. Since we are part of that world, whether we like it religiously, politically, or economically or not, we need to realize that our attitudes and actions can make us every bit as endangered as the spotted owl.

Frankly, if critics find an arrogance and narcissism in the New Age movement, it is because that movement arises from our current historical and cultural context. Such critics would do well to examine that state of our whole cultural household as well—the "beam" in their own eyes, as Jesus would say. In the New Age movement, at least there is an openness to play with the idea that we are divine rather than hypocritically denying any divinity to the human person and then acting like gods flaunting our power over the earth.

Still, the arrogance and narcissism are there within the New Age and do act as a hindrance to an authentic and compassionate spirituality. Actually, the idea that we create our own world or are responsible for the world we experience grew out of psychothera-peutic process that sought to deal with feelings of alienation, disempowerment, and a lack of responsibility for one's own life—the tendency to affix blame for one's difficulties "out there," onto someone or something else. It is a valid and valuable idea. Likewise, we are only beginning to understand just what the human mind is capable of. A person need only look at some of the amazing phenomena of healing and mind-body interactions being studied in such fields as psychoneuroimmunology to realize that we have not even scratched the surface of the powers that lie within the human psyche.

However, to discover and develop innate human psychic and healing talents, as with developing talents for music or art or mathematics, is not the same as creating community, much less embarking on a spiritual journey or moving toward divinity. To equate them with godliness is, to my mind, as mistaken as saying that learning to play the piano will make me a more deeply spiritual person. Music may take me to the threshold of an epiphany, as might an experience of healing through the power of the mind, but music and healing are not the same as experiencing God.

Again, the tragedy of the "I am God" faction within the New Age movement (sometimes isolated and elevated by the media—and by religious critics—as being a central teaching of a "New Age religion: the search for the Cosmic Self") is that it is a blind alley. To turn the self into deity is to become imprisoned within the self. When the powers of that self fail, as ultimately they will, to deal with all the mystery that life can bring to us, where then shall that person turn?

One very good element that the psychological emphasis within the New Age movement has brought has been a growing willingness and ability to confront the shadow, the existence of evil, pain, suffering, and woundedness in the world and in ourselves. When I first encountered the New Age movement in the late 1950s and then throughout the '60s and '70s, the general emphasis was on becoming spiritual, filled with light and love and goodness. There was no attention placed on dealing with the inner and outer shadow. I addressed this need in a talk I gave at the Findhorn Community in the early '70s. Using Lucifer as a mythic image for the shadow, I said that if we were not to engage with the Christ in an imbalanced way and, indeed, before we could fully embrace and discover the whole-ness that Christ represents, we needed to face up to, acknowledge in a healthy way, and work with the capability within us to create pain and suffering in the world. I rather flippantly called this a "Luciferic initiation," which was simply the realization that if we were to heal ourselves and our world, we needed to face the darkness as well as the light. (Unfortunately, later fundamentalist writers took this phrase out of context and, with no reference to the content of the talk, simply said that I was saying that to be a part of the New Age a person had to undergo a "Luciferic initiation" in which he would sell his soul to Satan, and this proved that the New Age was really a Satanic movement!)

The issue of the shadow—the repressed, suppressed, painful content of our unconscious, as well as the existence of oppression and injustice in the world—is gaining much more attention in the New Age movement now, which is to the good, though at times again it is dealt with in overly psychological ways. Still, if there is to be an authentic spiritual path toward the divine emerging out of the New Age movement, it cannot just be focused on the light but must work out how to deal with the darkness as well.

The psychologizing of spirituality with the consequent elevation of the self as either the arena for spiritual work or the location of divinity itself forgets one important factor: the rest of the world. We all live in community, and much that defines who we are comes from our relationships. We are cocreated by our connections with land, with nature, with one another, with society, with culture, with the cosmos. The self is not a private, isolated entity so much as it is a community project. God is nothing if not present within the whole of creation, the radical Other who invites us and at times forces us to go beyond the comfortable and the complacent boundaries of our psy-ches to engage with what is not us, with what is different from us, and to discover the sacred in the struggle to create and embody commu-nity. God may be in the wounds that I feel within myself, but God is also in the wounds that we inflict on one another and on the world. Healing myself may be a step toward the divine, but healing one another and the world is the other step that ensures we are actually going somewhere and not just standing still with one foot in the air.

The irony is that in the '60s and '70s one of the principal manifestations of the New Age was in the creation of community. It is also ironic that the New Age idea itself grows out of a much deeper image, myth, or archetype, which is that of the sacred community: a civilization in which humanity, nature, and God are all in a mutually enriching and empowering harmony. This myth can be found in nearly every human culture throughout history, and the sacred community is called by many names and imagined in many ways. At its heart is the sense that we are not fully human until we discover how to engage with the world and with one another in loving, compassionate, and cocreative communion, understanding that the well-being of each is dependent on the well-being of all.

If there is a valid New Age movement toward the divine, it can be helped by the psychological dimensions and practices of that movement but it cannot be defined by them. The movement into self may be important for personal healing, integration, and wholeness, but it is incomplete in itself. It should not be construed as being a movement toward the sacred.

So, where should we look to find a path toward God within the New Age milieu? We look, I feel, toward the idea that in a time of transformation, a time when all the cultures of the world are converging and we are beginning to develop a true sense of ourselves as a planetary species, we may also be experiencing a revisioning of our image of the nature of divinity. It is not just discovering another way of moving toward the divine (most of the older, traditional ways are pretty effective when properly undertaken) but reimagining the divine toward which we are moving.

At this point, let us return to the image of the fair. My argument so far has been that we cannot define the spirituality of the New Age—the way in which the New Age may serve as a path toward and into the sacred—by looking at any of the tents within the fair. Many of the tents are secular in their content and makeup, some are concerned strictly with psychological and therapeutic issues, some are places of discovery and exploration, and others offer specific spiritual paths that already exist outside the fair, such as Buddhism or Christian mysticism. The error, it seems to me, of many commentators on the New Age and its spirituality has been to isolate one or two tents and to deal with them as if they were cathedrals covering the whole fair.

The fair is not a cathedral. It is a place whose architecture is horizontal rather than vertical; it is a context within which a great many diverse paths can find some tenting ground and where there are many sights and sounds to be explored and investigated. Not everything is of equal value; not everything is compatible or agreeable. There are contradiction and conflict, confusion and paradox, a riot of colors whose combinations at times are pleasing and at times hurtful to the eye. Still, the fair is an environment conducive to learning and to discovery, to permitting the emergence of new insights and attitudes which might have had a harder time being recognized within the imposing structure of a cathedral.

The cathedral offers single-pointedness, a soaring aspiration, a unity of intent, every part supporting and augmenting every other part. It is contained by a vision. When we enter a cathedral, its very architecture informs us what we should feel and helps us to feel it, lifting our spirits toward a transcendent divinity. There is a conservatism within the cathedral, its very solidity and grandeur suggesting immutability.

Yet, as I mentioned earlier, we live in a time defined by change. Transformation is all about us. In the face of these pervasive energies of change, the religious institutions and traditions of our culture, rather than giving guidance and leading the way by being exploratory and daring in their own right, represent conservative elements, especially in their fundamentalist forms, acting to preserve the status quo. This, of course, can be a service, criticizing change for its own sake and providing continuity in the midst of transformation. It can also be reactionary, leaving religion on the sidelines while other institutions and processes guide the transformative energies of our culture but without including the spiritual dimension. If the New Age movement proves attractive for many people, it may well be because they want to grapple with personal and social change in profound ways but find no space or support in which to do so within their religious institutions. They seek the permissiveness, the support for exploration, and the whole wildness of the fair. The New Age fair in its diversity really only mimics the larger fair that is life itself. Such a fair includes and honors cathedrals, but includes much more besides. The tenor of our times demands that we learn how to engage with our world as it is rather than just with the bits and pieces of it that please or support us.

The cathedral emerges out of a singular image of God. The New Age fair contains many images of God, some contradictory, including the image that there is no God at all. How, then, can the New Age offer any kind of coherent or unified path toward the divine? The point is that it can't, if we are thinking in traditional, cathedral-like ways. Some of the tents within the fair can offer us their specific image of God and a path toward the sacred, but that is a different thing altogether from saying that there is a path embraced by and representing the fair itself.

The image of the future that the New Age movement is increasingly upholding is that we are moving away from a world of cathedrals, noble and heroic in their isolation, to a world that is a fair, confusing and messy in its diversity and interconnections. The task is to discover what anthropologist Gregory Bateson called "the pattern that connects," the wholeness underlying the fair. In effect, this means moving from a mind-set that sees everything in terms of separate categories and boundaries—my family, my tribe, my nation, my religion, my species to the exclusion of other families, tribes, nations, religions, and species—to one that sees in terms of patterns, connections, wholenesses, interdependencies, and the like, a mind-set that thinks in terms of ecologies.

Looked at this way, the spirituality of the New Age lies not in discerning a particular path to the divine but in asking the question, What is the nature of an ecological God contrasted to a cathedral God? That is, what kind of god, goddess, or sacredness can encompass and embrace a Christian, a Buddhist, a scientist, a psychologist, a Jew, a Muslim, a neopagan, a mystic, a human being, a tree, a river, a mountain, a planet? What kind of God lives in the connections between things and in the wholeness of life rather than at the end of a particular religious path?

At its best, the New Age offers a vision of sacredness that does not separate the individual from the world or from everyday life. It explores a sense of holiness and wholeness that is life-affirming and world-affirming, intimate with nature and seeking out the spirit of God in the incarnate cosmos. It is this incarnational and ecological aspect that may make New Age spirituality seem "new" to many folk, but in fact this aspect is also present in the best of our historical spiritual paths, particularly in the mystical traditions of our great religions. In fact, the whole idea of a "new" spirituality emerging—a specifically "New Age" spirituality—can be overdrawn and overemphasized, creating a division with past traditions where none really exists.

Where a primary difference may lie between "old age" and New Age spirituality is not in the destination but in the manner of the journey. One of the characteristics of the New Age fair is that it embodies a global spirit. The journey is not confined within a specific body of teachings but is conducted with openness to all the great faith traditions, including those that have special affinity with the spirituality of the land, such as the shamanistic traditions of many indigenous cultures. This eclectic openness can lead to diffusion and confusion and obviously carries risks: bits and pieces of traditions can be cobbled together in a way that seems pleasing to the celebrant but which destroys the awakening and disciplining power of those traditions. A false synthesis or homogenization can lead us nowhere.

On the other hand, by exploring the boundaries where faith traditions touch and begin to commune with one another, one can begin to discern the primal voice of the Mystery from which all these traditions ultimately emerge, the God of the ecology as well as the God of the cathedral. Approached with respect and discipline, the convergence of religions and paths in a global and ecological sensibility can also begin to reveal a truly universal spirit, the global aspects of a spiritual journey that previously has mainly been walked within ethnic and cultural hedgerows.

Therefore, the spirituality of the New Age is ecological in its outlook, both literally in its growing concern for the spirit and well-being of the earth as a whole and metaphorically in its emphasis on context, pattern, interconnections, and interdependencies. It recognizes how everything depends on, defines, and cocreates everything else, an image familiar to mystics but now being profoundly reinforced by the findings and perspectives of modern physics and cosmology.

The implication is that the divine is not a point toward which everything converges, but a field within which everything is embraced, sustained, and given special meaning and value. Accordingly, we encounter the divine not just in a special place or at a special time or through a special revelation, but potentially in any and all places and at any and all times. Anything in our lives can be a source of revelation.

Of course, this implies learning to think and to see in field-oriented terms, to think in terms of patterns and wholenesses, interconnections and intersections. It means honoring the particular as a unique manifestation of the overall field, but not defining or limiting the field in terms of the particular. We can honor Christianity, for example, as a unique revelation of the sacred, but not as the only revelation of the sacred. Indeed, by looking at and exploring other possible revelations, we may discover new dimensions and depths in our Christianity that were not visible to us before, when we lived exclusively within the architecture of its particular cathedral.

To explore another metaphor, this image is very resonant with the notion of the emerging information age and with the fluid nature of information itself. In the first place, as information doubles every five or seven years, the ability to navigate through "information space" becomes more essential, lest we be overwhelmed by the sheer volume of data. This means that the science of informational navigation and mapmaking, which is really a science of discerning interconnections and wholenesses and seeing the "patterns that connect," becomes vitally important. In such a science, I cannot arbitrarily discard information because it happens not to agree with or suit my particular belief system of the moment. By so doing, I might unwittingly create large gaps where the pattern becomes incomplete, or lose access to connections that later may be very important. In either event, my ability to navigate and arrive at new, more holistic perspectives can be impaired.

We see the physical analogy to this in the concern over the loss of the rain forest and other bioregions. We have no idea what information lies untapped in the biochemistry of the thousands of plant and animal species that are being destroyed every year with the rain forests around the world. The very information we may need to cure cancer, transmute toxic wastes, reverse the aging process, enhance intelligence, or aid some other human or planetary need may be being destroyed right now in the pursuit of limited goals.

The fact is that where information is concerned, diversity and difference are a virtue. Information loses its value when it is hoarded, hidden away, or reduced. It grows in value and gives birth to new information and insights when it is shared and exposed to a wider pattern of interactions. Where, in the past, each religious tradition may have jealously guarded its revelations and seen itself as the only truth, the New Age perspective is that in the quest for divinity the difference contained in the other fellow's belief system may hold a key to unlocking new revelation in my own. To destroy the metaphoric rain forest of the varieties of human religious experience in the name of one particular dogmatic monoculture is to visit upon our spiritual ecology precisely the same destruction and terror that is being visited upon our planet.

It is in this regard that Father Thomas Berry, Passionist priest, theologian, and self-defined "geologian," writes in his book *Befriending the Earth* that "the salvation of Christians lies in the unassimilated elements of Paganism,"[4] in particular those elements that have a reverence for and a sense of the sacred within the natural environments of the earth. It is in this regard as well that part of the spirituality of the New Age—part of the journey to the divine—lies in reclaiming the threatened rain forests of human spirituality and seeing just what important elements, even life-saving elements, within the current context of our ecologically and socially threatened planet there may be in such wild and exotic growths as shamanism, occultism, paganism, and Wicca, as well as in the domesticated and well-cultivated farmlands of Christianity, Judaism, Buddhism, Hinduism, and Islam.

The movement toward the divine in the New Age is thus more a movement to explore and broaden our images of the divine than it is a specific practice or technique in the traditional sense. It asks us to see the sacred from a planetary perspective, one inclusive of the many faith traditions that share this world and also inclusive in a deeply ecological way of the nonhuman world. After all, the animals, the birds, the mountains, the air, the rivers, the ocean, the forests, and all the rich diversity of earthly life have their tents in the fair as well! Older shamanistic traditions had a keen sense of the sacred as seen from the perspective of a tree or a stream, a beaver or an eagle; our loss of that deeper ecological awareness, that sense of the primal sacred community that is the cosmos and all the lives within it, has not really brought us enlightenment from superstition. It has brought us to the brink of destroying the natural world and ourselves with it, in the pursuit of human interests often narrowly defined by greed and short-term economic ascendancy.

The New Age is basically a transformational context. It gathers together and supports an energy of revisioning, reawakening, and new creativity within a variety of human endeavors. To my way of thinking, the purpose of the New Age idea as metaphor rather than as prophecy is not to tell us what the new world will be like but to inspire us with the knowledge that we can cocreate a new world. Part of that cocreation may well be a revisioning of our images of God, a transformation of our religious imagination to embrace a deeper and broader definition of the sacred, one that is cosmic, ecological, cocreative, and wild in the sense of being beyond the control of human interests and preferences.

God should not be tamed in our minds and hearts, a known commodity to worship and adore and to use as a boundary against everything that is different from us. God is the radical Other, challenging us to move beyond the familiar and the predictable. God is love and compassion beyond our imaginings, but God is also wild, ecstatic, and utterly unpredictable. God *is* the New Age, the original and only New Age, the Spirit that makes all things new. Perhaps the spirituality of the New Age movement will be to reawaken us to this transformative sacredness always being born at the heart of life and to empower us to make room for that birth in our own individual lives as well.

6

The New Age: The Movement Toward Self-Discovery

CARL RASCHKE

The Western metaphysical tradition, and to a large extent the
Eastern doctrines of spirituality, are based on the *separation* of the
body from the spirit, or soul. This legacy over the millennia has gone
by many names—Platonic, Gnostic, Hermetic, Vedantic. The
Greek thinker Plato talked about the liberation of *psychē,* or soul,
from its material casing through the practice of philosophy. The
ancient Gnostics, who believed in salvation through the achievement of secret "knowledge" (Greek *gnōsis*), regarded the body as a
prison, or tomb, from which the divine "spark" of human consciousness must be released.

Classical esotericists and occultists, who followed the doctrines
of the legendary teacher Hermes Trismegistus and laid the ground-
work during the late Renaissance for what today are known as "New
Age" theories, took much the same approach. Their legacy con-
verged around the turn of the twentieth century with the so-called
"wisdom of the East," in what came to be called the theosophical
movement. Theosophical tenets were built largely on views prevalent in ancient Buddhism and Hinduism, especially the scriptures of
the latter religion that have been named the "Vedas."

Until the twentieth century the dominant ideal of self-discovery
within the world's religions, or the quest for "authentic selfhood,"

was informed by a suspicion of sense awareness and the experience of the human body. The Hindu goal of moksha, or freedom from the cycles of reincarnation and earthly suffering, strongly illustrates this attitude. Although orthodox Christianity with its faith in a physical resurrection never fully embraced a so-called "mind-body dualism," the Western religious heritage has always been decidedly colored by such thinking. Over the millennia the Christian expectation of the "kingdom of God" has been cloaked in otherworldly symbols, even though liberal theology has at times sought to reinterpret the concept in secular, or this-worldly, terms.

The New Age Perspective

New Age religion, as it has evolved in recent years, takes a considerably different tack. The New Age perspective centers on the achievement of spiritual identity through a process of self-discovery that comes through the labyrinthine pathways of personal adventure and experimentation with new kinds of religion. The term *New Age*, in fact, is a label that has been pasted onto a whole spectrum of novel types of psychospirituality and the life-styles that accompany them. The word itself first appeared promi-nently several generations ago in the writings of Alice Bailey, noted theosophist and founder of the Esoteric School of Chris-tianity.

Since the 1960s, it has been applied to what used to be called "alternative" or "countercultural" styles of religious behavior. An-other expression that has been synonymous with New Age all along has been "Aquarian," although that phrase has steadily dropped out of use in the past decade.

The New Age angle of sight has always been suffused with a sense that the disciple must not adhere dogmatically to one set of theological principles or forms of religious development, but is free to pick and choose among an expansive range of options. New Age religion has been rightly, and without disdain, called by Harvard theologian Harvey Cox a "spiritual supermarket." Within that su-permarket are "name brands" of multifarious spiritual undertakings and disciplines, all of which are directed toward the general goal of self-discovery or personal fulfillment.

The typical New Age seeker is enormously different from the average, semireligious suburbanites who routinely take part in the formal expressions of historical Judaism or Christianity, yet direct their own private lives toward very common and tangible aims—a college education for their children, a comfortable retirement, paying off the twenty-year mortgage, and so forth. This typical New Ager is bent on "having it all," in a profound sense. He or she can only be content with the acquisition of "cosmic" understanding that includes a plenitude of personal knowledge as well as the attainment of privileged, religious insight.

Like the classic Indian yogi, the typical New Ager recognizes that there are many spiritual highways and byways to be trodden, and that ultimately all roads lead to the same summit of truth, consciousness, and happiness.

Yet, in contrast to the ancient approach, today's New Ager endeavors to follow as many road signs as is possible in a lifetime. In short, the typical New Age seeker wants to ascend the mountain and to traverse all its crags, canyons, and scarred surfaces, and he or she firmly believes there are many routes to the summit.

For that reason the "New Age way" can be considered a giant compendium, an ongoing *National Geographic* of the means of self-discovery. The New Age way is also a multivolume encyclopedia of metaphysical notions, esoteric techniques, crosscultural religious themes, and to some degree "scientific" maps of the universe. The present-day "guide for the perplexed"—which can be envisaged metaphorically as the entire range of subjects and titles in a New Age bookstore—entails astrology, yoga, divination, shamanism, Wicca or white witchcraft, worship of the earth goddess, ecology, human potential psychology, community activism, animal rights, geomancy, ceremonial magic, Buddhist meditation, "planetary politics," Jewish cabala, the ethics of Christian monasticism, the Hindu belief in karma and reincarnation, channeling of spirit guides, communication with dolphins and extraterrestrials, "psychotronics," Tibetan pilgrimages, the search for the earth's ancient "sacred sites," holistic health, herbs, psychic methods such as clairvoyance and telekinesis, out-of-body travel, "win/win" business strategies, massage, energy vortices, Indian sweat lodges, hypnosis, and so on.

None of these endeavors can be rated as having priority over or more importance than others. New Agers seek to be nonjudgmental about the world's many different life worlds and religious undertakings. Each undertaking, in fact, is just one gem in the great, complex mosaic of private religious meaning. But it all comes together, or makes eminent sense, for the seeker.

New Age Grammar

Sewn tightly within the luxuriant texture of global spirituality, however, is a common grammar that tends to support most New Age discourse. We might call this common way of talking about matters the "metalanguage" of the New Age. New Age metalanguage frequently employs the language of science, especially physics. Such a metalanguage in practice can best be described as a modern-day metaphysics rather than as a system of reasoning acceptable to established scientists.

The fundamental category in New Age metaphysics is "vibrational energy." According to quantum physics, all matter and energy can be schematized as a tapestry of vibrational patterns. Atoms and molecules vibrate at certain rates. The energy of the universe, and in particular electromagnetic energy, exists in discrete bundles or "quanta" that have their own vibrational signatures. Vibrational changes are responsible for the play, or transformation, of physical phenomena.

Some theoretical physicists have speculated that consciousness is the key factor in organizing these structures of vibrational energy, and thereby postulate a conceptual link between mind and matter. But such a position remains largely theoretical, with few experimental applications, and persists for the most part as a metaphysical construct.

Ancient religious attitudes and techniques, however, hovered around the sense that mind and body not only could be understood, but could be altered, in keeping with this picture of patterns of vibratory energy. An esoteric practice known as Tantrism, which developed in India but has certain counterparts in other world traditions, derived from the notion that the expansion of consciousness is achieved through the raising of physical energy to ever-higher states.

An evident, but not completely appropriate, analogy would be the generation of colored light waves through the heating of certain kinds of salts. The light waves are produced through the "raising" of the atoms to higher energy states. In the same vein, tantric ritual depends on the alleged raising of the "kundalini," or "coiled serpent," of sexual energy, which is lodged at the base of the spine, through a series of increasingly higher levels, or states.

These states, corresponding to different organs or points on the body, are designated as "chakras." The chakras are "plexuses" of the so-called "etheric body" which surrounds its physical counterpart like a shadow. There are seven chakras, located along an axis that passes from the tailbone to the cranium. The highest state is the "crown chakra" (*sahasrara* in Sanskrit) on the top of the skull, which, when energized, affords total self-knowledge as well as cosmic consciousness.

Specific tantric religious practices have throughout history been carried out successfully only by a small number of trained adepts. And while tantric worship has always remained suspect in the eyes of the orthodox clergy, even within those circles where it is accepted it has been surrounded with warnings and cautionary tales for the frivolous or uninitiated.

Although the idea of Tantrism as "sex magic" may have a certain prurient appeal for the modern sexual thrill seeker, the reality is quite different. The wrong application of tantric psychology and ritual may cause deep emotional distress. Altogether, the tantric path of "kundalini yoga," as it is popularly called, reflects a philosophical perspective that identifies sexuality with the creative and intelligent power of the universe. New Age religion in its varying facets has affirmed the connection between sexuality and spirituality.

Recently, some New Age adepts have more and more embraced this linkage by adopting neopagan or earth-based forms of religious expression. Only a small percentage of New Agers, of course, have leapt unreservedly into neopagan religious practices, which in the past have been popularly, although not necessarily accurately, termed "witchcraft." Neopaganism rests on the primordial belief that earth energies, which scientists increasingly recognize as magnetic lines of force, can be harnessed and channeled for healing purposes or to socially beneficial ends. Human sexuality, including in some cases the use of nudity and ritual copulation in special, controlled settings, becomes an integral part of earth-based piety. Whereas Tantrism seeks to transmute the power of personal sexual desire into higher forms of spiritual illumination, neopaganism stresses collective ceremony and group experience.

Tantrism can be highly individualistic in its deployment, whereas neopaganism tends to emphasize the "tribal" dimensions of knowledge. In the main, however, both Tantrism and neopaganism constitute important slices of the spectrum of practice and belief that count as the New Age way. The New Age way can be defined as the effort to harmonize the state of personal ego-awareness with a consciousness of the global, if not galactic, totality.

An Evolutionary Model of Transformation

One of the overriding themes in New Age literature is "planetary growth," the evolution of the psychic and social capacities of the human race from simple, sentient organisms to superintelligent beings. In comparison with the traditional biblical picture of the creator God who brings the world into existence by God's own command, and its view of human life as creaturely and subservient to the will of one's maker, the New Age outlook rests on the premise that human beings are evolutionary products of nature and that the goal of the long-term development process is the realization of their innate divinity. Shirley MacLaine's assertion several years ago in her television miniseries *Out on a Limb* that she was "God" can be seen as a statement of this evolutionary standpoint.

The divinization of the individual cannot be dissociated from the emergence of "planetary consciousness" in the New Age scenario. In his book *The Global Brain,* Peter Russell talks about the earth as an intelligent organism that destructive human behavior and environmental pollution have inhibited in its growth. The context for the elaboration of the "earth-as-conscious-entity" theory has been the work of British scientist James Lovelock, who called the planet "Gaia" after the name of an old Greek earth goddess. Lovelock's "Gaia hypothesis" has been a broad source of inspiration not only for New Age mythmakers, but for neopagan practitioners and religious feminists. If the planet is a conscious female entity, then "she" is worthy of respect.

In addition, the Gaia hypothesis becomes in the New Age mind a kind of metaphysical warrant for the critique of the Judeo-Christian tradition with its masculine God and its patriarchal structure of authority. Gaian religiosity has not merely been cited for the defense of an extreme ecological ethic. It has also been construed as a way of envisaging a thoroughly terrestrial spirituality that highlights the nurturing side of women and culture while orienting the mind toward the inner mysteries of the earth.

In the summer of 1987, University of Colorado art historian and New Age theoretician José Argüelles announced a major cosmic event that came to be known as the Harmonic Convergence. Although press pundits and cartoonists were apt to make fun of the celebrations that surrounded the Convergence, the episode turned out to be a major historical rallying point for the New Age movement itself. Argüelles talked to the media about ancient Mayan calendars, great beams of light from stellar sources, the unlocking of the meaning of the myth of the Mexican savior-god Quetzalcoatl, humming and chanting by clusters of like-minded seekers around the globe in an effort to boost the "vibratory rate" of the planet.

One of the sidebars to the Harmonic Convergence was a sudden rise in interest within the New Age community in visits to the planet's "sacred sites"—places of "high energy" from the geomagnetic standpoint that had been the destination for religious pilgrimages and vision quests for untold centuries among the earth's indigenous peoples, including the native Americans. A sizable party of New Age votaries spent the days of the Convergence at Chaco Canyon in New Mexico and buried crystals in the ground in order to help "attune" the planet's vibratory patterns.

The underlying belief among those celebrating the Convergence was that concerted conscious action on a planetary scale would not only lead to peace and a reduction in political tension, it would also empower hundreds of thousands of individuals in their quests for personal wholeness and self-understanding. Some celebrators of the Convergence also made love with each other in order to assist in the new vibratory alignment of Mother Earth.

In an interview with the New Age magazine *Magical Blend* in 1987, Argüelles gave the following explanation for the planting of crystals, which he said had been ordered by the higher powers. It is "to create a field of attunement . . . with the Earth and to send a message to the Earth that there are certain members of the human community acting on behalf of the whole who are responsive to the needs of the Earth at this time."[1]

Argüelles went on to note that the "instructions" he had received for "crystal planting" involved creating a circle and burying six crystals no more than one pound "in the form of a six-pointed star, which is inscribed by a hexagon." At the center would be a seventh crystal made of amethyst, referring to the "violet ray" that Bailey had talked about in her writings. "This is, in a way," declared Argüelles, "ceremonial magic."[2]

The degree to which the actual use of, and of course the belief in, forms of occult magic are central to Aquarian practitioners is an item of controversy among New Age watchers these days. The twentieth-century traditions of "magic," as they have come to be called, were spread with the writings of British occultist Aleister Crowley (1875–1947). According to some interpretations, Crowley has had a significant impact on the formation of New Age notions, although the theosophical strains are much stronger. Crowley taught the art of self-realization—what might be dubbed one's own "private alchemy"—through a variety of magical means with origins in ancient Egypt, Masonry, druidism, and most importantly Tantrism.

It was Crowley's preoccupation with "sex magic" that helped win him a notorious reputation. Crowley called himself the "Beast

666" after the diabolical monster figure in the book of Revelation, and in turn he was described in the press as "the wickedest man in the world."[3] Much of Crowley's outrageous life-style would probably be regarded more tolerantly today. What Crowley achieved despite his notoriety was the translation of hitherto highly secretive, and hopelessly obscure, magical principles into an idiom for the more mainstream individual.

Crowley is the leading source for today's popular ideology of magic, and the pivotal New Age value of self-actualization through personal transformation probably owes a large debt to him.

Nonetheless, the destiny of Earth, according to New Age teaching, is not entirely in individual human hands, although it is also not under the direction of an all-sovereign, willful father God, as in conventional Christianity. Human history and planetary growth have been under the watchful eye of highly evolved beings who have gone by many names over the centuries—"ascended masters," "mahatmas," "guardians," and more. In some recent New Age writings these "masters" have been associated with aliens from outer space. The popularity of the writings of Whitley Strieber, author of *Communion,* which describes encounters with and messages from extraterrestrials, has reinforced this sort of impression.

Interest in conversation between the "masters" and human minds has been the main occasion for the popularity of channeling. Channeling is an up-to-date, New Age version of what in earlier generations were known as "spirit possessions" or "seances." Channelers themselves are those who used to be called "mediums." The one-time Hollywood caricature of an elderly female medium with a scarf tied about her head, seated at a table along with relatives of a dead person in a darkened room and using a Ouija board to evoke the words of the departed Aunt Augusta, has been replaced by slick, bright-room seminars of youthful, attractive, and well-groomed channelers with celebrity status who go into trance and let speak the voices of ancient kings, holy men, and warriors with such strange names as "Mafu" or "Ramtha."

Yet the principle remains basically the same. Channelers and their followers, who for a while in the public's perception *were* the sum and substance of New Age religiosity, become the psychic bridge between highly evolved spirit-entities and their lesser, mortal brothers and sisters. The channeler performs a kind of priestly function in the New Age religious community, even though many channelers—as with all clergy down through the ages—have been accused by detractors and skeptics of hoodwinking and fleecing their flocks.

The spirit entities, through the mouths of channelers, advise their followers about everything from marriage problems to strategic investments to everyday life in ancient Atlantis. The central motif of the channeling sessions, however, is to find the best way to authentic selfhood. Channelers often advise private sessions with their clients, or encourage them to read works of New Age literature or certain other texts.

According to David Spangler, one of the best-known spokespersons for New Age thought and a contributor to this volume, the "New Age" is a metaphor for the act of creative transformation. Spangler says that "creative transformation" signifies in considerable measure the act of "taking responsibility" for the life choices one makes and for the movement of the earth itself toward a "new paradigm" of politics, intellect, personal relationships, and attitudes toward our environment.[4] Other writers have characterized New Age as "choosing our future" or joining forces with others to bring about a new "creative design" for the world as a whole. For human beings collectively to assume the task of redesigning the world is a tall order, and such an ethic differs fundamentally from the traditional Christian notion of waiting for God to come down and intervene in human affairs.

In many ways, New Age can be portrayed as a kind of personal, spiritual style of eco-humanism with an emphasis on the salvation of the world through planetary action. New Age eco-humanism departs from the older, nineteenth-century modes of humanism because of its adherence to the notion of an ineradicable spiritual dimension to human existence. Earlier humanism stressed the primacy of the material universe and set human ingenuity and creativity over against the creative power of God. Human beings were essentially divine by virtue of their humanity, said the old humanism.

Theology must become anthropology, wrote Ludwig Feuerbach, one of the foremost nineteenth-century humanists, who exerted a crucial influence on the philosophy of Karl Marx. New Age eco-humanism, however, maintains that human existence is not an end in itself, but one great wave on the limitless ocean of consciousness. To become truly human is to manifest the potential of the universal mind. To become cognizant of one's own "godness" and to arrive at the fullness of self-discovery are tantamount to each other, so far as many New Agers are concerned.

The New Age worldview, according to bibliographer J. Gordon Melton, turns chiefly on a mystical and almost ineffable state of mind dubbed "the transformative experience." The transformative experience can be summed up as a sense of sudden release from all the problems and oppressions of life. The transformative experience bears some similarity to old-style Christian conversion, but the resemblances are for the most part superficial.

Whereas conversion arises out of a feeling of incurable sinfulness, which is all at once erased by the grace of an infinitely merciful and loving God, the transformative experience is an instantaneous break with all negative habits of emotion and thought. The "transformed" New Ager, observes Melton, is at once unbound from poverty, illness, boredom, purposelessness, and every conceivable instance of existential anxiety. Like the Zen moment of enlightenment, the transformative experience sweeps away all doubts, confusion, and criticism.

The transformative experience can also be seen as the final goal of the New Age immersion in countless religious and ordinary experiences. The model of the transformative experience can be traced back to the thought of Abraham Maslow, who was instrumental during the 1960s in developing what has come to be called "humanistic psychology." Maslow outlined what he called a "hierarchy of needs" rising from the simple requirements of food, drink, and sex all the way up to so-called "peak experiences"—mystical states of religious understanding or illumination. Maslow's concept of the peak experience prefigures the New Age notion of the "transformative" experience.

The theosophically minded have frequently spoken about the inevitable advent of a great New Age teacher. In Bailey's writings he was called "Maitreya" and "the Christ." The juxtaposition of the two titles is slightly ironic, because the name "Maitreya" comes out of the Buddhist tradition and refers to a Buddha from the future. Bailey's disciples are fond of reciting the Great Invocation, which in some circles functions as the New Age counterpart to the Lord's Prayer in Christianity. The Invocation calls for, among other things, the descent of the "Light" within "the Mind of God" to Earth and its dwelling in the hearts of human beings, whereby the mysterious "Plan" of the ascended hierarchy will be put into operation on earth.

According to some renderings of Bailey's teaching, Maitreya as the New Age "world teacher" is what the Hindus used to call the "avatar," or incarnate divinity, for our age. In 1972, a student of Bailey's writings named Benjamin Creme started to "channel" communiqués from the ascended masters. On the basis of these channelings, Creme predicted the "reappearance of the Christ" in the spring of 1982, which unfortunately came and went without the public recognition of the world teacher. Creme recorded and published Maitreya's teachings, which were received telepathically and sounded remarkably like the sayings of Alice Bailey. On March 11, 1980, Maitreya proclaimed that "the Son of Man walks abroad once more, that the Teacher for the New Age is among you, and that the Age has begun. Speak thus, My dear ones, and light a lamp for Me."[5]

Creme has repeatedly stated that he has met the world teacher, who is living incognito in the slums of London.[6] Creme has never made clear how the New Age belief in personal self-transformation and the epiphany of a world avatar can be squared with each other. Traditional East Asian Buddhism has taught that the "coming" of Maitreya is not a historical event, but a breakthrough to illumination and wisdom on the part of the seeker. That interpretation may be more in keeping with the spirit of the New Age than Creme's somewhat literalist eschatology would imagine.

The Social and Political Agenda

Although the core of New Age culture is the transformative experience, the New Age movement itself has from the beginning had a social and political agenda from which the goal of personal self-discovery cannot be divorced. The details of this agenda were laid out in the early 1980s with the publication of a book by Marilyn Ferguson titled *The Aquarian Conspiracy: Personal and Social Transformation in Our Time.*

Ferguson's book was really an opening gun, a thundering manifesto, for the New Age change makers. "A great shuddering, irrevocable shift is overtaking us," the book jacket proclaimed. "It is not a new political, religious, or economic system. It is a new mind—a turnabout in consciousness in critical numbers of individuals, a network powerful enough to bring about radical change in our culture." The author speaks to those who are experiencing a growing capacity for change in themselves and know that it is possible for others. This book gives heart to the tens of millions who sense the ripeness of our society for renewal and to those who despair but are willing to look at the evidence for hope.

The Aquarian Conspiracy offers its own expansive Wal-Mart of options for "personal change." It lists self-hypnosis, transcendental meditation, Sufi dancing, dream journals, the science of mind religion, mountain climbing and wilderness retreats, all the martial arts, humanistic psychotherapies, New Age music, pottery, biofeedback, LSD, the Congressional Clearinghouse for the Future, quantum physics, the U.S. Army, self-help networks, hospices for the dying, herbalism, Elderhostels, free universities, Tibetan Buddhism, Werner Erhard's hunger project, and the Unity Church as significant instances or players in the "Aquarian Conspiracy."

Even though all these seemingly disparate institutions or activities may not at one level seem connected, in Ferguson's survey they become "invisible beginnings" of a "revolution in consciousness" that leads to a "transformation of society." Ferguson sums up the political rendering of the Great Invocation, the "plan" for a new social order: "Let there be transformation, and let it begin with me."[7]

The value of personal transformation can apply even to the disabled. In her essay "Shattered Dreams and Transformations," Dixie Hummer Toelkes, who identifies herself as "head injury consultant and counselor," cites Shirley MacLaine's writings as support for Toelkes's view that her daughter Julie's serious brain damage should be viewed not as a family tragedy, but as a "lesson" to be learned by different "souls" in this particular earthly drama. "I believe our family made an agreement as a unit to experience Julie's injury," Toelkes writes, "to benefit on a spiritual level from all the pain and suffering we've experienced." Toelkes concludes that Julie's confinement to a wheelchair in a nursing home turned out to have "many benefits," the most compelling of which was that the family became "determined to help our daughter achieve her highest potential."[8]

The New Age "personal growth" ethic has spawned a growth industry in its own right. In the late 1980s, an organization known as Choices and Connections in Boulder, Colorado, launched a chain of "personal growth retail stores" aimed at providing a "unique focus on improving the quality of life." Each store was designed to offer "a carefully selected array" of New Age books, music, educational tapes, children's games, and other forms of merchandise. Each store also offered equipment to assist with relaxation and stress management.

New Age entrepreneurship, not just in retailing but in management consulting, has flourished in recent years as a result of the new "transformational" value system. The motivating philosophy behind New Age business ventures, according to its own exponents, is no longer material acquisition and the profit motive, but the "spiritual" attitude of self-structuring. Such a philosophy has become most familiar to New Age participants through what has come to be called "win/win" gamesmanship.

In normal business competition there must be both winners and losers. In a win/win situation, however, everyone is what management expert Sandra T. Adair calls a "win/win winner." Win/win winning is characterized by basing decisions on what will bring success rather than failure, on developing support networks, on making a commitment that the other person in a win/win field of play becomes a winner, maintaining honesty and fully disclosing all information, careful listening to the other person while staying grounded "in the present," taking total responsibility for what one "creates," staying open to new ideas, and what Adair terms "living your passion."

To live one's passion is the key to "organizational transformation," which in turn enhances personal transformative experiences. A well-functioning organization is one in which stress is minimized and cooperation maximized. The relief of personal stress through different forms of "psychotechnology" such as meditation, biofeedback, and chanting can make a significant difference toward this end. But the best stress reliever, according to New Age management precepts, is a pervasive climate of trust and commitment on the part of all employees that is propelled by a win/win point of view. An article written by Adair urges that all win/win players surround themselves "with people who share the same passion." Win/win winners must be "willing to become win/win in all [their] interactions."9

But the movement toward self-discovery in the final analysis must be founded on a cosmic transformative vision of life. It hinges on the essential idea that the species, and the planet, is on its way toward what has been called the "quantum leap" into a whole new domain of existence. An anonymous futurist named FM-2030, who has been described by *New Age Magazine* as having "the transcendental presence of a master," calls this state "the transhuman." According to FM-2030 in his book *Are You a Transhuman?* there are distinctive marks of the evolutionary sojourner en route to a transhuman metamorphosis. Pilgrims on the way to this metamorphosis are known as "upwingers" and are considered the avantgarde of evolutionary and planetary progress. They are reputed to have great intelligence and not to let their emotions interfere with judgment.

The movement toward self-discovery in the New Age context is never-ending. Individual transformation is an open-ended process. Whether god or guru, planetary activist or personal counselor, magus or metaphysician, massage therapist or manager, networker or "neuro-linguistic programmer," the New Age wayfarer is on the road to the Ultimate Somewhere. The New Ager does not fear taking the road not taken, because all treks converge at the Final Crossroads.

7

The New Age: The Movement Toward the World

VIVIENNE HULL

About ten years ago the first of several conferences on "The Earth Community" was held at the Episcopal Cathedral of St. John the Divine in New York City. It was an important and timely gathering, bringing together colleagues from various disciplines and the general public to share concerns and insights about the spiritual dimension of the environmental crisis. Among the featured speakers was theologian and historian of cultures Father Thomas Berry, who in the following years was to be recognized as one of the leading voices in the formulation of a new ecological cosmology and theology. Tom Berry had a profound impact on the gathering with his message:

> What is clear is that the Earth is mandating that the human community assume a responsibility never assigned to any previous generation. We are being asked to accept responsibility commensurate with our greater knowledge. We are being asked to learn a new mode of conduct and discipline. This is preeminently a religious and spiritual task, for only religious forces can move human consciousness at the depth needed. Only religious forces can sustain the needed effort. Only religion can measure the magnitude of what we are about. . . . Our task at this critical moment is to awaken the energies needed to create the new world, to evoke a universal communion of all parts of life. We must now respond creatively to the urgencies imposed on us

by an interior energy that holds the stars within the galactic clusters, that shaped the planet under our feet, that has guided life through its bewildering variety of expression. There is reason to believe that those mysterious forces that have guided earthly events thus far have not suddenly collapsed under the great volume of affairs in the late twentieth century.[1]

Tom, who has since become a close colleague and friend, at a later time shared his passionate conviction that our generation is one of destiny. What is needed is a compelling vision that will capture the imagination and commitment of people, evoking sufficient energy to meet the great challenges of this time in history.

The New Age, at its best, has represented to many just such an entrancing vision. It has grasped and inspired the imaginations of men and women who have taken to heart the seriousness of our situation and the importance of the choices we make in this crucial era. It has drawn those with deep spiritual hunger, those for whom religion failed or offered only an inadequate response to the search for life purpose, foundational ethics, and meaningful participation in shared community. It spoke to those who sought confirmation that some great and good force indeed continued to guide human affairs in spite of all very real evidence to the contrary. It offered a new context in which to view our period in history as the threshold of a new planetary era in which the future depends on our capacity to live beyond self-interest and on behalf of the common good. Most significantly, it defined the common good as the well-being not just of the human community but of the Earth community, the whole interdependent community of planetary life. It linked personal well-being with corporate well-being and brought to light what may be the foremost ethical challenge of our time: the responsibility to recognize that personal values, choices, and actions profoundly affect the quality of life of all people and all species, and the lives of all future generations.

This is not, of course, what the New Age symbolized then or now to everyone. Even at the time of the first Cathedral conference, the New Age was receiving considerable attention in the popular press, and usually in its most outlandish and dismaying aspects. Mixed together, with little assessment or discernment, were important and

pioneering efforts in the fields of ecology, health, community, appropriate technology, psychology, science, education, agriculture—in
short, almost all fields of human endeavor—with an eclectic spread of
activities from psychic channeling and moon rituals to crystal power,
aura balancing, past life regressions, meditation practices, and a
steady stream of gurus, from East and West, some authentic, some
not. The New Age wheat had not yet been separated from the chaff,
so to speak, the true wisdom from the spiritual junk food, the guiding
vision from the glittering light.

Underneath the perplexing and mostly benign assortment of
ideas, programs, and therapies identified as New Age ran a deeper
transformative current marked by two important convictions. One
was the belief that this time in history is unique, a watershed era,
marked by a radical shift in how we understand human nature and
our interdependent relationship with our environment. The second
was that if there is to be a viable future at all, then our social,
political, and religious institutions must reform themselves in light
of this new relationship.

What the critics did not fully consider was that the New Age
movement represented in itself an important response to the perceived failure of mainstream values and institutions by many people
who were seeking answers to the issues affecting both personal life
and the fate of the planet. For example, in many of the intentional
communities popular in the early 1970s men and women worked
hard to counteract what they perceived as wrong or inadequate in
conventional social forms. They experimented with non–materially
dependent life-styles, consensus decision making, nonhierarchical
forms of leadership, self-responsible health care, economic cooper-
atives, and a variety of efforts in both rural and urban settings to heal
the environment by emphasizing the importance of organic garden-
ing, urban permaculture, the protection of regional biosystems,
"living lightly," and the mandate to "think globally, act locally."
These efforts were not at that time given much thoughtful consideration or assessment by social critics or the mainstream press.

For reasons not fully understood to date, the conservative
Christian church took to the road in condemnation of the New Age.
The accusations came not from liberal or progressive Christian

communities, which remained mildly suspicious or mildly interested, but from the conservatives who saw the New Age, along with a host of other things, as a threat to the traditional values and beliefs of historic Christianity as defined by their own interpretation of scripture. At the heart of the reaction were serious concerns such as the loss of the centrality of Christ and the manipulation of the individual by cults. Surfacing again, however, was the old fear of the devil, the Antichrist, the "satanic conspiracy" suspected to be hiding in liberal causes and "left-wing" social or religious movements. These fears typically resulted in acts of categorical dismissal. By labeling an array of diverse activities, programs, ideas, and people as New Age, and with New Age judged as a threat to Christ, then nothing and no one in the movement was to be taken seriously, and everything was to be equally dismissed.

The mainstream Christian community failed to challenge the conservative reaction and speak out for open-hearted respect for diversity of belief and practice. In retrospect this served to convince many men and women drawn by the inspiration of a New Age vision that the institutional church had little to offer their search for authentic spiritual life, or to guide their response to the challenges facing the global community in the last decade of this century.

With most of my colleagues I welcomed the thoughtful critique of the New Age by informed people, though I regretted the controversy. The variety of activities that had come to be associated with the New Age seemed increasingly superficial, opening people to new ways of thinking and to new experiences but not adequate to sustain mature personal, spiritual growth, nor to promote committed and strategic responses over the long haul to the mounting social, ethical, and environmental problems before us. Many of us soon disclaimed the New Age label or worked to redefine it. We certainly looked for other ways to name the deeper creative current moving in our society. We talked then, as we do now, of a new global order, of a planetary age, of the consciousness or transformational movement, of the postmodern world.

The New Age can be seen as a mixed bag, its excesses and superficialities obvious to note. While it is important to look at its serious shortcomings as a strategy for personal and social change, and the ways in which it may fail to promote truly creative and responsible action, it seems more important to me not to do this first—not until we have taken a serious look at the positive contributions of the New Age movement to our society and to the lives of many caring, intelligent, and deeply spiritual people who are committed to being of service to the world community.

It is in this spirit that I would like to identify what I believe are the contributions of the New Age, or the transformational movement as I prefer to name it, to the formation of a new social, spiritual, and ecological vision and mandate.

I would like to set a context for my perspective on the New Age by sharing a bit of personal history, for two reasons. First, I believe the New Age is all about "story," the story we tell about who we are, why we're here, what we believe, what is the nature of our time, who and what we serve. Second, because the formative experiences of our early lives, though not made conscious or integrated until much later, may provide the motivating energy for our most critical life choices. This is certainly true for me.

Born in Northern Ireland in the "old age" of the 1940s, I grew up in a working-class Protestant family whose beliefs, habits, preferences, and prejudices were strongly determined by the teachings of a conservative Presbyterian church. I was reared in a Christian community whose major concerns were, first, the salvation of my soul and, second, that I would in no way or at any point, ever, be influenced by Catholicism. My childhood was constricted by prejudice and overshadowed by the fear of those who were different, by boundaries that one did not question or cross, by battle lines drawn both theological and actual, in the name of Christianity and Protestantism. Even as a youngster I wondered about all this and knew in my bones that something was not right.

In marked contrast to the rigid sin, redemption, and anti-Catholic orientation of my church, my own inner experiences of God were accompanied by a pervasive sense of lovingness and grace, of somehow being known, part of, and needed in the greater order of things. I was also touched by a bit of the old Irish magic.

For in Ireland, then and now, the stream of an ancient spiritual tradition still runs as a strong mystical undercurrent to the conservative orthodoxy of the day. Though the ancient Celtic mysteries and contemporary Protestantism did not fit well together, and I lacked an adequate theological or intellectual framework in which to interpret my experiences, I knew that in this realm of spirit lay the key to overcoming the barriers and superstitions that shadowed my Irish world.

In retrospect I can see that the driving motivation in my life has been for an understanding of Christian spirituality and theology that honors the integrity and authenticity of our personal experience of God, that assists people in recognizing and confronting prejudice and dogmatism, and that enables people to live beyond self-interest in order to forge a future where the needs of others in the shared community of life may be honored and met.

As I grew up and out of conservative Christian Ireland, and came to know and appreciate other cultures and traditions, I continued to be a committed and involved member of the Christian (Presbyterian) church, though my inclinations obviously drew me away from anything dogmatic and rigid and into more liberal and activist circles. While fortunate as an adult to be part of a vital, caring, and engaged church community, I came to see that liberal Protestant Christianity, while more generous than the conservative church in its acceptance of diversity and allowing greater variation in theological interpretation, nonetheless also drew the line of judgment defining who was within the circle of God's grace and who was not. It was of course a much wider circle. But outside it lay the unchurched, the non-Christian world, and all of the natural order. However, in spite of growing theological discomfort, growls of conscience, and occasional protests from my Celtic soul, I remained properly "Christ-centered, biblically based, and socially relevant" in viewpoint. Then came the 1960s, a watershed period in American life, a deeply disturbing and unsettling era characterized by a profound opening up of consciousness and conscience and a radical alteration in many people's views of the world and its future. Including mine.

This to me is the ground in which the seeds of the present New Age movement took hold, born out of a profound personal disturbance about the viability of our social, political, economic, and religious institutions to address the issues of the day, energized by the personal search for meaning, values, and an adequate worldview, and inspired by the possibility of new ways of thinking about and engaging our world.

Many people at the time were criticizing Western industrial society as failing to offer a viable vision of the future with the power to give meaning to present action. They believed that imaging the future only as a further extrapolation of present material, industrial, and secular trends could offer little or nothing that inspired the imagination toward new possibilities. Joseph Campbell in an early interview with Bill Moyers echoed this sentiment, saying that until the middle of the twentieth century viable myths and images of the future held society together and provided a shared framework for value and meaning. Such myths and ideals were what the religious dimension of life was all about. Their loss marked the failure of religion to keep measure with the development of human experience corresponding to the changed realities of history. Campbell perceived that society evolves according to the energizing images and stories informing and inspiring its people. Today, this is what we lack. We are in between stories. We hunger for a new guiding myth that gives our lives meaning and helps us to be at home in the universe. We need, as Tom Berry says, an entrancing vision commensurate with the realities of our time.

It was in the light of these concerns and our perceived need for new approaches to spiritual formation and religious education that my husband, Fritz Hull, and I "broke pattern" and in 1972 left our work in the institutional church. We formed the Chinook Learning Center as a learning environment and covenant community dedicated to the "personal integration of religion and life." We did not see ourselves as leaving the Christian community, nor as joining a New Age counterculture. Rather, we were motivated by a powerful inner experience of God's calling and our sense that a vital new movement of Christ's Spirit was out and about in our world and making itself known within and outside conventional religious circles. This was, in fact, what the New Age first meant to us personally. We saw it not as a movement, and certainly not as a religion, but as a "new story," a metaphor, a way of describing the shift from a narrow worldview to a planetary perspective. It was a way of imagining a hopeful and compelling vision of the future. It called for the revitalizing of spiritual life and affirmed the ongoing presence and participation of God's Spirit (by whatever name) in the evolution of planetary life. It linked inner personal transformation with responsible action and service in the world. It was for us another way of talking about the "kingdom of God."

It was about this time that I stumbled into a wonderful thing. The search for innovative models of Christian community had taken us to the Island of Iona in the Inner Hebrides of Scotland as guests of the Iona Community. Founded in the 1940s by George MacLeod, a visionary leader of the Church of Scotland, the Iona Community had become a highly acclaimed international, ecumenical order of men and women linked together by a commitment to the work of peace and justice and to the renewal of the inner contemplative life. With its emphasis on education and service, the Iona Community became an inspiration and model as we created the Chinook Learning Center.

Iona brought another gift. Here, on this lovely island known since ancient time as a place of unique beauty and spiritual power, something remarkable had happened which bore unexpected relevance to the issues of my own life. Its contribution to the New Age movement would later be apparent.

It was here I discovered the story of Celtic Christianity and the influence of the Irish monastic schools, of which Iona in the sixth century was among the most renowned. I learned how Christianity developed in Britain from the first century for almost a thousand years with its own unique theology and form. I learned about the contribution of strong, visionary women and men with powerful spirit and flamboyant style, for whom Christianity heralded nothing less than a new order or a new age of the Spirit. This little-known stream within Western religious history became not only a vital resource in my own spiritual formation but a reminder of the rich diversity of belief and practice that historically lies at the heart of the Christian tradition.

As I set out to learn more, and found few reliable sources, I was troubled that such sparse attention had been paid in conventional theological education and church life to the contribution of the early Celtic Christians. Such a rich tradition would be ignored only if its theology and practice presented a clear challenge to the prevailing orthodoxy. Fascinated by the hint of controversy, I plunged into a long-term study of the "alternate path" along which Christianity had developed in the West.

A bit of history helps tell the tale. While common belief holds that Saint Patrick brought Christianity to Ireland around 432, recent scholarship confirms that in fact Christianity was well established in Ireland more than a century earlier. By most accounts Christianity reached Britain before the end of the first century, carried by traders, soldiers, or members of early sects escaping persecution. The "new story" of Jesus and his teachings took hold and spread rapidly in Ireland, where it was taken up by scholars and priests and adapted into the central teachings of the great learning centers that existed throughout the society. By the sixth century it was said that the saints of Ireland "numbered more than the stars in the heavens."

By Patrick's time the Irish Christians already had a reputation on the Continent for their contrary theology and practices. Many scholars have concluded that Patrick was sent to Ireland not as missionary but as reformer. His task was to bring the errant Celtic church under the doctrinal and ecclesiastical authority of Rome. That it took several more centuries for this to occur indicates the vitality and tenacity of the Irish Christian pattern.[2]

Christianity flowered in Celtic Ireland because its central story was seen as a further elaboration of the existing spiritual orientation and cosmology of the culture. It developed with an emphasis on both scholarship and mysticism, maintaining a rare dance between a highly sophisticated theology and an intuitive, imaginative spirit. Within a relatively short period of time the existing scholastic learning centers were molded by the abbots and abbesses of the early Irish church into great centers of monastic life and training. New schools proliferated, some growing into large cultural centers. Into these flowed a steady stream of the privileged classes from throughout Europe, and out of them came the teachers, scholars, monks, poets, and artists whom history would credit with keeping learning, art, science, and the devotional life alive throughout the dissolution of the Roman Empire and the centuries known as the Dark Ages.

Other unique elements contributed to the vitality of Irish Christianity. Most notable was a cosmology that perceived the spiritual world as interpenetrating the physical universe and accessible through the practicalities of everyday life. In both theology and practice emphasis was on understanding the immanent presence of God in all things. The natural world was regarded as a primary manifestation of the Divine. Christ showed the way; he was the model of the fully realized human, the one who could "go back and forth between the worlds," and yet who lived fully present to the struggles and longings of the common folk. Profoundly devotional, the Celtic monastic schools stressed the development of the inner contemplative life, the importance of individual experience over doctrinal belief, the sacramental nature of everyday life, a great love for the natural world, and the call to a life of hospitality and service.

Needless to say, confrontation with the developing orthodoxy was inevitable as traveling Celtic philosophers and monks made themselves known in the Roman world. Charges of heresy (denial of the Fall and original sin) and pantheism (God was too much in nature) were matched by eloquent argument on behalf of humanity's "inherent dignity and capacity for moral choice" and the sacramentality of the natural order. At issue also were the role and authority of women in the Celtic church, the refusal to recognize the authority of bishops appointed by Rome, the adherence to the path of John rather than of Peter, and more subtle annoyances, including style of dress and tonsure. In spite of censure, Celtic Christianity continued to develop in its own fashion and for many centuries remained an influential presence on the Continent and an irritant to the prevailing Roman Church.[3]

The early New Age movement made no particular mention of Celtic spirituality. It is understandable, however, that with the recent resurgence of interest in spirituality and in the Western esoteric and mystical traditions, the Celts would be "discovered." Soon, within certain New Age circles, a fascination with Celtic culture and mythology grew almost to faddish proportions. The spiritual mecca of the West some called ancient Ireland; while for others Celtic civilization became the idealized model of nonpatriarchal, partnership culture supported by a highly sophisticated esoteric knowledge of the universe. Myth and history intertwined, and imagination readily filled the gaps left by an incomplete scholarship. Yet some great spiritual hunger was being fed as the wisdom of the Celtic Christian tradition became accessible again. At a time when many people had concluded that a life-celebrating, nondualistic spirituality was not to be found in Christianity, the recovery of the Celtic Christian story resulted in their renewed interest in and respect for the Western spiritual heritage. For some it meant "coming home" at last.

In developing the Chinook Learning Center we were clearly inspired both by the contemporary Iona Community and by the bright witness of the Irish monastic schools. Though different in form, Chinook represented to us a complementarity of spirit and purpose across time. In this critical era of the late twentieth century it was, in a sense, a contemporary "monastic school" where a "new story," a fresh understanding of the great pattern of meaning and purpose linking humanity, the Earth, and God could be learned and lived.

We soon found that we were not alone but part of a growing network of educators, theologians, therapists, environmentalists, artists, scientists, and economists, many of whom had left conventional professions in order to engage in pioneering work. We were inspired by their high level of scholarship, their willingness to take risks, to try new approaches, and to be willing to live outside the "mainstream" in order to try out new ways of thinking and acting. Cultural historian William Irwin Thompson, writing in the early 1980s about such social innovators and experimental models, noted the power of what he called the "catalytic enzyme" or "evolutionary deme," the creative yeast in a society which, though barely noticed, has the potential to have great influence and impact. Not all such experiments survive. Some remain marginalized and inadequately developed, particularly if they are born out of reaction rather than from vision. Their value, however, is not necessarily determined by longevity but by their power to aid society in imagining new possibilities.[4]

Imagining new possibilities, however, depends entirely on how we read the signs of our time. What is happening? How serious is our situation? What is our best response? In an affluent society, what motivates people to make different choices and change behavior for the sake of others? Can we learn to live on behalf of "the seventh generation," as native American wisdom teaches? Faced with the magnitude of the challenge, we can feel ineffectual and disempowered. What enables us to believe that as individuals we can have any impact at all? And what is the deepest motivation for our actions? Are we responding primarily from fear and the threat to our own life-styles, or are we stirred by hope, love, compassion, and a new vision of what is right and possible?

The New Age is an attempt, I think, to make some response to these concerns. It is in no way a unified movement. It lacks a cohesive social or political agenda. It can be criticized as naive about "evil" and systemic injustice, offering "positive thinking" as a remedy for everything. The majority of activities with which it is identified are overly focused on personal growth and self-help, without a complementary emphasis on service to others and the serious engagement of issues. Nonetheless, in that the New Age represents a deeper transformational movement in our society we can look at the pattern as a whole and identify the significant areas where the New Age movement has made a positive contribution.

The first contribution, and for me the most essential, is the emphasis of the New Age movement on the renewal of personal spiritual life. In its best sense the New Age promotes the spiritual dimension of life as offering the greatest reservoir of power, imagination, and courage for meeting our time in history. It promotes a creative spirituality which overflows rigid and time-bound forms and belief systems that no longer meet the spiritual, emotional, psychic, and intellectual longing of people today. While not very concerned about institutional religion, the New Age has accelerated the search for authentic spiritual experience and has turned people on to the importance of spiritual discipline and practice. Though lacking any one theological orientation, the New Age consistently

132

emphasizes the immanence of the Divine. It recognizes the Sacred in and through all life, and has consequently helped people overcome the deeply ingrained dualism of Western Christianity which has inordinately emphasized the transcendence of God and minimized the immanence of Spirit.

The new spiritual resurgence has also brought a lively interest in and appreciation for the spiritual traditions and practices of other cultures and indigenous peoples and recognizes the active presence of Spirit in a diversity of forms, languages, images, and rituals. While the awareness that "all paths lead to God" may be accompanied by a lack of spiritual discernment and theological depth, it brings a welcome openness to and nonjudgmental reception of the rich diversity of ways people have always named and celebrated the Sacred.

This deep sense of respect and appreciation for the beliefs and wisdom of others, born from the vitality of one's own spiritual life, has the potential to transform the way we regard the needs and rights of those who are different from ourselves and therefore our response to injustice, prejudice, and abuse. This is, I believe, one of the most important gifts of the New Age perspective.

With the renewal of spiritual life and the discovery and recovery of the wisdom of other traditions and cultures has come a severe critique of conventional Christianity. Most notably the New Age has challenged the dominance of a redemption-oriented theology and has given rise to a new creation-centered and nature affirming spirituality. Dominican priest and author Matthew Fox has been the pioneering voice in formulating and popularizing a creation-centered theology, and by tracing its roots within historical Christianity, including Celtic Christianity, has encouraged many people in a renewed appreciation for the rich diversity of the Christian heritage. *Original Blessing*, which he published in 1983, was widely acclaimed in New Age circles and became for some a prophetic banner, a way of declaring that a new life-celebrating spirituality was on the move. *Creation Spirituality*, published in 1991, incorporates a cosmological perspective and links creation spirituality with the human justice concerns of liberation theology. In writing of creation spirituality as both a tradition—for it is not a "newly invented" path but a "newly discovered" path—and as a liberating movement of Spirit, Fox says:

> As a movement, creation spirituality becomes an amazing gathering place, a kind of watering hole for persons whose passion has been touched by the issues of our day—deep ecologists, ecumenists, artists, native peoples, justice activists, feminists, male liberationists, gay and lesbian peoples, animal liberationists, scientists seeking to reconnect science and wisdom, people of prophetic faith traditions—all these groups find in the creation spirituality movement a common language and a common ground on which to stand.[5]

In addition to Fox, there are many other voices within the church, particularly those in process theology, who are advocating a more generous and inclusive interpretation of Christian history than a narrow Fall/redemption bias permits. The most noted voice in the New Age movement itself is that of David Spangler. Writing from the perspective of the Western mystic and esoteric tradition, Spangler has for many years promoted a new theological understanding of the integrity of the creation and the cocreative relationship of God, humankind, and nature.[6]

The new emphasis on a creation-celebrating spirituality has led many to reject the rigid patriarchal system of thought and practice dominating much of Christian history with its denial of the legitimacy, integrity, wisdom, and creative power of women and its corresponding repression of pre-Christian, Earth-oriented spiritualities. In the search to claim and name an authentic spiritual life, many women have ransacked historical tradition and reached farther back in time to recover the feminine archetype in human experience. Jean Houston, popular transformational psychologist, talks about the "rise of the goddess" as a phenomenon with profound implications for the way we define both human nature and the Divine. In *The Search for the Beloved* she writes: "Denied and suppressed for thousands of years, the goddess archetype returns at a time when the breakdown of the old story leaves us desperate for love, security, for protection, for meaning. It leaves us yearning for a nurturing and cultivation of our whole being, that we might be adequate stewards of the planetary culture."[7] Other feminist writers and theologians support the view that religion, without an active, creative feminine principle, is seriously inadequate and unable to guide the mature development of either women or men today. While a goddess orientation in and of itself is as incomplete as a male-defined and -dominated religious system, it offers an exceedingly important corrective. The recovery of the feminine archetype has enabled women to celebrate the integrity and authenticity of our own spiritual development and to challenge rigid images of God and male-reflecting forms of worship, and is helping both women and men rediscover and create rituals that celebrate the birthing, nurturing, and relational dimensions of the Sacred.

The second important and timely contribution of the New Age is its affirmation of the sacramentality of the natural world. This perspective celebrates God's presence in and through the created order. It sees all life, everything in creation, as sacred.

As our work at the Chinook Learning Center unfolded, this understanding of nature is the area where we found it difficult, until recently, to build bridges with the church. From the beginning environmental concerns and the relationship of God and nature have been central to our work. In the early 1970s, as concern for the global environment and the "fate of the earth" became more widespread, we were surprised and troubled not only by the lack of awareness or response within the mainstream church, but by the severity of reaction to any suggestion that God could be known in the natural world. The New Age regard for the sacramentality of nature and the affirmation that God is in all things (as well as beyond all things) brought to the surface the deeply rooted fear of pantheism in the Christian tradition and concern that reverence for nature will turn people away from God, bypass Christ, and result in the worship of the creation and not the Creator.

The recognition of sacred presence in nature is certainly not a new idea. Native peoples have always understood this. They speak again today with the voice of wisdom and authority about the importance of knowing the presence of the Sacred in the life of every aspect of creation. They say that as we learn again to listen to the voices of nature, God will be enlarged, not diminished, and we will gain a renewed compassion for all creatures and a new level of accountability for how we live within the greater family of life. In the well-known words attributed to Chief Seattle: "Every part of this earth is sacred . . . every pine needle, every sandy shore, every mist in the woods, every clearing and humming insect. . . . We are all part of the web of life. What we do to the web, we do to ourselves."

The search for sources of wisdom within the Christian heritage that affirm nature as an expression of the Divine has uncovered the stories of women and men not heard for centuries. Philosophers and mystics of the early medieval period are among them. So are the Celts. John Scotus Eriugena, the brilliant ninth-century Irish scholar who some say may have been the most original of the great Scholastic thinkers of the Middle Ages, argued in his greatest work, *On the Division of Nature,* that all creation in its wonderful diversity is "a living theophany, a manifestation of the Word."[8] Nature and scripture were for him the two shoes of Christ. "We ought not to understand God and the creature as two things distinct from one another," he wrote, "but as one and the same. For both the creature, by subsisting, is in God and God, by manifesting Himself in a marvelous manner creates Himself in the creature."[9] Hildegard of Bingen is another. This remarkably gifted twelfth-century abbess saw the earth as vibrantly alive with God. The Holy Spirit to her was greening power and Christ was greenness incarnate.[10] Best known, perhaps, is the thirteenth-century mystic, Meister Eckehart. "Apprehend God in all things," he wrote, "for God is in all things. Every single creature is full of God and is a book about God. If I spent enough time with the tiniest creature—even a caterpillar—I would never have to prepare a sermon. So full of God is every creature."[11]

The response from conservative church circles to the suggestion that God can be experienced in nature indicates just how deeply entrenched is the fear of substituting nature for God. Yet many within traditional Christian institutions are working to redress the obvious lack of a Christian ecological conscience and the exclusion of nature from mainstream theology. As the church in recent years has taken the environmental crisis more seriously, new statements representing an ecologically informed theology and liturgy have been drafted and discussed in several denominations, and some local congregations have formed study and action groups. Some would say this is too little, too late, motivated from being found wanting, rather than from an inherent concern and advocacy. Yet in many Christian circles there is a new listening for the revelatory presence of God's Spirit acting freshly in our time, revealing what we have neglected to see, inspiring in us a love for what we have neglected to love, and encouraging our confidence that humankind can learn to live responsibly and in harmony with the natural world.

For many people associated with the New Age movement this renewed sense of the sacramentality of creation and the interdependence of humanity and nature energized a profound commitment to work on environmental issues. Some began to refer to the New Age as the "ecological age" or as the age of the "Earth Community." Several New Age communities in this country as well as in Europe, Australia, and India undertook experiments in sustainable agriculture, appropriate technology, reforestation, species protection, and pollution cleanup, and also promoted environmental issues through educational and public awareness programs. Though these efforts may have remained on a relatively small scale, nonetheless they point to a significant way in which the New Age emphasis on the sacramentality of nature served as the motivation for a new environmental advocacy.

In recent years as the magnitude of the environmental crisis hit more and more people, some New Age centers began to make this issue a major priority. Most notably, the Findhorn Foundation in northern Scotland, which gained an international reputation in the 1970s for remarkable gardens grown in cooperation with "nature spirits," has now turned major resources to the building of ecologically sound housing, power generating windmills, and the replanting of the ancient Caledonian forest.

Personally, having come to believe that the environmental crisis is preeminently a spiritual crisis of the greatest magnitude, my husband and I have formed a new work called the Institute for Earth and Spirit. The Institute will focus directly on the spiritual dimension of the environmental crisis and the linked issues of theology and ecology. Like many of our friends, we are determined to make a new and creative response to the urgencies of our time.

The third major contribution of the New Age to a new way of

engaging our world is its affirmation of the value, uniqueness, and integrity of the individual person as a member of the interdependent community of planetary life.

In marked contrast to the fear by some fundamentalists that the New Age is a cult in which the individual is denied freedom of belief and action, it has been my experience that the New Age actually is the opposite. It calls forth a high vision of each human being as a responsible and creative member of the planetary community. In fact, it may be one of the first modern social movements to stress both individual personhood and the vision of a planetary community. In so doing, the New Age has been a voice honoring the diversity of cultures and creeds. In emphasizing what might be called "kinship ethics" it has also inspired many people to move beyond self-interest and to seek to live in responsive service to the greater whole.

This vision of unique personhood within a larger interdependent community of life is articulated beautifully by Buddhist scholar Joanna Macy. She believes that we are living in the midst of a changing definition of the self, from the notion of the separate, contained, and competitive individual which has dominated Western society to what she calls the "ecological self or the eco-self, coextensive with other beings and the life of the planet." She regards this awakening consciousness of the self as a unique part of an interdependent world as "the most fascinating and hopeful development of our time." She writes:

> This is hardly new to our species. In the past poets and mystics have been speaking and writing about these ideas, but not people on the barricades agitating for social change. Now the sense of an encompassing self, that deep identity with the wider reaches of life, is a motivation for action. It is a source of courage that helps us stand up to the powers that are still, through force of inertia, working for the destruction of our world. I am convinced that this expanded sense of self is the *only* basis for adequate and effective action.[12]

This larger and more generous sense of who I am and to whom I belong and to whom I am accountable results in a heightened sense of the importance of individual choices and actions. Everything we do impacts the rest of life. No action is too small to matter. The more conscious we are of our influence and effect, the more possibility there is that we will make choices that contribute to the healing and well-being of the larger community of life. Though perhaps naive in just what it will take for such a "paradigm shift" in individual consciousness to take hold, the New Age nonetheless holds up a high vision of human potential and encourages our belief in the inherent dignity and worth of every person. In light of the patterns of violence, suffering, and injustice deeply imbedded in the fabric of our society and reflected in our environment, it seems to me far better to believe in our highest potential, and to call it forth, than to decide that we are incapable by nature or circumstance of a creative and compassionate response.

To be sure, this expanded sense of selfhood is not a quick or guaranteed stage of human development. It is, rather, a vision of what we can become. It requires that we have in place a strong sense of our own individual identity and gifts as well as understanding that we are needed in the greater community of life. The ecological self, for me, is a way of imagining freshly the individual person as part of the body of Christ. It calls us back again to the basic Christian mandate to "do unto others as you would have them do unto you," and by "others" to mean everything with which we share the gift of life. To paraphrase W. H. Auden, "Everything becomes a You and nothing is an it."[13]

The fourth area in which I see the positive contribution of a New Age perspective to the issues of our day is its understanding of the power of positive vision, hope, and love as the motivation for our action and service in the world. In other words, it emphasizes the belief that positive change and true healing and transformation come when we act on the basis of our deepest hopes, inspired by what we love, rather than when motivated by fear and reaction to what we believe is wrong.

This is tricky ground. Clearly, the facts of life in the 1990s require our willingness to face up to all that is wrong and to act with far greater courage, wisdom, and boldness than we have shown to date. But the question posed by a New Age perspective asks us to be clear about our vision for the world and its future. What are the deepest values we embrace? What do we most love? How do we resist and say no to all that is wrong, in ways that are congruent with our highest vision and most cherished values?

Intrinsic to a New Age or transformational perspective is the awareness that what we think, what we imagine, what we hold in our consciousness may largely determine what happens in our personal lives and in the world around us. The image of a New Age, or of the possibility of a new order of life breaking into human experience, is in itself a positive, guiding, and energizing thought form. To "hold the light," in New Age terms, on behalf of a positive vision of the world, and to do what we can in our daily lives to align with and manifest that vision, brings an important sense of empowerment as we face challenges of such enormity that individual action can seem totally ineffectual. When "two or more" gather in that spirit, then the potential to affect the world is all the greater. In this regard the New Age supports the Christian understanding of the power of prayer in the life of both the individual and the gathered community.

In facing the magnitude of current problems, the New Age recognizes that true healing and transformation do not come about easily or quickly. It calls us to attend to root causes rather than to engage the symptom level only. Thus the emphasis in New Age circles on "changing consciousness" and perceptions of reality. It asks that while being alert and responsive to the pain of the world we do not become so immersed in the struggle that we lose connection to the larger transformative vision and are unable to maintain hope, buoyancy of spirit, and confidence. By acting from the inspiration of our hope, and of all we love, we may be better able to maintain the level of commitment and vitality needed as we engage the incredibly difficult and complex issues of our time.

While this perspective is clearly at the heart of the New Age, many critics have pointed to a lack of social consciousness and earnest engagement in critical issues by many people associated with the movement to date. Some say that the emphasis on personal healing and growth often results in people simply becoming enamored of themselves and failing to engage the issues affecting the larger world. I find this critique in some measure valid. There is a strong tendency in our society toward overly personalistic concerns and the substitution of ideals and rhetoric for concerted action and service. This is as true in New Age circles as anywhere else. We too easily forget the truth of Jesus' teaching that to find myself I must "lose my life," or in Joseph Campbell's words: "The ultimate aim of our quest must be neither release nor ecstasy for oneself, but the wisdom and power to serve others."[14]

In summary, as I think about the journey of my own life, and about this decade and what is ahead for the planetary family, for our "generation of destiny," I feel that the New Age movement merits our very serious consideration and our respect. In spite of its excesses and trivialities, it has been one way to talk about the deeper current of change that characterizes our time. Its emphasis on the renewal of a vital personal spiritual life, its affirmation of the sacramentality of the natural world, its recognition of the value of the individual as a member of an interdependent planetary community, and its understanding of the power of positive vision, hope, and love as the motivation of action and service cannot be undervalued.

Though the term itself may no longer be a viable label, the New Age has been a way of naming the upwelling of spiritual consciousness and conscience in our culture. It has opened up a new conversation among people in all disciplines about who we are as a human family, about our relationship to the community of planetary life, and about the story we tell and the vision we hold for our common future. It has called for no small change of mind, but a metanoia, a turning around, a transformation of heart and habits and economics and politics. It has indeed grasped the imagination of many people as an entrancing and empowering vision. By whatever name, nothing at this time in our history may be more essential. My old friends, the Celts, would certainly agree!

SECTION THREE

NEW AGE SPIRITUALITY: AN ASSESSMENT

This final section attempts to assess the value of New Age spirituality. It has met the needs of a great many people and been a constructive force in our culture and beyond. But the movement also has its limits and liabilities. What is clear is that people in this postmodern age are seeking a new spirituality.

8

New Age Spirituality:
A Positive Contribution

LISA N. WOODSIDE

Introduction

The positive contribution of New Age spirituality is the new emphasis on health and healing and on interconnectedness, which provides a balancing force for stress and specialization in the modern Western world.

Examples and applications of New Age thought from authors who favor the New Age, or attempt to remain objective about the New Age, are cited in this chapter. Authors who are cynical and critical of the New Age are not cited. They can validly point to fads, fakes, and quackery within the movement, or even can question the movement in its entirety. That the New Age stretches from exploitation to idealism and from naïveté to sophistication does not set it apart from other human endeavors. Nevertheless, by the 1970s Western society had moved to a position of overvaluing compartmentalized knowledge based on reason alone. The New Age offers an affirmative, compensatory view by valuing intuition and spirit.

The thesis on which the New Age rests is optimistic and positive in its own right: From whole and healthy people come thoughts and actions that will transform the world. It is this thesis that will be explored and described.

The "old age" will transform into the New Age. The goals of the transformation are spiritual wholeness and health for individuals, society, and the world. Even now, physical, mental, and spiritual health are a seamless web for each person. As each person transforms and progresses toward wholeness of self and higher spirituality, inner conflicts are resolved. The current fragmented world is a result of fragmented persons. A whole world will be a result of whole persons, wherein cooperation will become more and more prevalent. Networking will continue to replace hierarchical and bureaucratic institutional forms for government and business. Additionally, self-wholeness and spiritual enlightenment reduce alienation from nature since, indeed, one's interconnection and oneness with nature are realized. The current environmental problems will diminish as better decisions based on true self-interest emerge. The worldview is holistic and positive.

The New Age

The core concepts of the New Age are three. The New Age is a new religion; it is a current social movement; and it is a projection of a planetary transformation.

As a new religion, New Age thought is intimately personal, affecting the individual. As a social movement, it is organizationally dynamic, affecting social issues and enabling new models. And as a possible planetary transformation, it potentially affects the status of nations, their interactions, and planetary perspectives.

How does this "new" personal experience of religion relate to new social change? And how does social change make a New Age planet? New Age writers and activities believe and discuss how societal changes add up to a planetary transformation.

What follows here presents examples of each level—personal, social, and planetary—showing relationships between levels, where possible, as represented in New Age thought. The positive side of the themes of healing and interconnectedness will be apparent, as it is in much of New Age thought and activity.

New Age as Religion:
Personal Transformation

At the heart of the New Age is the spiritual thirst that has become prevalent in our secular, postindustrial society. We place high value on science, technology, competition, specialization, and material acquisition. We have benefited greatly from these values and the accomplishments of our society. They have been remarkable and mostly welcome. However, the devaluation of the intuitive and the irrational, the lack of regard for subjective feelings, nurturing values, and the natural environment, and disregard for spiritual reality cannot be tolerated by an increasing number of people in Western society. Although we find that some New Age practices go overboard in the other direction by imbuing irrational and illogical occurrences with too much meaning, many are corrective to the long-term imbalance in our society.

A usual comment among New Age followers is "I am spiritual, but I'm not religious." This comment reflects the fact that the new religious movement does not have a particular doctrine or belief system. There is no dogma, no accepted body of authoritative texts and tenets. The movement is built, rather, on personal vision and experience, and, especially, it is built on personal transformation.

What is this personal transformation? The biological transformation process of a butterfly can be seen in its body from egg to winged adult.

A person's spiritual transformation occurs in the human psyche. It is seen in the relationships and actions of the person. The individual's psychic movement is from dependence to independence to interdependence with others. Interdependence is the ability to relate to "the other" with a truly independent, authentic self.

No matter how old we are in years, most of us have dependencies that we need to relinquish to become mature. Healthy dependency is appropriate for infants and children. But as their bodies grow, they need to grow psychologically too, and assume inner autonomy. No one does this automatically. Meeting emotional and spiritual challenges and resolving them must occur if individuals are to grow. Only fully mature individuals with psychological maturity can be genuinely interdependent. What, then, is also possible is relationship with the divine. A direct relationship with the divine is, in fact, the goal of a New Age seeker.

Direct relationship with the divine remains a gift. We can prepare for an enlightened state but not necessarily arrive. It is not sure to happen. Like many human endeavors, however, the process of preparation itself can have great meaning and thus elevate the quality of life. This process of personal transformation allows us to explore the inner life, to discover psychic abilities and discover unknown potentialities, and to experience a sense of community and society transformed.

If personal transformation leads to a direct knowing of the divine, there is no intermediary. Thus, it is a mystical transformation—the sensation of being touched by a reality that transcends ordinary life. Much of the experience is indescribable in direct, linear language. When people try to explain it, they describe a oneness-in-all, a connectedness, an intercausality, and a unity of the universe. The laws of logic and reason do not apply. The feeling and sense of it seem best expressed by paradoxes and poetic images.

How does one reach this experience? The process and work of attaining progressive levels of self-awareness and then cosmic awareness are, in fact, much of what the New Age phenomena are. Psychological and spiritual practices of all sorts—with various equipment, teachers, classes, camps, therapies, and instructive materials—abound.

It may be helpful here to clarify the use of the terms *psychological* and *spiritual*. Psychology is a behavioral science, which studies the mind with its mental and emotional processes. Scientific emphasis is often on behavior that can be defined and measured. The Western therapies are aimed at helping the individual attain a fully integrated personality by working through emotional blockages and self-misunderstandings. When, through disciplined effort with some school of therapy, the blocked emotion becomes part of consciousness, this is felt as an "expansion of consciousness," or sometimes described as a step toward "higher consciousness." If and when developmental blocks have been integrated into the personality and a person has attained an autonomous, stable self-structure, the client will have reached what has been considered the level of "wellness" by traditional Western societal standards. There are also Western therapies that concentrate on helping people "act well" with the help of external cues and learning devices rather than trying to deal with mental, emotional, and "inner" states. Acting well can lead to being well, at least in some cases. More and more, in dealing with psychological problems of development, psychologists find that working exclusively with "inner" or "outer" criteria is not as helpful as working with both.

When a reasonably well-integrated personality has been achieved, accompanied by self-understanding and self-acceptance—which in fact can certainly be attained without the aid of any therapy—levels of "higher consciousness" lie beyond this state. Such an area of psychic life is where the possibility of direct contact with the sacred, spiritual experience seems to exist. Here is the focus of the spiritual which, unlike the psychological, does not fit as clearly in the Western paradigm of scientific measurement. Various psychic phenomena, abilities, and powers may also be in this area, which, again, are experienced by the individual as a "place" or "state of altered consciousness."[1] Some individuals seem to move easily into various levels; most use transformative techniques to help themselves.

Discussions of states of consciousness (and the psychological and spiritual) tend to make the mind sound like a layer cake or a set of stairs to walk. In fact, anyone who has done any introspection at all with different modes of intellect, emotion, contemplative states, and skilled activity knows a personal sense of self and not-self. On the other hand, descriptions of both psychic and spiritual experiences from many centuries and cultures have similarities that are recognized as valid by those who experience them. Each person has a personal and unique, subjective sense of psychology and spiritual life.

Some of the transformative practices have come directly from the East—the group of practices of meditation and that of yoga. The purpose of meditation practices is to train the attention in order to bring mental processes under greater voluntary control. The control is then used to cultivate mental qualities, such as awareness, concentration, joy, love, and compassion. The ultimate goal is deep insight into the nature of the mind and development of mental well-being.[2] This focusing of one part of the mind on another is characteristic of most "psychotechnologies," as Marilyn Ferguson labels them. She mentions many processes that can shift consciousness or call into question conscious assumptions, bringing awareness to be aware of itself: sensory overload, biofeedback, music, chanting, self-help groups, hypnosis, Sufi stories, dream journals, theosophy, logotherapy, course in miracles, t'ai chi, rolfing, Alexander, encounter groups, wilderness retreats, and many, many more.

No transformative process works in quite the same way for each person. An achievement of various states of clarity or of vision may occur only rarely. The transformation is a continual process after the initial experience or "entry point" that has led the person to acquire the identity of a spiritual seeker. The commitment to a spiritual path or journey takes shape in the individual with varying degrees of urgency. Working on a continual personal transformation means choosing, for a period of time, practices taught by a single spiritual teacher or tradition, or trying various transformative practices and making an individualized way. This commitment does not necessarily bring smooth progress. External and internal factors may provide difficulties. Confusion from misunderstanding and from possible exploitation may originate from the external environment, and the inner voice is not always clear and discernible. On the other hand, glimpses of a more meaningful dimension and contact with individuals who also seek can provide encouragement.

The New Age movement recognizes the claims of many spiritual and religious movements that some kind of energy is at work in creating transformation. This energy is not energy in the form of heat and light as recognized by Western science, but a universal energy which goes by many names—healing force, psychic energy, prana, Holy Spirit, orgone energy, *chi'i*. This is the force that causes psychic healing, cures pathological conditions, and expands to more transitional consciousness which allows the individual to experience the sought-after level of mystic reality. Here is the experience of wholeness, oneness, and interconnection of all life and matter.

The attention to self and the grooming of inner life so prevalent among spiritual seekers have led critics to accuse the movement of unhealthy narcissism and me-ism. The question of whether this is justified needs to be analyzed case by case and considered in context. An introspection and self-discipline that promote wellness is hardly unhealthy. On the other hand, a game-playing attitude and a passivity that somehow expects some external agent to solve life's problems are not productive and could be considered a form of selfish narcissism.

From Personal to Social Transformation

In her book based on a case study approach, *Ordinary People as Monks and Mystics,* Marsha Sinetar describes clearly the influence of individual psychological growth on wholeness and integration and its relationship to social action. After personal transformation, the transformation of society is the second vision of the New Age. Societal transformation is based on the actions of persons changing through their personal transformations: From whole and healthy people come thoughts and actions which will transform the world.

Marsha Sinetar is an organizational psychologist and mediator who studies adults who fulfill their potential. The case studies documented by Sinetar show a link between personal transformation and positive social action. She describes the increasing sense of rightness and the need to express oneself in positive action as one becomes increasingly psychologically healthy. It is this phenomenon the New Age too addresses. The New Age is, in part, a social movement with impact on medicine, ecology, business, education, societal organizational patterns, and other areas.

Marsha Sinetar claims that ordinary people can and do grow to a state of psychological wholeness and completeness, which, she reminds us, Maslow described as a state of self-actualization. Sinetar's emphasis is that self-actualization is not a rare occurrence. It is relatively common that everyday folk attain their full authenticity, wherein they are conscious of and receptive to their innermost self. They respond to an "inner law" and a "vocation" which may mean living life outside, or not in accord with, conventional standards or expectations. As they attain a more mature and whole-thinking attitude, ego interests and preoccupations tend to be less pressing. A desire for relatedness to others, a sense of community, and a generosity of spirit—in other words, aspects of a type of love— develop.

Sinetar adopts the concept of stewardship from the Judeo-Christian tradition to describe the sense of social action that the mature personality feels. Stewardship originally meant "servant-hood," or service. It referred to the care and management of God's material and human resources. Thus, in this tradition humankind has a dominion over the earth, but must take responsibility for the consequences.[3]

As Sinetar describes it, stewardship has three qualities. First, discovery of a *core sense of self* with a sense of objective separate-ness, then expression of one's unique talents. Work is an integral part of self and is the preferred activity, not just a means to money, power, and status. Anyone may feel this—teacher, carpenter, pot-ter, housewife, politician, manager.

The sense of cohesion between self and work leads to the second quality of stewardship. This is the *feeling of relatedness to others.* A clear sense of self is maintained while realizing that the other is much alike. This is the feeling of interconnectedness and kinship.

As maturity and enlightenment develop, relatedness is lived through various parts of life. The individual continues to work on accepting characteristics within the self that are seen outside the self. Sinetar goes on to say that the third quality of stewardship, *genuine caring about others,* is a natural response. Some feel a sense of duty to work ethically in a service profession, but not yet desiring actively to give. Others reach a level where they have a strong desire to give. Life is service. Work and leisure merge. The pleasure of concentration, purpose, and meaning in life strongly motivate the individual.[4]

Sinetar's case studies show the link between personal transfor-mation and social transformation that the New Age espouses. When hundreds and hundreds of persons have well-developed, mature personalities and are acting in society through their unique talents in a related way, society is affected. Enough self-actualized individu-

als working as "stewards" of their talents in a related and cooperative endeavor could transform society from the level of the individual. Thus, Sinetar's book is a study of the statement I formulate
thus: From whole and healthy people come thoughts and actions
that will transform the world.

There are, of course, individuals who cannot or will not take on
the interior journey to transformation. Some New Age proponents
believe that when a "critical mass" of individuals reach a certain
level of enlightenment, the correct idea will spread through the
human race. This ability to spread through the race seems to be
based on the holistic view of reality that typifies New Age thinking.

Holism

The vision of the whole and the interrelatedness of its parts is
the goal of mystical experience that is so sought after by those of the
New Age. But also, New Age thinking accepts holism as a societal
and biological reality, not only a spiritual one.

> Holism sees the universe as a complex set of whole systems. Philo-
> sophically considered, the universe is the ultimate whole system,
> which includes a number of other systems at differing levels. All
> systems are intricately connected and interdependent, with each part
> reflective of the whole. And though the whole consists of all of its parts,
> it is believed that the whole is always more than the sum of its parts. In
> like measure, the parts of the whole reflect the whole, because each
> part is also a whole system.[5]

The holistic view of reality, related as it is to the vision of
ultimate reality, is seen in major practices and transformative activities and structures in society identified as New Age. Beginning with
the person, the body is seen as a total system—mind, body, and
spirit—rejecting Descartes's eighteenth-century dualism of mind
and body. Societal structures favored by the New Age are communes and networks, not the traditional hierarchical or bureaucratic structures; the natural environment as well as life on earth is
seen as an interlocking, interdependent entity, with even a sense
that the planet is itself one self-regulating organism, not an anthropocentric world where humanity should rule nature.

People do not have to decide whether to adopt fully the New

Age worldview and drop another. Contributions to the understanding of health, social issues, and planetary well-being have entered our culture from New Age thought, and the opportunity is there to support or reject them based on evidence and evaluations.

Mind, Body, and Spirit

The New Age concept of the human being as a total interactive system of body, mind, and spirit has implications for medical concepts. Consider the following examples of medical phenomena, which look at the mind-body interactional point of view, not the dualistic position which sees the mind within the body but a separate entity from the body.

The Will for Wellness. Norman Cousins, then editor of *The Saturday Review,* literally laughed at death and won twenty-six more years of life.[6] In 1964 he was diagnosed with an irreversible, crippling disease which attacked his connective tissue. He had six months to live. Cousins did not accept the verdict. He decided to take responsibility for his treatment, in large measure, into his own hands. He based his plan on the ideas that positive emotions have a positive effect on body chemistry, that pain is affected by attitude, and that vitamin C helps to oxygenate the blood.[7]

Cousins watched old shows of *Candid Camera* and movies by the Marx Brothers. He found that ten minutes of a good belly laugh acted as a natural anesthetic, and he could sleep. The nurse read him humorous stories. He took massive intravenous doses of vitamin C in the form of ascorbic acid. Dramatic and quick improvement followed within eight days. He had been so ill that it still took many months before almost total recovery took place, with essentially full mobility and no twinges of pain in the joints from sudden movement.[8]

Cousins was completely convinced of the therapeutic value of the will to live. The will to live, laughter, and ascorbic acid seemed to be the treatment that saved him. No specific physical intervention saved him. Moreover, he believed that he would not have recovered under "normal" medical practice.

Cousins repeatedly credited his doctor for his willingness to consider his patient as a respected partner in the treatment. Cousins also made it abundantly clear, however, that he deeply respected traditional medical skill in diagnosis, clinical evidence, and the systematic thought of the scientific method.[9]

Cousins's basic message is that each person needs to take responsibility for maintaining health, and even, if possible, to participate in treatment plans if ill.[10] This concept is current in New Age thought and health care.

Placebo Effect. One hypothesis that Cousins mentioned for his remarkable recovery was the result of the placebo effect. The traditional concept of a placebo has been the "sugar pill," a harmless pill offered to a patient merely to humor the individual. It has also been used in experiments as a control on the results for testing medications. The placebo, however, is apparently much more than an item that looks like a medication—it *acts* like a medication. This is the concept which is in accord with New Age thought. The power of belief that medication has been taken mobilizes the body's healing defenses. As recently as spring 1991, on the television series "The Search for the Mind," an experiment showed the power of belief, the placebo effect, to control pain. Apparently the patient was able to release endorphins, a natural opiatelike chemical, to control pain. The patient who believed that a painkiller was given influenced the body's system of regulation. The New Age concept is not incompatible with Western scientific processes of measurement. The measurements, however, do not tell us why.

It is equally important to note that placebos can produce physiological damage if the patient fully believes that the given substance is toxic.

Cousins remarked that the placebo can be thought of as a process, not a pill. It begins with confidence in the doctor and extends through the functioning of the patient's own immunological and healing system. The process depends heavily on the quality of relationship between doctor and patient. If the placebo is known to be a sugar pill, it will not work. But if the patient-doctor relationship is one of confidence, seriousness, and respect, the patient's body is able to transform the will to live and be well into tangible, biochemical change. Reaching out for help and believing the help to be there in the form of a trusted medical agent prompt the body's "internal doctor" to do the job.

Now, a third example of mind-body interaction, which is significantly different, follows. The patient need not consciously believe in the efficacy of the treatment or even know that the treatment is supposed to work.[11]

Therapeutic Touch. A nurse walks into a room where the patient is suffering from an acute tension headache. The nurse gives a friendly smile and says that she is giving a checkup. Then, unbeknownst to the patient, she fully prepares herself for the intervention known as therapeutic touch. She quietly centers her mind through meditative concentration, then focuses on her intent to heal. She passes her hands about eight inches from the patient, without touching the body, and brings her hands to rest close to the head or solar plexus. The patient, then, sits quietly for about five minutes, breathing deeply. Feelings of tingling, warmth, and relaxation arise. The headache disappears. Several hours later the headache is still gone or greatly diminished.

What happened? The technique of therapeutic touch has as its main spokesperson and practitioner Dr. Delores Krieger, RN. Therapeutic touch is based on holism and systems theory, which are basic themes in New Age thought and are represented in nursing science by the theory of the unitary person. Systems theory states that each person, and indeed the universe, is composed of complex interactive fields of life energy. The healer is able to channel energy to the patient, who, in turn, internalizes it to create healing through a self-process.[12]

The three major effects of therapeutic touch are reduction of anxiety, relief of pain, and facilitation of the healing process. Experiments have been conducted using casual touch (pulse-taking), placebo touch (no energy transfer), and therapeutic touch with and without direct skin contact. Therapeutic touch produced significant results whether it was by direct touch or by the noncontact method. In another experiment, both therapeutic touch and a placebo simulation of therapeutic touch reduced tension headache. But the actual intervention, therapeutic touch, resulted in much stronger positive results.[13]

The essentials of therapeutic touch are: (1) the intent to heal, and (2) the conscious transfer of energy. Since the therapist's only tool is the self, and empathy and desire to help are necessary, skeptics have claimed that response to therapeutic touch is based on the placebo effect even though the experiments control for placebo effect.

How did Krieger begin serious study of this modern version of laying on of hands? She witnessed Oskar Estebany interacting with patients with a light and relaxed touch. Krieger was startled at the significant number of persons who improved, and decided to study the phenomenon in detail.[14]

Krieger reports that she did not find any clue in Western sources to how the benefits of laying on of hands are accomplished. Since she has a background in comparative religion, she turned to the East and consulted Sanskrit texts, where she found a possibility. In Eastern texts the interaction between healer and subject is based on a state of matter for which there is no translation. In Sanskrit the concept is "prana," and our closest concept would be "vitality," or "vigor." The texts go on to say that a healthy person has an abundance of prana and an ill person too little. The deficit is the illness. "*Prana* can be activated by will and can be transferred to another person if one has the intent to do so. The [Eastern] literature also states that *prana* is intrinsic in what we would call the oxygen molecule."[15]

Krieger went on to conduct experiments measuring hemoglobin levels in subjects before and after treatment with this modern version of laying on of hands, therapeutic touch. The level of hemoglobin rose significantly. Whether this is the primary chemical basis for the healing or simply a sign of various changes needs study.

When Krieger conducted her experiments on relative hemoglobin values, one of her controls was to use nurses who scored high on a specially designed test to measure self-actualization. The nurses participating in the experiment were "inner-directed, self-supportive, freely expressive of feelings, possessing a high sense of self-worth, accepting of themselves in spite of weaknesses, and having a positive capacity for intimate contact."[16] Apparently Krieger believed in 1975 what Sinetar shows by case studies in 1986—that there are many among us who are at high levels of self-actualization.

Both Cousins's and Krieger's experiences with wellness are attributed by some to the placebo effect. Although it has a name, the placebo effect is still a mysterious process. We know that the body's physiology can be triggered by belief, and specific examples of the effect seem to be documented. Is "placebo effect" simply another name for the "healing force"?

Coincidentally, both Cousins and Krieger worked with the oxygen level in the blood, which Krieger states is associated with prana in Sanskrit. Perhaps additional experiments with oxygen will reveal more information about the role of oxygen in the physiology of healing.

Societal Change:
Medical Models—Disease, Interactive,
and Holistic

Positive emotion, the will to be well and to live, and energy flow between organisms—these are concepts and practices that are more at home in the mind-body interactional position and holistic medicine than in the disease model of medicine. Like many ideas labeled "New Age," this generation often rediscovers knowledge long understood and adapts it to modern thought.

One of the early advocates of a kind of interactional model was Hippocrates, about 400 B.C. He suggested that four different body fluids, called "humors," tended to determine the personality type: black bile for melancholia; blood for optimism; yellow bile for irritability; and phlegm for listlessness.[17]

The major and most noted proponent of dualism is, of course, Descartes. When within this philosophical context nineteenth-century discoveries of diseases caused by germs became known, the disease model became strongly entrenched and trusted. The concept provided information that allowed great advances through sanitation and vaccines.[18]

The medical profession did not ignore the interactional position. Freud, of course, emphasized that mental health influences physical and emotional health. Even John Watson, who was a strict experimental behaviorist, endorsed the role of psychological influence on disease processes. During the 1800s and until recently in the 1900s, however, action and training based on the disease model were extremely effective in ridding society of infectious diseases. Additionally, the information about the interactional mind-body position was mostly anecdotal and from case studies. Little research was conducted to provide persuasive evidence that elements other than biological should be considered in medical treatment and practice. And, then, there was general satisfaction with the model both within the medical community and by the public.[19]

Important changes in recent years have challenged that picture and have begun to change it:

1. Problems with infectious diseases are much less significant than chronic diseases, such as heart disease, cancer, and hypertension. The basis or aggravation factor in most chronic disease is stress. The psychotechnologies of New Age seekers have a common denominator of decreasing stress, quieting the mind, and increasing concentration. Thus, these practices agree with the concept of pursuing physical health through good psychic health.

2. Additionally, chronic diseases often have a slow onset rather than a dramatic one as caused by bacterial or viral diseases. The issues of quality of life and medical ethics for individuals suffering debilitating diseases pose new questions.

3. Research on psychological states and health-maintenance practices has provided strong correlations to longevity. For instance, the practices of regular exercise, low or no alcohol consumption, no smoking, regular sleep, and proper weight maintenance are correlated to longer life for both men and women.

4. A pressure on the traditional medical system has been the rising dissatisfaction with cost and delivery.[20]

Against this backdrop, the model that has gained most acceptance, departing from the biomedical (disease) model, is the biopsychosocial concept of health and illness. This concept maintains that a person's health is a matter of complex interaction among biological, psychological, and social determinants.[21] This more holistic approach to health is compatible with New Age thought with its practices of seeking physical, psychological, and spiritual health.

There are also many current medical practices, which have essentially merged with the New Age movement, that are called simply "holistic." The use of the term "holistic health" is often confused with any practice that does not fit the orthodox Western mode. Various examples of such treatments are macrobiotics, reflexology, aromatherapy, gestalt, and radionics. A true holistic approach supports treating the patient physically, emotionally, and spiritually. The acceptance of the holistic approach that spiritual discipline has medical value is often the crux of clashes between the traditional medical approach and New Age beliefs.

Societal Change: Networking as
an Organizational Form

The most important and prevalent organizational form for the New Age is the network. Not a new form, it has become very popular and powerful. A network is a loose structure of people and organizations who share a common interest, goal, or values, They are connected by a mailing list or directory giving name, address, and phone number.

This simple form can be remarkably effective. It is leaderless, but each member may be a leader. It can work strenuously on a task, then self-destruct, to be replaced by some new network arising for another issue. Local groups of any size can quickly transmit information about successful activities in many directions, to a receptive audience eager to learn. Networks may have a common cause, such as peace, ecology, or animal rights. Their successes can and do shift power from other societal structures, the more traditional hierarchical ones. Networks may also be self-help groups such as those for life transitions (widowhood, divorce, death of a child) or for addictions (gambling, drug abuse, alcoholism, compulsive overeating) or self-development (various diets, spiritual disciplines, and exercise).

Networks are expressions of grass-roots problems and concerns, of people in transformation and people transforming society. Networks are cooperative, not competitive. They link up and spin off in new combinations. An important point to realize too about the networks is that they keep a dynamic image of growth in the eye of the public and engage participants in the New Age goals who do not, or who perhaps would never, consider themselves part of the movement.

J. Gordon Melton et al. in the *New Age Almanac* explore the history of the network directories and networking periodicals.[22] The first network directories during the 1960s were informal and were connected to the growing number of Asian teachers in Europe and the United States who had begun to establish centers of converts to Hinduism and Buddhism. By 1972 book-length volumes appeared, professionally prepared and backed by one of the Asian religions. *The Year One Catalogue* by Ira Friedlancer appeared that year, and 1972 is a year that has been called the beginning of the New Age movement. However, the roots of the movement in the United States and in Asia go back many years.

The early 1970s also saw networking periodicals emerge, first little more than newsletters. *Common Ground* of San Francisco introduced a format of categories, calendars, and advertisements that became the model for other developing periodicals. Many of the periodicals are free in bookstores and food outlets, with revenues coming from advertising. Melton lists eighteen of the most successful networking periodicals active in the '80s. Their concerns deal primarily with health, ecology, politics, education, personal and spiritual growth, and global issues.[23]

During the '80s, the scope and diversity of the directories burgeoned, following the active growth of networks themselves. There have been several national directories of organizations, services, and people, with annual updates that are important to the movement because of the volatility of the networking system and the mobility of people within the movement.

Also, local directories have increased and have become numerous and specific in cities with well-developed New Age communities, such as San Diego, Los Angeles, Denver, Chicago, Detroit, and Washington, D.C. Additional topics of interest in such directories include crystals, communes, music, and in-depth coverage of holistic health services.[24]

Some directories now blend into sales catalogs, shifting away from people, services, and transformational groups to jewelry, cosmetics, ritual objects, and advertisements for amusement. The directories and periodicals will continue to be popular and to develop their own genres as long as the decentralized movement continues to prosper in its networking organizational form.

An excellent New Age source for a detailed discussion about networking, covering such topics as networking as an expression of holism, inner networking, global networking, and networking with computers is Lipnack and Stamps's *The Networking Book: People Connecting with People*.

Planetary Transformation: Planet Earth and the Gaia Hypothesis

Transformation comes in various ways. Often it is simply a new way of seeing what has always been. A kaleidoscope turns, and new colors and a new pattern appear. Sometimes the change is so great there seems to be a new kaleidoscope. Thus, the scientific hypothesis of Gaia was new to the science community. When Apollo beamed back pictures of Earth as a "shining blue pearl" suspended in black space, an intuitive jolt had some people say, "Yes, the planet is alive." But is there life on Earth, or is the Earth alive? Moreover, if Earth is alive, what is the human function? What matter is personal transformation for each individual? What does the human species contribute or take away?

Gaia Hypothesis

In 1979, J. E. Lovelock published *Gaia: A New Look at Life on Earth*. His idea had its origins in a problem he was trying to solve for NASA—how to recognize life on Mars, if it exists. Since Mars has no oceans, Lovelock decided to analyze its atmosphere chemically. He reasoned that life forms would have to make use of the atmosphere. A static atmosphere would imply no life. An atmospheric test was particularly suitable because it could occur at any landing site.[25]

Lovelock used Earth as his model. Test results from Earth's atmosphere, however, did not accord with accepted geochemical thought of the mid-'60s. The general belief was that Earth's atmosphere is the end product of the planet's liberation of gases. Under this belief, for example, oxygen comes from the breakdown of water vapor and the escape of hydrogen into space. Oxygen is left behind in the atmosphere.[26] According to chemical laws, Earth's atmosphere is improbable. The improbable nature of Earth's atmosphere would be explained by a chemist as a "persistent state of disequilibrium among the atmospheric gases."[27] Lovelock's explanation of disequilibrium is the one he believes to be the only feasible one: Earth's atmosphere is being manipulated from Earth's surface on a day-to-day basis, and the manipulator is life itself.

Consider Lovelock's example regarding oxygen. Methane and oxygen exist together in Earth's atmosphere. Sunlight causes these gases to react and produce carbon dioxide and water vapor. Methane and oxygen are thus used up. To sustain the known rate of reaction, about a thousand tons of methane must be introduced into the atmosphere each year, and twice as much oxygen. To keep Earth's atmosphere constant with this mixture is improbable to one hundred orders of magnitude, without life to alter it. Therefore, he reasons, biological processes are maintaining the atmosphere. As Lovelock puts it:

> Disequilibria [of gases] on this scale suggest that the atmosphere is not merely a biological product, but more probably a biological construction: not living, but like a cat's fur, a bird's feathers, or the paper of a wasp's nest, an extension of a living system designed to maintain a chosen environment.[28]

The Gaia hypothesis, simply stated, is that life creates and maintains precise environmental conditions favorable to its existence. All that is the planet is not alive. It is, rather, like a beehive where life maintains an abode appropriate to its need. If Earth is not quite an organism, yet it surely is, Lovelock claims, a self-regulating, self-sustaining system, which adjusts chemical, physical, and biological processes to support life and to continue evolution.

Another statement of the hypothesis, more poetic and giving a sense of the enormity of the implications, is this:

> The entire range of living matter on Earth, from whales to viruses, and from oaks to algae, could be regarded as constituting a single living

entity, capable of manipulating the Earth's atmosphere to suit its overall needs and endowed with faculties and powers far beyond those of its constituent parts.[29]

Gaia: Fully Alive

Four years after the Gaia hypothesis was published, Peter Russell published *The Global Brain: Speculations on the Evolutionary Leap to Planetary Consciousness*. He acknowledges that his book is a vision, not a prediction or scientific proof.

Russell's New Age idea is this: Gaia is alive. Gaia is an organism. She has been alive for centuries but without full consciousness. Now the human species is becoming Gaia's organ of consciousness.

Russell envisions the human species' relationship to Gaia as analogous to what the brain cortex is for an individual. The cortex is the newer part of the brain in evolutionary terms. It controls judgmental and self-awareness functions. Global consciousness, literal world consciousness, would allow judgments on a global scale. Russell sees each human as a nerve cell, cities as nerve centers, and the communications devices—telephone, computers, mail systems—as the interlocking network of Gaia's brain. Here is the world's greatest network!

Russell provides supporting evidence for his New Age vision in his book. He applies the concepts of general systems theory (of which holism is a popular explanation). General systems theory looks at the world as an interconnected hierarchy of matter and energy. Nothing can be explained on its own. Each thing is part of a system with interrelating, interacting parts.[30] Russell's vision is yet another version of the mystic vision and of holistic thinking.

In *Living Systems*, James Miller uses general systems theory to describe the nineteen critical subsystems for living systems. Using Miller's book, Russell compares examples of the nineteen subsystems to a human body, to the human society of a nation, and to Gaia's biosphere. Gaia satisfies the nineteen subsystems characteristic of a living system. But so does an automobile. What is, of course, different is that a machine wears out, while life is able to repair and regulate itself. The nineteen systems are apparently necessary for life, but not sufficient. The Gaia hypothesis provides the missing piece of sufficiency. Gaia is able to manipulate her own systems. She is self-regulating and can maintain an internal order. Thus, Russell puts the nineteen critical systems for life together with the ability to self-regulate. He considers Gaia to be a fully living system in her own right.[31]

Russell's book is structured in two parts: (1) past, present, and future evolution of the world and society, and (2) inner evolution of the self and its effect on society. He makes an explicit connection between inner enlightenment of the individual and an advanced, healthy society. He too would say: From whole and healthy people come thoughts and actions that will transform the world. The species has evolved to it.

His is a positive, utopian vision. Russell briefly acknowledges that a negative, "cancerous" future is also possible, but that is not his hope or interest. In the possible society that can evolve, Russell sees a collective behavior change. He envisions decreased violence and emphasis on spiritual values, personal growth, and education as a lifelong process of holistic health practices, along with a better use of natural resources.[32]

The New Age does not have dogma or a specific body of doctrine. Visionary and optimistic works like Russell's stimulate, integrate ideas, and act as beacons. One must take care whether to accept a literal interpretation or to think in metaphorical terms. The New Age thought that encourages each person to take responsibility for self, growth, and actions is a grounded and sober thought. Utopian visions, however, can provide inspiration to maintain a personal discipline to work for growth.

Gaia and Ecology

Ecology is a word based on Greek *oikos,* which means "house." Ecology is, then, a study of habitats or abodes. Somehow, with the concept of Gaia as a living planet, a house becomes a home. The idea of rocks, plants, animals, humans, oceans, and sky being at home together, and being a home together, provides a sense of connectedness to the environment. Here is a positive contribution of the New Age.

Increasingly in recent years the media have been reporting that an environmental crisis exists. Consider the following:

Hundreds of miles of beaches in Prince Edward Sound are covered with crude oil that has actually permeated three to four feet down into the beaches. The tides wash back and forth with poisonous hydrocarbons which are preserved by the glacial coldness of the sound. Fish, birds, and mammals not killed outright are poisoned and die. The entire food chain is affected. Those animals at "the top" of the food chain—eagles, bears, and humans—are at risk. The self-regulating systems of Gaia will go to work, but what was before may never be again. In planetary regulation, species come and go.

Far to the south, Costa Rica's rain forests are essentially gone— hundreds of acres that could have produced fruits, textiles, nuts, dyes, herbs, medicines, meats, and leathers. Hundreds of species no longer exist. This is no result of Gaia's self-regulation, but of humans' changing planetary ecology without accounting for the long range—the results that interconnectedness may bring.

Western society faces what are now referred to as third- generation environmental concerns—alarming rates of population growth, habitat loss, and species extinction; global warming; and threats to the stratospheric ozone layer. The 1970s saw concern about air and water pollution, which are "first generation problems." The '70s and '80s went on to recognize toxic and hazardous materials as thought-provoking problems with widespread consequences. Now we have arrived at the third-generation problems. They are global, long-term, costly, and controversial, and seem intractable. Western and international laws and regulations are still struggling with first- and second-generation problems.[33]

The popular programs on cable and public television that aired the drastic concerns of Prince Edward Sound and Costa Rica also tell of Californians working patiently day after day cutting off gill nets from the necks of sea lions and treating the wounded animals to save their lives. Ranchers in Venezuela have made artificial lakes that have stabilized into habitats for their cattle and for wildlife living together. The farmers also benefit from killing a small percentage of the caiman of the properties and selling the skins. The Royal Bengal tiger and, of course, all other species associated with its habitat are again well established in India through specific efforts.

Such successes help, but they are far from enough. The first Earth Day was April 22, 1970. The twentieth Earth Day has come and gone. Although there have been activity and education for a new popular issue, the environmental situation is worse by any measure.[34]

In his article "An Activist's Perspective: The Inner Nature of the Environmental Crisis," Richard Myers, poet, naturalist, and director of the Sierra Club in eastern Pennsylvania, discusses the implications of the Gaia hypothesis, named for the ancient Greek earth goddess, which evokes a sacred dimension. But Myers aptly quotes Spangler, agreeing with the statement, "Turning Gaia into a mythic or spiritual idea may be inappropriate or premature, leading both to misplaced concreteness and misplaced spirituality. On the other hand, Gaia can be an *inspirational idea.*"[35] Myers and Spangler agree that modern Western people are cut off from nature, perceiving it as something separate from humanity and unable to feel and know the true sacred dimension of Gaia.[36] Myers espouses the tenet:

> Individuals wishing to create a more whole and healthy world face a dual task—we must work for change in the outer world through involvement in the issues each person feels drawn to, while simultaneously doing our own inner transformative work and helping others to understand the need for inner work.[37]

This is Myers's statement of the basis of this chapter: "From whole and healthy people come thoughts and actions that will transform the world."

Myers discusses four environmental movements that are addressing issues ignored by the mainstream. The four he mentions are deep ecology, bioregionalism, ecofeminism, and the Green movement. He indicates that although the movements differ in emphasis, all appreciate the need for inner, transformative work plus the need to focus on outer activity. Deep ecology reintroduces the concept of the ecocentric, not anthropocentric. Bioregionalism provides a place for action for each person: Live consciously in the local environment; understand the sense of the place, wherever that is for each individual. Ecofeminism celebrates wholeness and the human connections to nature. The Green movement concentrates on political and environmental problems.[38]

The concept of Gaia adds a new dimension to traditional environmentalism and highlights the concept of human-nature relationships more clearly than any of the new movements in the following way: Traditional environmental concerns maintain an anthropocentric viewpoint; concerns are focused on human health. The Gaian sense of health is focused on natural ecosystems, not on individual species.[39]

The Gaian perspective mirrors the mystic vision of oneness, intercausality, and connectedness. The human potential for relating to this vision, being part of it but not being subsumed in it, is unique and an epitome of spiritual experience.

From this reminder of intercausality also comes the idea that "from healthy thoughts and actions come results that will transform individuals." The New Age thesis can be reversed. Perhaps the New Age ideas come around to "Know thyself" and "Do good works." These ideas are "old age," even "ancient age," but if not felt as alive and vibrant within the self, do not have personal meaning.

Conclusion

The words *health* and *whole* are related linguistically, and they are perpetual partners in New Age thought. The reaction of the New Age is that scientific, specialized, centralized, competitive, authoritative, and rational values have gone too far. This essay has reviewed a book of case studies of individual transformation; the concept of mind, body, and spirit with impact on medicine; social manifestation of interconnectedness through networking; and planetary perspectives—both utopian and actual environmental concerns. The worldview of holism pervades New Age concepts.

If the New Age takes its own message seriously, overreaction will be remembered as unhealthy too. Wholeness is a balance. The mystic vision brings the sense of oneness, but not sameness. Within the vision, the self is retained as a discrete entity to experience the vision; rationality, too, is important. The New Age message—heal self; heal society; heal the planet—is a positive and optimistic call to those who value the spiritual life.

9

New Age Spirituality: A Critical Appraisal

HARMON HARTZELL BRO

The able church historian and president of a Methodist seminary in Ohio, Leonard Sweet, has often and publicly observed of the
New Age that there is an entire "ecstasy industry" out there, and
mainline churches are ignoring it. As a rubric, "ecstasy" would
hardly capture the commitments of many in the New Age effort for
a right relation with the environment, nor for holistic health, nor for
replacing strident patriarchal values in institutions ranging from the
family to shops to government. Yet it rightly accents the longing for
a direct personal relation with the divine which is at the heart of so
many New Age activities and speculations, from meditation, to
devas of plants, to soul development through successive lives, ever
with an eye to illuminative states of consciousness.

And the category of "industry" hardly does justice to the rich
congeries of teachings and techniques, networks and publications,
workshops and jargons, nutritions and rites, that express the vitality of
the New Age swirl in our midst. Yet the accent on entrepreneurship is
essentially sound. Many are fishing for followers in mall fairs, in those
breezy New Age periodicals full of self-serving ads which appear in
every metropolis, and in the bazaars of ideas that run just down the
street from staid clinic, campus, or church. It would be premature to

call all this bustle and chatter a full-blown movement, although theological conservatives and evangelicals target it mercilessly as an organized threat to the church, whether in Pat Robertson television programs or in slick exposé books and manuals with titles such as *The New Age Rage,* or *New Age or Old Lie,* or *Confronting the New Age.*

But something of weight is in fact happening among us when millions of New Agers (defined by activities and convictions more than by self-labeling alone) who claim the divine is within them have helped to generate thousands of health food stores as well as created a section in bookstores everywhere, and when one quarter of Americans and Britishers incline to accept reincarnation as reality, and far more think they have experienced telepathy or contacted the dead, or use astrology with friendly good humor. Only a smug church could afford to pretend that nothing much is going on. The citizens of the self-proclaimed New Age are not 1950s Zen fans, or 1960s flower children and potheads; they are generally middle-aged—early or later—and middle-class, willing to read books and to hear tapes, as they are ready to put their money and time where they see hope for personal and social change.

As a psychologist of religious experience and behavior within the history of religions, East and West, who has taught at five seminaries and been the dean of one, I have long felt that God is quite capable of speaking to groups and peoples from outside established religious institutions. I am appreciative of Paul Tillich's method of correlation, where the culture poses questions to the faith, and I even suspect that voices from the culture can propose fresh answers to the faith. So in recent decades I have written at times for New Age readers, and lectured often at conferences of New Agers in a score of cities reaching across the United States and Canada, as well as in Europe. For despite the chaotic social and intellectual scurrying of the politely apocalyptic New Agers, I am convinced that they are onto some deep themes of signal importance to themselves and to the churches.

Yet their efforts carry self-defeating thrusts, as we shall see, and need engagement by discerning church leadership if all of us who hope for a new time are to be found doing God's work, not just tending our own ecstasies and pitching our own wares. How shall we in the churches begin to evaluate all the New Age striving for self-transcendence, which is what *ecstasis* really means, and all this busy experimenting and hawking that make church suppers and Bible classes look stuffy?

We can claim, as scholars so often do, that what we see is nothing new, and be partly right. For assuredly there are strands in the New Age of very old astrology, alongside ancient shamanism and modern pop spiritualism, together with familiar theosophical consulting of channeled masters, and New Thought sententious metaphysics, as well as fascination with Hindu and Buddhist notions that long ago engaged the proper New England Transcendentalists; there are also bits of lost LSD glory from a nearer period, not to mention end-time speculation on pole shifts and the coming of a cosmic Christ, which are in principle as old as biblical eschatology. But today's New Age folk are not disfranchised ethnic or social minorities (except that many are women), and not college rebels. They are neighbors to proper churches, as Princeton-trained theologian Lowell Streiker points out in his introspective little book, *New Age Comes to Main Street*. And, as he affirms, they are clearly chewing on a new cosmology and ethic, with its attendant spiritual practices, however indigestible some of the combinations they try. In a way we can claim they are allies of the churches, when they reject a mechanical universe and shallow civic religions, as well as challenge daily routinization that substitutes the melodrama of politics, the addiction of erotic-violent-trivial television, and the rites of shopping for the deeper longings of heart and soul.

We can claim that the current throbbing of arcane messages and techniques is merely a ferment, not worthy of being called an Age of anything, and be partly right. Little has yet emerged that is compelling enough to die for. For New Agers have been so busy rejecting established Western traditions, in favor of the novel, or the exotically ancient, or the supposedly Eastern or native American, or the airily higher in consciousness, that they typically step out of history rather than continue it in a new epoch. Yet many of the themes they pursue are surprisingly like those Harvey Cox lists as definitive of a "postmodern era" (the respectable way to say New Age in church circles) in his post-Bonhoeffer *Religion in the Secular City*.

Or, seeking to get a fix on this often brash and busy spirituality, we can cite regrettable extremes in its brief history, and make these our basis for hoping it will just wear out or go away.

Excesses and Extravagances

Most of us who are church people would be aggrieved to have the entire life of the church judged by doubtful practices of certain TV evangelists and other religious crusaders and exploiters. Yet we would grant that a shallow ethic usually comes from a shallow gospel and accept the responsibility for testing the congruence of our faith with our public behavior. So, too, we can rightly note the reprehensible and trivial features of the New Age, if we agree to go on and examine the theological anatomy of the creature, to see whether and, if so, how it may systematically foster the distressing outcomes that it has sometimes produced.

It is difficult to avoid seeing *greed* at work in the high fees for consultations that have built elegant, chandeliered horse stables for the medium who channels a supposed thirty-thousand-year-old Atlantean warrior. And one marvels at the costly conferences around the country, through which a talented movie actress has become an affluent high priestess of the New Age. Or there is a suspicion of avarice when a California psychic charges well to produce wisdom direct from the minds of dolphins. Many have raised questions of *manipulation* when a national group conducts intensive sessions that take the usual New Age slogan, "You create your own reality," to a crippling extreme that hammers on guilt for bringing cancer or job loss on oneself. And while the New Age is not just a cult or collection of cults, it does get itself tangled up at times with apparent brainwashing in centers like the open-sex ashram in Oregon whose charismatic guru got deported. There is *fraud.* The two lover-operators of a New Age center in Wyoming (which I knew well) simply absconded in midseason with all the cash, leaving staff and lecturers and conferees, as well as vendors, stuck with their consciousness aspirations and not much more. A very large self-proclaimed New Age organization (which I also knew well) raised a million dollars from members and friends to do "controlled, objec-

tive research" on astrology, and then simply mailed out commer-
cially bought horoscopes with some questionnaires, hardly approaching the touted research and pocketing three quarters of the
money for other purposes. And the levitation at the maharishi's
university in Iowa turned out to be a kind of hopping, not much like
what was proclaimed in the media.

There is the appearance of *self-deception,* or worse, when a
channeled being named for a minor biblical prophet, with a considerable following in the western United States that includes a respected former member of the Episcopal clergy (and a number of
my damaged counseling clients), proclaims that in a prior existence
he taught Jesus everything the Galilean knew, including the means
used to pop off the cross before dying and go marry an Egyptian
woman. And the indiscriminate promotion of the widely studied *A
Course in Miracles* as literally the words of Jesus, which it proclaims,
overlooks the obvious Vedantist substance of the teaching (which
denies the crucifixion and ultimately the reality of sin and evil), far
from the New Testament, and robs students of a legitimate but
disciplined encounter between Eastern and Western treasures approached in their own integrity and depth.

There is *doubtful morality,* of course. A widely respected New
Age psychologist and author abruptly dumps his wife and family to
marry a self-proclaimed psychic, even before the actress who made
New Age a household phrase describes her torrid affair with a
British M.P. right along with her cosmic soaring. One of the most
respected New Age physicians at age seventy suddenly announces
that he needs to discard his physician wife, so he can have more time
alone to be a spiritual leader—but soon after marries his younger
nurse, after "turning within" for guidance. There is *narcissism* in the
claims of walk-ins (those I have known) supposedly taking over
someone else's adult identity, as there is in such shrines to esoteric
wisdom as the New Age seminary where I have lectured, which
replaces the usual holy emblems in a lavender-decorated chapel
with a bas-relief of a woman salvifically embracing the world—a
woman who looks strikingly like the resident guru. And there is
unending *trivialization,* in pitching conferences and publications to
soul mates, or the wonders of prehistoric Egypt or Atlantis (why

neglect India's Mohenjo Daro?), or touting crystals and pyramids, as well as techniques for tuning in a higher self that require no metanoia, in a world without homeless or a Holocaust.

Perhaps it is not surprising—though certainly sad—that the signature of the New Age in *art* is so often stylized figures amid an auric haze of shafts and swirls of light and color, minus shadows of serious evil, and without evocations of prized values in conflict. Or that New Age *music* is so often mere musing with trivial, repetitious harmonies and avoidance of meaningful dissonance or strong minor keys in favor of half-conceived melodies and toying with timbres. All is relaxing and preparation for elevation of consciousness toward a divine Reality which demands little serious change. Surely neither mystics nor prophets can find a home in such an Oz. It should not be surprising that the gutsy wounded in AA and related movements have stayed out of the New Age, or that the older, sophisticated innovators in Steiner's Anthroposophy, with their fine sense of art and dance, as well as their Waldorf schools, have done the same.

The Death and Rebirth
of Key Symbols

But the very extravagance of a try-almost-anything wave of effort at transcendence in our midst may point to dynamics that help us to understand it. More than half a century ago, Carl Jung wrote an essay on the predicament of modern man (today we would say modern person), which gave the title to a small but widely read book of his essays, *Modern Man in Search of a Soul.* In this paper, he wisely disavowed omniscience, but offered his own analysis of a coming flood of interest in theosophy, the occult, parapsychology, and Eastern religions, set in a larger context of reevaluating matter, the feminine, the psyche, and the divine. He saw the emerging ebullience of seeking in terms that match surprisingly well what now is called the New Age. What led him to this prescience?

In his view, the deep, rich energies of the psyche in every era seek expression in forms that carry the inner vitality (ever differentiating new richness of potentials and trying to integrate them) into outer activity: rites, roles, institutions, social and cosmic schemata, technologies, credos, causes, artworks. In some epochs the match of outer forms and inner archetypal thrusts is reasonably stable and effective (Jung specifically illustrates from the Middle Ages). But in other periods certain crucial symbols—in the broadest sense of cosmology, myth, rite, custom, tale, and art—begin to erode and collapse, as they are challenged by critical thought, by comparison with impinging cultures, by calamities, by sustained social evil, or by other prods to social change. Key symbols, by which life is to be lived and sacrificed for a worthwhile destiny, lose their bite and become quaint. What might work for Arthurian society won't cut it for industrious burghers of a later Calvinist capitalism (to make the point). Crucial to any epoch are those symbols which shape the sense of the life-renewing holy, in relation to vocation, to stages of life, to loving, to gender roles and social class, to orderly social change. Much more than customs shift. The perceived cosmos, and all that is duty and opportunity and ecstasy, become problematic, though not all at once for everyone.

In such a time of wavering structures and values, as Jung described the process in this essay and others, the libido or natural vital energy of the psyche strikes inward or regresses in many people. If the image is not taken too literally, it may be said to "flood" to the depths of the collective unconscious, stirring up all manner of strange patterns from times past or possible. Forgotten worldviews become permissible alternatives. Ancient rites become appealing. The inner world of archetypes, so laden with witches and angels and alchemy and magic creatures, becomes the stuff of dreams and cults and movements, while the times await leaders who can pull the sword of order and discrimination from the stone of blind fate. Meanwhile, witches are burned or celebrated, crusades mounted, and opportunities lost, as the collective unconscious disgorges its untempered alternatives. For Jung, the emergence of Nordic mythology in rites of Aryan supremacy that drove the Nazi movement illustrated the extremes of such a process.

Jung's thesis may well be sound. If it is, then the New Age may not simply be a conspiracy of the Antichrist (as some theological literalists see it), nor an excrescence of decadence and indulgence, nor a hodgepodge of escapist fantasies. More likely, it may be the chaos that precedes serious shifts in contemporary worldviews and ethics and faith, for better or worse. During a preliminary period we get a jumble of paganism, mantras, sexual adventures, gods and goddesses, skinheads, shamanistic drumbeats, past lives, folk cures, yogic postures, and true mystical illuminations, tumbling out in expensive séances alongside Greenpeace ardor, together with resurgent fundamentalism and military adventurism. What will be lasting depends on our discrimination and imagination, gifted by grace in an atmosphere of humor and humility. The task of helping choose the treasures to keep and develop is worthy of a thoughtful church in such times, using its charts from history, but steering more to the hopeful eschaton than back to its own ecstatic Eden.

Are we in the West living in a time of death of key organizing symbols? Every age claims this, as unfailingly as commencement speakers do. Yet we have reason to think that the death of forms in us and around us is widespread and important. Courtship and marriage have had their biggest jolts in centuries, and the answer to how to manage two-earner families still dances just out of reach. We are strung out on drugs as few if any societies before us. Class and race and gender discrimination are still with us, although changes have been large and dear. Sports are often incredibly commercialized, and the less-noted underpinnings of teams and lodges, clubs and Scouts and unions, seem to wobble. Life-span transitions yield their wonder to rites of convenience, and the church year is quietly replaced by the shopping year, from January white sales to summer barbecues to December Santa binges. Ethnic and regional character becomes merely colorful and quaint, as we prowl our terrain in expensive cars, wondering if all our world is interchangeable Coke and Pepsi and malls and video-primed dancing. Billboards and commercials trivialize our aspirations into everlasting coveting. Bankers and brokers falter as fast as politicians and preachers; who is to be trusted to lead?

Behind all this smash and tumble and seediness lie faltering worldviews and duties and hopes, by which we try to live. Most of us no longer plan on going to medieval heaven or hell. But where shall we head, as pilgrims without promise? What is worthy of lifelong discipline? What can command our largehearted sacrifice? Who or what can renew us when we burn out?

Jung argued in assessing his "modern man" that the runaway love of rationality, a huge overvaluing of consciousness, is our root problem, which the psyche would try to correct with corresponding deluges of irrationality. His thesis is matched today in essays of those who question Western technology in love with itself, or see patriarchal exclusivism and dominance as a dangerous dead end.

Especially when meaningful events and seasons of initiation and transformation fail us, we lose the delicate interplay of structure and anti-structure in *rituals* of dedication and renewal which the anthropologist Victor Turner has so carefully chronicled as essential to the balance of I-it and I-Thou relations in culture after culture (he notes his indebtedness to Buber). We lose the sense of how to go apart and find transcendence, managing only how to go on and on. Can stylized Sunday worship, supplemented by a few festival events and some pleasant discussions among peers, really redeem such a time?

Whatever else New Agers have come upon, they have rediscovered the *weekend apart* as a vital retreat time for workshops and seminars and conferences, as well as for sweat lodges and silence, dancing and drawing. Taking time, taking on each other, huddling close to nature, passing around treasured sayings from other cultures and times, trying to build or garden, they begin the incubating that may finally distinguish the birth from the afterbirth, as the unconscious inundates us. For Protestants without a monastic heritage for backup, the pressure to go apart, fashioning authentic communal vehicles for shared depth in our times, is huge. We have to reinvestigate missioning, orders, retreats, academies, and pilgrimages. Without some invention of events and vehicles, along lines in which New Agers are pioneering, we in the all-too-proper churches may have to go through the bitter pruning that upright Job encountered, until the raw archetypal unconscious shook him awake with its terrifying grandeur, under the finger of Yahweh.

Yet, *process* alone is not enough. There must be viable *content* of conviction and commitment, tested by old and new criteria. Every society needs its saving secrets, verbal and nonverbal, to command loyalties, fire imaginations, toughen wills, provoke vows. Some of the secrets are "closed secrets," reserved for initiates. The

New Age explores many of these, in its rites of firewalking, in its proffering of channeled beings, in its myths of sunken Lemuria, in its parading of near-death experiences, in its cross-legged postures and chanted Om. But it also knows something about "open secrets," which are only secret because too good to be believed. The astounding immanence of the divine to ordinary people who seek with good hearts, the precious life of creatures, the love that honors the stranger and empowers the marginal are more than interesting paradigm shifts, such as fascinate Marilyn Ferguson in her New Age manifesto, *The Aquarian Conspiracy*. They are the stuff of faith itself, and deserve careful examination, which we can at least suggest in this chapter by examining four themes: truth, matter/body, the psyche, and community.

Verifiable Truth

Many of the central issues that New Agers address belong properly to philosophy and religion, where questions of human nature and destiny, the oneness of force and energy, the fitness of rite and ethic, the possibility of evolution in consciousness as well as in species all have their place. Yet New Age books are found in their own section in bookstores. Why? Likewise, many of the disciplines that New Agers espouse, from relaxation and visualization to consulting the I Ching, and on to reverence for creatures and espousal of feminine values, with planetary politics, belong in psychology and in self-development shelves, or in history and social criticism. Yet, New Age authors and groups have their own corner of books, where Sybil Leek of witchcraft is perched beside psychic Jane Roberts and seer Edgar Cayce, and the dead medium Arthur Ford speaks through journalist Ruth Montgomery (having known both Ford and Montgomery well, I doubt it), while the shelves groan under expected earth changes that will dump California into the sea, or under the burden of stars that tell secrets of fate and romance. What do all these have in common to make a marketing category, not only in bookstores but in hotel conferences and living room study groups? Surely, it is their espousal of private authority for truth, bypassing critical norms of disciplined inquiry.

As William James long ago warned, it is ever tempting to validate truth by roots rather than by fruits. If a teaching or practice can be shown to come from a trance or automatic writing, or is presented as from an evolved master on another plane, that makes it fascinating to the mind vulnerable to the brewing unconscious, and to a life searching for shortcuts in an age of canned entertainment and politics of expediency, beset by handgun crime and ambient AIDS virus. The church is no stranger to this strategy for identifying truth, whenever it claims that the Bible (or the pope or the historic church) offers authority that need not be questioned, tested, or set in the marketplace of ideas. Behind the too-glib assertions of revelations by New Agers lies the church's own proffering of revelation, in shelves just one aisle down. Gurus only ape preachers, all too often.

But what is the church's actual teaching about verifiable truth? It has historically distinguished between *inspiration,* which is private, and *revelation,* which is corporate and time-tested, in the household of faith. New Agers blur the distinction at their own peril, when, for example, they propose Helen Schucman's miracles course as authoritative just because it came from a voice giving "inner dictation" and claimed to be from Jesus, or when they violate Edgar Cayce's firm strictures to test every teaching from his prayer-inspired trances by their fruits in daily life, and to measure them by scripture and norms of prized community.

Further, the church has balanced revelation with reason. Matthew Fox once observed that New Agers seem to have been missing when left brains were passed out. How has the church valued the uses of critical *reason,* in the various disciplines of study that use the left brain? While the church has at times exploited reason only to unpack and organize its authoritarian revelation, the mainstream of church thought in recent centuries has taken on reason (with all its empirical inquiry which today we summarize as science) as giving us truth *in tension with revelation,* where neither wholly captures the other. This is not to say that for Christian reflection disciplined reason only wars with revelation, so that left brain and right brain make tumult in the corpus callosum, and in human judgment. In a pregnant phrase, Tillich has written of revelation as "the depth of reason," and unfolded its compelling quality by using Jung's concept of archetypes in the collective unconscious as mediators of the divine self-gift (a position foreshadowed by William James as he saw the "subliminal" presenting the divine in religious experience). But it is to say that serious religious thought in the West has used reason and revelation in patterns of checks and balances, not abandoning the left brain for the latest amazing pronouncement from some inspired or dazed spokesperson for the Holy. For the best of New Age thinking, the tradition has here some healthy warnings and invitations—to be critical, to use canons of inquiry, to try the spirits, to report not only what somebody announces but what careful testing in practice has shown, in left-brain modes and communities that allow further investigation and improvement.

For revelation in the long experience of the church is *communal*. Sometimes this has been merely institutional, with dogma from a hierarchy and punishment for divergence, against which New Agers rightly rebel (many, as preliminary studies have shown, are ex-Roman Catholics, although ex-Jews, ex-Baptists, and other former Protestant faithful are well represented too, alongside those who have never found such communities appealing at all). But in its better forms, the church has clung to checks and balances, to keep its sense of revelation holy and vital. Three components of revelation have been treasured as needing each other in every generation, to point to God's ever-renewed self-gift, not just to a neat body of creedal or catechetical teachings. The three are: *scripture,* the *church* as community with its historic traditions, and the working of the *Spirit* in religious experience. Any of the three alone is dangerous. Scripture by itself can become mere fundamentalist bibliolatry, lending itself to recipe morality and rigid scenarios of salvation. The church with its several streams of tradition, allowed to run ahead of scripture and the Spirit, can become tyrannical as the tool of self-serving clergy and political or class or gender authority alike. And the Spirit without tempering wisdom from compacted and cherished scriptures, or without more sweeping perspectives of the community in its history, can fly into fragmented theosophies and ethics of self-indulgence.

Viewed against this tripod meant to give footing to revelation which can continuously enrich reason, the New Age shows up poised and swaying on one shaft, dancing on one toe: the Spirit. Affirming radical newness and openness, New Age devotees want raptures and illuminations like the most precious revelations in traditions of East and West, or of ancient Egypt and modern shamanism, without having to buy into any particular community. Yet that is like loving women or men in general but not wanting to marry one. The deepest mysteries and empowerment of spirituality may only be available to those who invest in a particular tradition, who learn to sing its songs, tread its processionals, bury its dead, own its confessed evil, speak its hushed names of the divine, and wait in its hallowed places. As New Testament scholar Wayne Rollins has traced in his penetrating study entitled *Jung and the Bible*, spirituality worth having comes in interlocked chains of archetypes. Those who seek the ecstasies of the Spirit apart from particular scriptures, rites, and communities of East or West may not find them—or may find only flashes that dazzle and beguile, yet transform neither person nor society.

Does this mean that to become a serious Christian or Jew or Buddhist, or a disciplined partaker of some other rich tradition, requires shutting out the treasures of the others, as New Agers so fear (partly because of the narrowness of church history, which Presbyterian theologian Richard Drummond has shown in his epochal *Towards a New Age in Christian Theology* to be true to neither the Bible nor the church fathers and mothers, not to mention the Christ)? Quite the contrary, many of us would affirm. Deep calls unto deep. Those who walk one path in patience and humility and hope can find again and again the gift of daring and depth and delight in another path, while those who commit to none find the secrets of the Holy hidden from their raids of ambitious spirituality.

But let us be fair to New Agers. The work of the Spirit has hardly been a vital stream in recent American Protestantism, though it has eddied in prayer groups and movements and soared in a few mystics. Instead, the Spirit has often been cramped into the biographical space allowed for conversion, so featured on the American frontier. All that the church has in other times meant by sanctification—the slow but precious growth into whole-souled closeness to the divine (into what some of the mystics have called "the godded life")—has too often been jettisoned in favor of simply being saved, the redemptive work that is part of God's ever-fresh gift, but surely not all of it.

Wherever the New Age is truly a quest for life-transforming and world-transforming ecstasy, not just for evanescent peak experiences, then it comes as both a judgment and a promise to those churches which have buried the Spirit under conventional rite, Bible-prattle, and propriety. The gift of sustained silent and image-less mediation to a busy-busy church may be priceless. God-talk that is regularly trimmed by the humble practices of the Via Negativa, abstaining from rattling on about majesty and glory we hardly dare guess, can spring us loose from pretense. Having to think about God as Mother, or nature as copilgrim with us, can dump our neat compliance with a God who seems to ask only obedience to left-brain rules but never asks entrance to the dark spaces of dismay and suffering that are both tomb and womb for rhythms of love that mere churchmanship never guesses.

Insofar as the New Age, with its everlasting relaxing and getting ready, is a restless hunger for genuine transcendence and visitation, then its pilgrimage is to be welcomed, though not without challenge to engage the fullness of reason and revelation in potent wrestling together. Especially in its bold insistence on empirical investigation, heady at times but capable of rousing somnolent faith to honest passion for God, it is full of promise.

Finally, we need to note that the exasperating New Age indifference to verifiable truth, in favor of ravishing experiences and mind-boggling pronouncements, may indicate something not unfamiliar to serious Christians: a longing for a *relationship* first, and for *propositions* later. That posture is at the heart of faith, so long as it does not degenerate into love of holy-sounding experiences in place of love of the Holy itself. Some of us in the church will continue to greet with affection and hope those in the New Age who go apart into the wilderness of nature, and into the wilderness of their own surging unconscious, in an era when the church at times takes up offerings more readily than it takes up the dangerous Presence.

Matter and the Body

In his essay on the predicaments of modernity, written sixty years ago, Jung did not stop with his surmise that the psyche would exact a kind of revenge from the unconscious on the overrationality of consciousness, by boiling up with all manner of theosophical, Oriental, occult, and psychic interests—a menu of much of what we today call the New Age. He insisted, in closing, that the revolution would reach all the way to the relation of matter (and the body) to spirit, no longer allowing matter to be seen as enemy of the spirit, nor allowing it to be merely neutral stuff which could be manipulated at will. Some twenty years later he wrote more explicitly of the "psychicizing" of matter that he saw coming. In a graphic and penetrating essay on the mother archetype, and then in his impassioned cry to God (written in two weeks while he ran a fever) called *Answer to Job,* he laid hold of the current papal pronouncement of the Assumption of Mary, raised up in her flesh, as symbolic evidence of the necessary reevaluation of matter as twin to the spirit.

In New Age circles, few views are as widely held as the affirmation that matter, and therefore all of flesh and created nature, partake somehow in the being of the divine, and answer to it with a high place in cosmic destiny. In its least-developed forms, this affirmation becomes pantheism and vague nature mysticism. Conservative Christians can then cry monism, and bewail the confusing of God and creation. But, in richer modes, the new and higher evaluation fits into panentheism, as Matthew Fox is fond of pointing out, where the divine is not equated with all that is in nature, but rather nature is somehow *in* God, even as God is *in* it. Edgar Cayce, the seer with a biblical faith (often sadly hucksterized since his death), once used a formula from the Eucharist to suggest the relationship: God as in, with, and under all creation, not just the loaf and the cup.

How to think about matter and the body in new metaphors has much exercised New Agers. Often reference is made to "vibrations" or "energies" that might proceed from the One, not only at the beginning of creation, but continuously. Some opt for versions of Gnostic emanations which sell out the qualitative distinctions that Christians have sought to preserve by insisting that creation was made from nothing at all that might exist apart from God. Whatever the images, some strong statements are being made, and ethical principles derived, which must interest thoughtful Christians.

For clearly there is a new comradeship with matter—with oceans and ozone and creatures and ecological systems—coming up from somewhere in the human depths of our times. Some call it resacralizing matter, as the first step toward a world capable of numinous Presence, which it began to lose when the Goddess of Reason was enshrined at Notre Dame during the height of the French Revolution. If the sacralizing goes on to outright venerating, we are back in a world of druid trees and Egyptian animal-headed deities, identifying with and patronizing what Christians and Jews would rather encounter in hallowing—which is finding that we can say "thou" to and be addressed by matter that shines in God's light, as truly as we can with one another.

In a rehallowed natural universe, we can no longer locate evil simply in matter and the flesh, where even today monastic life of West and East often seems to place it. We can no longer use imagery from the Gnostics and others, of sparks of the divine needing to be freed from matter. Human passions, so like those of the animals, are no longer the great threat to spirituality, so much as misuse of our creative imagination and free will in living *to* the flesh while we are *of* the flesh.

Paul's poignant imagery of all creation groaning and struggling with us finds its echoes in the groans and songs of whales whom we now seek to protect, just as we do spotted owls and Serengeti lions, and the caribou of the oil-pipe tundras. On a worldwide scale there is evidence of a kind of awakening to tender regard for our cradling environment and its species, alerting us to threatened rain forests and warning us of obscene piles of near-eternal discarded plastic. Although we cannot yet seem to spontaneously cherish children of other continents, faiths, and races enough to feed and heal and educate them together, we may be on our way to exactly such love—by beginning with love of the nonspeaking beings, and of the ambient elements that give us all life.

If, in fact, we are all wandering, however uncertainly, on a new pilgrimage in loving, which can one day stretch from creatures to children and farther on to adults, even strangers and enemies, then the preoccupation of New Agers with reengaging the creation is important, though oddly expressed in native American medicine wheels, or in the chants and spells of Wiccas and covens. (I once found six former members of covens in one seminary class I taught.) Pleasant little church school hymns that tell how this is my Father's world do not come anywhere near the blazing mysteries of nature that made Job clap his hand on his mouth. Nor do they approach the stupefying drama of the Buddhist bodhisattva, who resolves after eons of lifetimes not to enter nirvana until every blade of grass has found its fulfillment. There are Christian resources to enable us to think about the cosmic destiny of blades of grass, as Santmire has shown in his brilliant history of Christian thought on the subject, *The Travail of Nature.* And they do not require that we simply discard nature in favor of more highly evolved structures, as he points out, despite the appeal that Teilhard de Chardin has had for many Christian environmentalists. Wherever imagery of the exodus and a promised land has gripped Christian imagination, instead of the static and hierarchical Great Chain of Being which theologians long have announced, there is hope that Christians can journey with nature, not away from it, to the messianic time.

One of the modes for "psychicizing" nature among New Agers may be found in their widespread agreement on the reality and—to some extent—cultivatability of psychic experience, both as cognitive and as kinetic. Conservative Christians sometimes link everything psychic to divining and witchcraft, to be condemned. Yet the New Testament abounds with dreams, guidance, telepathy, and healing, which suggest elements of worthwhile psychic processes, just as do certain experiences of judges and prophets in the Toroh (analyzed with skill by the gifted British scholar Alfred Guillaume in his *Prophecy and Divination Among the Hebrews and Other Semites*). This is not the place to examine the huge mound of modern research data supporting the likely reality of psychic processes, for which adequate theories are still the sticking point. But we can well note some of the implications.

Matter itself, for example, is relativized as a category, if the mind can directly engage its structures, both for data and for control. And, in turn, the body is no longer a skintight monad of flesh, if someone's distant thought can penetrate its systems with telepathy or with healing currents. The consequences include exciting new ways of conducting daily life in a world where everything is a kind of music, however inaudible, that vibrates in clashes or consonance with other music, in complex fields of vibrations, sometimes mediated by chakras. Prayer and meditation as practiced in churches, with perfunctory Sunday blessings on this week's hospitalized, may be far out of touch with what Jesus manifested in healing, as he linked it to fasting and to moral purpose.

Unfortunately, the modern and thoroughly American love of technology often corrupts the cultivation of worthwhile psychic processes by emphasizing power and knowledge at the expense of rich values which in fact best elicit what we quaintly call the paranormal. Separating telepathy and clairvoyance, psychokinesis and precognition, from love and patience, courage and wonder, may only trivialize and hide them.

If the body is an instrument to be played with and for others, not just a lump to be prodded and distracted and medicated, then the New Age preoccupation with holistic health is appropriate and a real challenge to churches. Christians have caught on to the linkage of soma and psyche, enough to breed a whole generation of psychiatrically wise pastoral counselors. But stretching the equation to include the spirit is not yet a commitment in church-sponsored medicine, even in typical Presbyterian, Methodist, and Lutheran hospitals. Were the spirit taken seriously, it would be unthinkable to treat illness without confession and forgiveness (as AA knows)— which New Agers are often as slow to engage with healing as are church people. But the winds of the times blow in this direction. Matthew Fox has nicely urged that now and then a church have a Liver Sunday, in which the artwork and the music and the liturgy celebrate the gift of a particular organ and confess our abuse of it, in the larger tapestry of matter which serves creation as truly as does poetry.

How we shall engage matter, including the raw elements as well as creatures and our own saltwater blood, in rites of cleansing and renewal is a riddle that biblical faith has confronted ever since its first shudders at Baal fertility ceremonies. We know we cannot find the answer in Greek idolization of the body, nor in Roman strutting. But neither are we likely to find it in Hindu mortifying. An ascesis, an athletic training, in flesh that spends itself in high-spirited creating with and for others in need, must be found where medieval piety offered chiefly only sublimation. New Age adventures in acupuncture and Vedic medicine, as well as in Sufi movement, in hot-tub sharing, in touch therapy, and talking to plants, can be seen as invitations to thoughtful exploration by church people who affirm that even dead cells and organs can dance to a fuller Reality, despite a brutalizing cross.

The Psyche

While the New Age is busy rescuing the realms of matter and the body from centuries of doubt and exploitation, and industriously examining contemporary physics for models, it is also upsetting centuries-old Christian images of the self or psyche as inherently blighted, needing massive intervention from the divine even to start growing in a healthy and generous manner. For some, this new, higher view of human nature is expressed by seeing humans as the self-aware nervous system of *Gaia, the evolving planet,* which has been developing in self-regulating modes ever since the "big bang." The admittedly exciting drama of natural processes patiently reaching toward self-aware unity with the divine, in what some are calling the "new story" and new myth for humankind, replacing old teachings of the Fall and redemption, does not easily, however, capture the sense of a profoundly personal divine, tenderly or fiercely beckoning to each person.

For those in the New Age who see personhood as a precious . cosmic reality, dear to the heart and even the nature of God, models for thinking about human nature may sometimes come from *psychiatry,* although there is often a surprising gulf between New Age reflection and medical model making. For much of a century, since Freud published his *Interpretation of Dreams* in 1900 (at about the same time James did his lectures on varieties of religious experience), psychiatric thought has relied on the distinction between two kinds of operations in the psyche: secondary process, which does all the conscious coping and planning, and primary process, where wish and myth and basic drive offer both imagination and compulsion, often preverbal modes. But these days it is possible to speak, guardedly, of tertiary process as a hypothetical possibility, pointing to some center in the psyche that carries a sense of full humanness and tries to actualize it, through the other processes. Carl Rogers contributed to such explorations with his client-centered therapy which suggested that troubled people really know at some nonsurface level what is wrong with them and how to cure it. And Jung's affirmation of a Self with a German capital "S" made its own connections with the Western image of an undefaced soul and with the atman of Hindu tradition, as well as with affirmation of a Buddha nature unfolding in all sentient beings. Other streams in both psychiatry and transpersonal psychology stretch the image of selfhood by incorporating the banished feminine. Some of the New Age proclamation that human beings have a higher self in direct touch with the divine comes from such thinking.

But actual experiences of engaging the transcendent in ecstatic ways, or seeming to do so, have probably contributed more to the New Age affirmation of a high view of human nature. Five types of such experiences must be noted. *Psychic encounters* carry their own sense of wonder and sometimes wholesome creativity which stimulate the New Age seeker. If one can know the thoughts of another person, at times, why not know the thoughts of God? To have such knowledge, even in fragmentary ways, requires considerable congruence between the two participants: a person and the divine. So a view of human nature emerges that does not fit well with images of fallen humankind, waiting forlornly for redemption. Further, psychic currents may provide an unseen mode for connecting all individuals and nonhuman reality as well, leading to a cosmology that emphasizes ultimate Oneness, and a high estate for personhood.

Second, the rediscovery of *mythological motifs* at work in

ordinary people in many cultures, seen in dream and vision and patterned behavior trends, lights up the inner world of humans with the glowing faces of goddesses and gods. While there is no easy jump from finding that one behaves like an Athena or a Hermes, in remarkable degree, to claiming potential divinity within, the explorations of Campbell and many others, and of students of shamanism, have opened up the issue of essential human size and nobility trying to express itself.

Third, the cultivation and study of *altered states of consciousness,* in which mystical moments of states seem to come within reach of ordinary people, have contributed decisively to rethinking human nature as not so inherently twisted as Western faith has seemed to affirm. Starting with dreams, adding hypnosis and the suggestive stimulus of powerful guided imagery, and going on to drug-related or fasting-related experiences of transcendence, as well as to near-death and out-of-the-body events, the wide probing of altered states and their implications has been a major social current in our times. One might expect churches, which keep affirming the transcendent consciousness of prophets and reformers in times of prayer and worship, as well as the action of the Spirit on ordinary folk, might welcome all this exploration into altered states. But the leap that New Agers make, to affirm that these ecstasies tell us who we really are, in our final design, works to put off those church people gripped by an image of fallen humanity, fixed on original sin more than on what Matthew Fox has called original blessing.

Fourth, the New Age interest in *reincarnation and karma* has taken a different direction from its classic Hindu versions, where being reborn in human form is regrettable and getting off the wheel of rebirth is the goal. While New Agers hold various fuzzy views of what might be happening in the rebirth process, they generally affirm a position not too far removed from centuries-long Christian views of purgatory: God has more growth in store for us than one lifetime can possibly hold, and will continue to stretch and empower and transform us after death. Karma is often presented as retributive and purging, much as was suffering in older views of purgatory. But more sophisticated New Age views, like those carefully worked out by Buddhist Ken Wilbur (who does not list himself as a New

Ager), or suggested by Edgar Cayce (whose deeply biblical worldview hardly qualifies him to be a New Ager), also find in karma the flowering of talents and opportunities for service of one's fellows, as well as the qualitative enrichment of personhood toward its destiny of conscious unison (not necessarily union) with the divine. The practical evidence for possible reality in karma is multiform, ranging from dream content to hidden talent, and including peculiar patterns of attraction or repulsion, as well as origins of meaningful disabilities and suffering. However the rebirthing drama is sketched, for those who profess a continuing and formative interest in reincarnation (apparently one person in four in any American supermarket), the issue of the nature and destiny of the soul is back on the spiritual agenda after an absence from mainstream theological reflection for two centuries of modernity. And it is there in a mode that does not see human beings as trapped in unfortunate bodies, but as pilgrims in a long journey, which is worthwhile because full-sized humans are worthwhile to God. Church people can rightly protest that such a viewpoint is not explicitly biblical, but they must not too easily fall into the trap of denying in advance what empirical inquiry into recesses of the unconscious can find—for such denial of investigation on biblical grounds did not work well with Galileo, Darwin, or Freud.

Fifth, the New Age affirmation of *self-responsibility*, that "You create your own destiny and circumstance," flows naturally from a perspective that affirms the just and patient workings of karma. However, New Agers hold to this notion on the more practical basis of observing how we bring on ourselves what we fear or hope, in New Thought processes where "mind is the builder." Partly, this is an affirmation of radical possibilities by getting rid of gloomy and constrictive mind-sets, which contains sound psychological counsel. But the doctrine often goes farther, to become "You create your own reality," suggesting self-responsibility not only in illness and hardship, health and prosperity, but in the whole way the cosmos appears to us and therefore works with us, as friendly or antagonistic. When pushed to an extreme, this ebullient posture borders on paranoia, of course, and can generate guilts over failures as great as the exhilaration of release. But the outlook undoubtedly contributes its own strand to the emergent high view of human nature and destiny in New Age circles.

Here we must enter some warnings. American popular culture, with its love of technology and gimmicks and its pursuit of instant gratification (the theme on which psychiatrist Scott Peck opens his influential manifesto, *The Road Less Traveled*), can easily take the above five strands and turn them into shallow psychotechnologies, which depart so far from the deep drama of transformation in the great religious traditions as to be both preposterous and dangerous. Psychic experience and attainment can be made a kind of ladder of spirituality without moral reference, where seeing auras means that one is evolved, and getting messages by channeling means intimacy with the divine. In the same way, plundering one's unconscious for patterns that resemble this or that goddess or god or heroic saga of mythology can become mere technique, in which there is no Olympus and no pain—quite overlooking the terrible price that Prometheus had to pay for stealing fire from the gods to give to mortals (an emblem of all consciousness-making). The pursuit of altered states, in the hopes of finding ecstatic visions, can be canned into flotation tanks, packaged vision quests into the outback, ritual chanting or sweating, and dream capturing which offers a higher consciousness that knows nothing of crucifixions and self-giving for others. We have noted the shallowness of much New Age art and music, which affirms the reachability of higher consciousness through endless relaxing and musing, without engaging one's shadow side and the deep perversity that dogs human nature. Reincarnation can of course be made the vehicle for narcissistic speculation and "readings" about one's remarkable past, or for escaping responsibility to respond to the suffering of others because it is their karma. And even taking responsibility for one's life and affairs can degenerate into mechanical affirmations of potency and peace, which dodge the divine call in situations where poverty of circumstance and spirit is the greatest strength, and miss the divine outrage over situations where there should be no peace. The call to solve the world's hunger problem by merely visualizing a lack of hunger, put forth by an influential New Age organization, represents just such trivialization into psychotechniques.

The issue that most deeply troubles church people, however, in all the elevating of human nature and destiny that the New Age has sought to bring about, is surely the handling of evil. It may be that dour Calvinism and frontier revivalism have overstated the case for being "a wretch like me" who receives "amazing grace." But to go to the opposite extreme of reveling in how godlike we all are, even affirming that in principle we are God, looks past pervasive human sin and evil in ways that make the New Age appear shallow indeed. Scott Peck, who rather carelessly identified God and the unconscious in his first book, at least took a hard look there at laziness as a deep human propensity. Then in his second work, *People of the Lie* (much less popular in both New Age and church circles), he more carefully examined personal and social evil, even proposing it (unwisely) as a psychiatric category. Here he added narcissism to laziness as a pervasive human problem, enriching his account of evil in ways that approach the biblical account of two levels, grounded in misuse of the imagination and the will, that Buber developed in his searching though demanding little volume, *Good and Evil.* As the psychiatrist in charge of investigating the American atrocities at My Lai, Peck speaks with penetrating authority on how distancing of responsibility and participation in modern society leads finally to real social evil on the part of all of us. And he goes even farther to identify transhuman evil, in recounting exorcism, raising an issue that has New Testament roots.

All of these are themes that easily get buried in New Age enthusiasm, sundering it from compelling fiction and biography, as well as from scriptures of East and West. Any method of channeling your higher self without really having to forgive, sacrifice for, or cherish your spouse or your neighbor or your enemy becomes a hollow promise. And it is a promise that finds no real support in the literature on the richest of altered states, just as it does not in historic mysticism.

Yet the New Age, for all its excesses with respect to the persistent darkness in human nature, may be seen as redressing some balances in contemporary spirituality. The tension between *obedience* and *gnosis*, which runs deep in faith traditions, is one of these. Put in stark terms, biblical faith has stressed obedience and the bending of will, while those traditions springing from Hindu roots (not unlike their Greek counterparts in Indo-Aryan spirituality) have stressed overcoming ignorance in favor of salvific illumination, which is the basic meaning of gnosis. It is possible that obedience and gnosis always need each other, lest keeping the commandments becomes legalism and seeking transcendent wisdom becomes morally bankrupt. Insofar as the best of New Age efforts have incorporated Hindu and Buddhist themes of transcendent vision as universally important and accessible, they may be bringing vitality to churches sunk in conformity without the hope of the beatific vision, in this life, that always changes what it fully illuminates.

Community

For many of us in church life, a crippling weakness of the New Age is its handling of community and tradition, where cheerful pluralism and relativism may sell out to novelty, gimmickry, and guruism. Attending endless workshops and conferences and New Age fairs produces a kind of togetherness, to be sure. And undergoing rites of drumming or dancing or visualizing can generate real intimacy for a time, just as can a vision quest in the wilderness. Gathering with the like-minded to defend dolphins from tuna fishery ships, or enrolling in the growing number who change the sexist language in hymns and prayers, can motivate powerfully for a time. But lasting community, grounded in tempered tradition, is needed to provide full accountability, both in disciplined thought and in moral effort, to limit the excesses that we cataloged at the start of this chapter. And it is needed for worshipful humility in speech and manner, as it is to hold out a graded way of spiritual growth, with definite stages and realistic processes for evaluating progress.

For many in the New Age misunderstand spiritual growth as something that will proceed automatically, once one has been "awakened." The need for dogged retraining of all our pettiness and meanness, and the need for regular celebration of each gain in generosity and patience, has not often gripped New Agers to the extent of calling forth new social structures. To be sure, small study and search groups have emerged that have enduring promise, although they are often narrowly psychological and consciousness-oriented in ways that look hopelessly narcissistic to third-world people in circles of liberation theology, such as those which have invented Christian base communities.

The Aquarian flower children of the '60s tried communes, which were not new on the American scene, though new for college youth. By contrast, New Agers are older, with jobs and institutional roles, as well as plenty of broken marriages in the current social turmoil; for them, inventing social groupings for their gospel comes harder. But the hunger is there, as seen in rallies for a Harmonic Convergence or in solemn peace assemblies on New Year's Eve, as well as in awed delight at native American ceremonies to unite earth and air and all creatures that occupy them. Like the rest of us, New Agers seek structures that can be both corporate in organization and activity, and yet convenantal in character because they respond to a Center which is transparent to the divine.

The groupings that will work must get past many temptations to abort the real sharing process, as Scott Peck points out in his *The Different Drum,* and must avoid temptations to engage in local ecstasy without political and social change on a larger scale. Further, they must finally address the nagging issue of what to do with the Christ and the Buddha in a thoroughly pluralistic time. Benjamin Creme's widely publicized New Age announcement in newspapers around the world that the Maitreya Buddha, who is also the Christ, is now alive and living in London, takes its bearings from theosophical elitism that does not compel many.

It is fashionable in New Age circles to affirm a "Christ-consciousness" that slumbers in every person, waiting to be awakened and capable of making the person Christlike—in terms reminiscent of Pauline "putting on Christ." Yet the Christ so claimed is often cut off from community and traditions, teaching and rite, until beyond specification. One may find some resonance to the image of the transcendent, formative Logos in the New Age, but not having to take up the wounded or lonely or alienated in the kind of concreteness that Christians have found in Jesus and Saint Francis, carrying on the traditions of the prophets and the suffering community of faith. What kind of Christ New Agers seek, and how this Christ might seek them, remains a prime riddle for generating New Age community. Part of that riddle must surely be the issue of the Christ's redemptive intervention in individual and corporate life, which can be conceived in reincarnation terms, as carefully suggested by the able theologian and historian of religions Richard Drummond, in *A Life of Jesus the Christ* (identified as New Age by the publisher). Can we get to a New Age, or to new maturity of selfhood and shared life, without radical aid from beyond ourselves? Or is that intervention already at work in ways seen and unseen that may outstrip church rituals and proclamations, wherever selfless loving and spirited training are at work? New Agers, with characteristic boldness, have sought to spring Christ loose from his church. In so doing, they remind us all that he is no prisoner of the faith, in any generation, though they also risk dissolving him into an archetype.

The contribution of the New Age to our times is likely to remain the kind of ill-defined ferment from the unconscious that Jung described, until ways are found to embody the vision in everyday community, not only of a religious body, but of the family and the workplace, the PTA, and the precinct. Some of us suspect that the wheel will turn and attention come back to the church and its analogues. But the Christian spiritual community for the next century may not be a one-pastor parish, rehearsing all the old tales and moralisms, singing tidy four-stanza hymns while the children learn about Joseph's many-colored coat and Jesus' seamless robe. It may be far more a joint creation, doing theology from the ground up, in worship and in study and in service, engaging members periodically in much larger time-frames than Sunday niches. It may find its life by losing it in forays of social change, and in shared spiritual sabbaticals of training and travel, not for ravishing utopias, but to take up one good cause or idea after another, year in and year out. It may speak a tongue of humility that claims treasures of spirituality from around the globe, because it knows how to keep close to its own stream of the Mystery that beckons to us all. If that kind of community emerges, today's ecstasy industry, despite its extravagances and often unrepentant shallowness, may have done more to prepare than to hinder an adventurous new time in faith.

10

Spirituality
for a New Era

MATTHEW FOX

The subject of "New Age" is one that raises deep feelings in our time. New Agers are the new bêtes noires of the fundamentalists, who don't have the Communists to kick around any more; but the New Age challenges the more mainline and liberal theological establishment as well. In our time, given crises of ecology and rich-poor divisions, a critical need for metanoia, or change of heart, presents itself to our species, and a serious awakening of human consciousness beckons us. The New Age phenomenon speaks to this awakening either directly or indirectly. In this chapter I would like to treat the following issues: What is New Age? Why is there a New Age movement in our time? What are the strengths and the weaknesses of the phenomenon we know as New Age? What are the elements of a spirituality for a New Era? And what role does the New Age movement play in that New Era; what challenges, for example, does it put to the churches and the transformations they need to undergo in preparation for a third millennium of Christianity?

What Is New Age?

The chapters in this book testify to the diversity of meanings surrounding New Age. Some authors, Carl Raschke for example, define New Age as a religion, yet David Spangler, who is a longtime guru within the New Age movement, rejects the notion that New Age is a religion. I side with David Spangler, for I see New Age as a transition movement in a time of great transition. New Agers are seekers after experiences and values that we usually identify as religious, and thus they both critique religion and offer an alternative to the present forms of religious practice we have in our churches and synagogues. New Agers share in common a seeking for spiritual experience and for mysticism, from which they hope to derive a vision and a focus that matches their yearning for a healthier worldview.

Many New Agers I have met have given up on the religious tradition of their birth which, they often feel, has failed to teach them mystical practice and a mystical inheritance. Many of these persons are angry at their religious tradition (they may be Jewish, Roman Catholic, Anglican, or Protestant), and New Age allows them to let go of what they perceive as the failure of their religious heritage. Many of them may be "recovering" Catholics, Baptists, Presbyterians, Jews, and so on. It is because of the failure they perceive in the current religious practice of the West that they are drawn to what David Spangler picturesquely calls the "county fair" of New Age attractions which, because of their common denominator of promising some spiritual experience, become a kind of oasis to religious seekers who are feeling a call to *experience* Divinity instead of just hearing *about* God or *about* God's commandments. It is my experience that there is much pain within the New Age movement (as there is within our whole culture), but that much of that pain is so deep--being the result of religious abuse—that it rarely gets exorcised or dealt with. This is why many New Agers overindulge in the "light" energies the movement offers them and tend to shy away from the wounds, the darkness, the suffering of others brought about by realities of injustice in society. It is because they have not been able to deal with their own suffering that this denial of the dark often holds appeal. For rare are the forums where people are able to speak out about the way they feel their religious upbringing has failed them.

I know a Franciscan parish priest in New York City who, a few years ago, put a small classified ad in the *New York Times* inviting persons to come to church on a Tuesday night if they felt wounded by the Roman Catholic Church, in order to discuss it. He was expecting perhaps thirty-five people to show up. In fact, 450 showed up the first night! (Far more than attend Sunday liturgy, one might add!) The statistics on mainline churches' declining memberships in America and the near-demise of church life in Europe—where 2 percent of Anglicans practice in England; 3 percent of Lutherans in Scandinavia; 4 percent of Catholics in France and 7 percent in Germany—point to the truth behind this story of recovering Catholics in New York City. There are far more people wounded by the church, feeling deserted by church, or simply fed up with the lack of spiritual nourishment from church than there are those going to church. New Age has been for many of these people a kind of haven. Were the churches to reground their theologies and their seminary training (a point Morton Kelsey wisely makes in his chapter in this book) so as to allow its vast wealth of mystical and prophetic energy to flow into their worship and education, then New Age would have contributed to a great accomplishment: the reawakening of the churches whose spiritual powers have been effectively lying dormant for some time.

One of the finest efforts to define New Age appeared recently in the *Religious Studies Review*. It is a sign of our times that this review, published by the Council of Societies for the Study of Religion, felt the New Age phenomenon was a serious enough matter to publish the article it did on "Literature of the New Age: A Review of Representative Sources." The author, Dr. Mary Farrell Bednarowski, teaches at the United Theological Seminary of the Twin Cities in New Brighton, Minnesota, and she lists the major themes of New Age thinking as the following:

> An insistence on the need for a new cosmology that will embrace and restore to wholeness the dualisms that are considered the products of outmoded Enlightenment worldview—science/religion, body/spirit, matter/consciousness, thinking/feeling, male/female, etc. Another is the insistence on the immanence of the divine or the Absolute in every atom of the universe along with its correlative proposition—the interrelatedness of all things. A third is an intense optimism about the possibility for individual and social transformation. A fourth is a

concern with ecology and the need for planetary rather than a national or even international consciousness. Underlying all these themes is an assumption of the cosmic pervasiveness of the evolutionary process, however defined and interpreted by particular groups.[1]

I appreciate Bednarowski's lucidity at naming some of the deep issues behind the New Age phenomenon, for, as the articles in this volume attest by their diversity, defining "New Age" is no easy task. One reason it is so difficult is that New Age is, as Spangler points out, a movement and not a religion of doctrines and dogmas. Yet Bednarowski does manage to name several of the key ideas that bind this movement together. I question her notion of the "intense optimism" about transformation, however, and wonder if perhaps she is missing this subtle pedagogical point: when we are faced with the truly *apocalyptic* issues that confront us as citizens on this planet today, the response is one of exhorting and urging. This exhortation may appear to be optimism, whereas it is in fact the effort to awaken hope in a time of despair. Hope and optimism are vastly different energies.

Why Is There a New Age Movement?

Every millennium movement brings a kind of psychic happening in its wake. Poet Bill Everson says that a millennium is not just a turn of a calendar page but a "psychic awakening." This was the case in the year 1000 and certainly the case in the millennium two thousand years ago into which Jesus Christ entered. Indeed, a strong argument could be made that the early church derived some of its spirit or *pneuma* experience from the millennial hopes and fears of the times. In our own times religious leaders like Pope John XXIII have called for a "new Pentecost." His Second Vatican Council and the advances in the ecumenical movement, the World Council of Churches, the role of women in ministry, the open debate about sexual minorities in ministerial roles, liberation theologies, and the urge for mysticism have not gone unheralded in the churches in spite of obvious setbacks in all these movements in various church bodies.

New Age is as much a response to culture as it is to church or to the churches' failures. And the issues in our culture that are crying out for attention will not go away with more updated versions of the welfare state or of capitalist democracies, any more than they were able to be resolved by industrial socialism in the East. I speak primarily of the ecological crisis, which is no respecter of persons or of nation-states. Whether you are wealthy or poor, white or Black, East or West, North or South, matters not a bit if the air you and your children breathe or the food you eat or the water you drink or the forests you depend on or the animals you delight in are suffering from a growing acquired immune deficiency. The hole in the ozone layer is no respecter of ethnic, religious, class, racial, or sexual differences. The fact that every man, woman, and child living in Mexico City today is breathing the equivalent of two packs of cigarettes a day due to the toxins in the air means that in a generation or two libraries and universities will be a thing of the past, since the minds of the children are being so polluted by the toxins that as adults these people will not be able to read or to think.

The reality of life for the citizens of Mexico City is an issue for all of us. They might be considered the canaries in the mine— remembering how, before electronic devices were invented to measure toxins in the air in mines, canaries were sent ahead of the miners. If they sang, all was well. If they died, a warning was given. One might ask of our species today: How many more warnings are necessary? We have Chernobyl; we have Love Canal and Times Beach and now the Sacramento River in our country. What are these warnings about? They are about grief, about death, about the extinction of our species along with others far more ancient than ourselves (whales have been here fifty-six million years longer than we, and a rain forest can never be duplicated or revived once destroyed).

Above all, the warnings of these events are about our relationship to things, indeed to God's creation. They are about our sense of the sacred, and the responsibility we take for it. They are about the depths of our love for God and God's children for untold generations to come—which is all of creation. Therefore, they are about our outrage and the depths of our prophetic willingness to respond effectively to the killing of the planet. They are about what Jesus preached: metanoia, change of heart, change of ways, transformation. And none of our institutions—not religion, not education, not economics or politics or art—can go untouched in this call to change of heart and conversion. We are talking about a religious crisis and a religious opportunity, a spiritual awakening that is far more demanding than the Reformation times of the sixteenth century. For reformation is one thing—it implies the reshuffling of the forms we have—but renewal is another. And renewal implies a new beginning, a new spirit, a new energy unleashed, a new paradigm, a new way to see the world. Enter the phrase "New Age."

Is the idea of a "New Age" all that new? By no means. In the biblical tradition it is a constant promise of the prophets, and the Christian scriptures used this prophetic sense of an eschatological hope as the basis of their theology of the Spirit. (Indeed, I believe that a good argument could be made that the New Age movement got its name from Teilhard de Chardin, a Jesuit priest and scientist and poet who, in turn, got it from Saint Paul.) Consider the prophet Joel, for example, from whom Peter borrows in his sermon at the first Pentecost.

> After this
> I will pour out my spirit on all humankind.
> Your sons and daughters shall prophesy,
> your old men shall dream dreams,
> and your young men see visions.
> Even on the slaves, men and women,
> will I pour out my spirit in those days.
>
> I will display portents in heaven and on earth,
> blood and fire and columns of smoke.
> The sun will be turned into darkness,
> and the moon into blood,
> before the day of Yahweh dawns,
> that great and terrible day.
> All who call on the name of Yahweh will be saved.
> (Joel 2:28–32, author's translation)

Notice the cosmology in these prophecies—sun, moon, light of day, earth and heaven alike will all be affected by the coming of the Spirit. It is striking that in the Jerusalem Bible, which was put together by French biblical scholars at the renowned École Biblique in Jerusalem in this century, the passage we have cited from

Joel is entitled "The New Age and the Day of Yahweh." This title, inserted by biblical scholars, appeared long before anyone had ever heard of the term *New Age* as we use it in the present volume.

In the New Testament, Jesus is depicted as bringing new life and as the sender of the Spirit who will make all things new, the bearer of a "new covenant" such as the prophet Jeremiah had written of, wherein the law of love will be written on people's hearts (Jeremiah 31). Paul calls Christ the "new creation," and Luke has the same image in his depiction of the birth of Jesus. Paul urges the followers of Jesus to "put on a new self" (Col. 3:10, JB). The final book of the Christian Bible ends with a vision that is cosmological and, like Joel, speaks of a new age.

> Then I saw a new heaven and a new earth [cf. Isa. 51:16; 65;17; 66:22]; the first heaven and the first earth had disappeared now, and there was no longer any sea. I saw the holy city, and the New Jerusalem coming down from God out of heaven, as beautiful as a bride all dressed for her husband. Then I heard a loud voice call from the throne, "You see this city? Here God lives among the people. God will make the divine home among them; they shall be God's people, and God will be their God; God's name is God-with-them. God will wipe away all tears from their eyes; there will be no more death, and no more mourning or sadness: The world of the past has gone."
>
> Then the one sitting on the throne spoke: "Now I am making the whole of creation new." (Rev. 21:1–5, author's translation)

Is this cosmological and apocalyptic language "New Age"? One can see by this question how confusing a time we live in. Clearly the New Age impulse has origins in the biblical tradition (among other places). Clearly the biblical tradition urges us to an eschatological vision and renewal, and this especially in an apocalyptic historical moment such as we live in today and such as the writers of this late-first-century document were undergoing in their day.

Our spiritual ancestors have always included a sense of eschatology, or New Age, in their mystical theologies. Thomas Aquinas wrote that "Christ is the primary source of newness and renovation" and that "Paul prohibits what is old and encourages what pertains to the new."[2] Meister Eckehart taught that the first gift of the Spirit is newness and that God is "Novissimus," the newest thing in the universe.[3] Newness is a part of the mystical experience; indeed this very notion is captured by Jesus when talks of "rebirth" and "being born again," as for example in his conversation with Nicodemus in John's Gospel (John 3:1–21). Paul in his letter to the Romans connects newness to the resurrection: "Just as Christ was raised from the dead by the glory of the Father, so we too might walk in newness of life" (Rom. 6:4). The New Law calls all Christians to a sense, not of tiredness, but of newness.

Newness, then, is no strange idea to Christian theology or spirituality. In fact, its absence is what is strange. An eschatological energy has been lacking in mainline Christianity for some time now. Because teaching of mystical practice, and therefore of the experience of newness, has been so rare during the modern period of church history, a void was presented which the New Age movement has entered and partially filled.

But it is not only our religious tradition that urges a sense of newness and eschatology upon us. Today's science is doing the same. Indeed, it is doing it with much more conviction and clarity of purpose than the churches are doing, for it is *consciously* seeking to change paradigms or worldviews, while the churches are still acting for the most part only *un*consciously in this effort. The movement from Newton's machinelike universe to Einstein's mystery-filled universe constitutes a revolution of thought greater than that from Aristotle and Ptolemy to Copernicus in the sixteenth century. We are all undergoing this shift of worldview, whether we be scientists or laypersons, for we live in a culture that honors science and considers its spokespersons to be the elders behind our educational, political, economic, military, and even religious worldview. All religion depends on a worldview of some kind—as Thomas Aquinas put it in the thirteenth century, when there was a revolution in paradigms almost as immense as our own, "A mistake about creation results in a mistake about God." We derive our notions of God from creation as well as from scriptures, for both creation *and* the Bible are sources of revelation. As Aquinas taught, Revelation comes in two volumes: Creation and the Bible. To find out what nature is telling us, we naturally go to those who study it, that is, to scientists.

One of the spokespersons for the scientific paradigm shift is the English biologist Rupert Sheldrake who, in his recent book *The Rebirth of Nature: The Greening of Science and God*, addresses, among other issues, the topic of a New Age consciousness. Notice the very title of this book—a scientist daring to use the word "God" in the title of his book! And notice the topic of "rebirth." These facts are indications of a paradigm shift that is affecting many scientists, especially younger ones, who are not content to separate their craft from their living of life nor their love of nature from their study of it. Sheldrake writes: "The approaching dawn of a new millennium in the Christian era will inevitably create a sense of the beginning of a new age and the end of an old."[4] Far from seeing this as "intense optimism," Sheldrake puts this new age in a context of moral repentance and renewal that is, in fact, deeply biblical in its very prophetic tone. He writes:

> The recognition that we need to change the way we live is now very common. It is like waking up from a dream. It brings with it a spirit of repentance, seeing in a new way, a change of heart. This conversion is intensified by the sense that the end of an age is at hand.[5]

We have left behind the notion of an "objective science," which carries no moral responsibility with it. On the contrary, repentance and a change of heart are in order precisely because the ways we have been living our lives as a culture, based as they are on the ways we see the world through science, have been destructive and indeed sinful in the traditional sense of that word. Ignorance may have partially mitigated our responsibility in the past, but this is no longer any excuse. Sheldrake writes:

> Faced with this sense of impending doom, we need a spirit of repentance that is not just individual but collective. The imbalances that threaten the world are not the fault of a few greedy systems that have proved so destructive. At the very least, our attitudes and political and economic systems will have to change radically if we are to live in greater harmony with Gaia.[6]

With language like this coming from a scientist, it is clear we have a new paradigm in the making.[7] Not only is the new science deeply mystical, it is also becoming keenly ethical, demanding as it does a change of ways. But the ethic is not one based on Kantian or Calvinist *duty*—it is more one based on the preservation of the awe and wonder and gratuity of creation (called "Gaia" by Sheldrake). It is prophecy coming from mysticism. This emerges from the best traditions of Western spirituality.[8] For example, Thomas Aquinas taught in the thirteenth century that the "primary and fundamental meaning of redemption is to preserve things in creation." And Rabbi Heschel says that there are three ways to respond to creation: by enjoyment, by exploitation, and by awe. It is responding from awe that is the mystical perspective. And the new stories from science about our common sacred origins and about the singleness of the universe fill us with awe.

The paradigm shift we are all undergoing today has been characterized as our moving from the modern era to the postmodern era. The former period, so indebted to Newton and Descartes, saw the world as individualistic atomic pieces embroiled in a competitive struggle for survival. Today's emerging worldview sees interconnectedness as the basis of the universe; all things are bound together by interconnectedness. Philosopher David Ray Griffin of the Center for a Postmodern World writes about this in the volume he edited called *Sacred Interconnections*. He believes that what most characterizes a postmodern spirituality is the theme of interconnectedness—a law of the universe that mystics have always recognized and that forms the basis of the practice and theory of compassion, as I have indicated in my book *A Spirituality Named Compassion*.[9] In addition to the law on interconnectedness, Griffin names other themes as basic to a postmodern spirituality:

> A nondualistic relation of humans to nature and of the divine reality to the world; the immanence of both the past and the future (albeit in different ways) in the present; the universality and centrality of creativity; postpatriarchy; communitarianism (versus individualism and nationalism); the "deprivatization" of religion, meaning the rejections of the autonomy of morality, politics, and economics from religious values; and (specifically) the rejection of materialism, in the sense of economism, meaning the subordination of social, religious, moral, aesthetic, and ecological interests to (short-term) economic interests.[10]

In the volume that Griffin edited I present a summary of the issues at stake in the paradigm shift in spirituality as we move from a modern to a postmodern spirituality. The list looks like this:

1. From anthropocentric to cosmological.
2. From theistic (and deistic and atheistic) to panentheistic (God is in all creation).
3. From left brain (analytic) to both left brain *and* right brain (synthetic).
4. From rationalistic to mystical.
5. From patriarchal to feminist.
6. From the quest for the historical Jesus to the quest for the cosmic Christ.
7. From knowledge to wisdom.
8. From the three paths of Plotinus and Proclus to the four paths of Creation Spirituality.
9. From linear to spiral.
10. From a modern naming to an inclusion of premodern, modern, and postmodern spiraling.
11. From climbing Jacob's ladder to dancing Sarah's circle.
12. From obedience as the dominant virtue to creativity in birthing compassion as the dominant societal and personal virtue.
13. From the sectarianism and piecemealness of the Newtonian parts-mentality to the deep ecumenism of an era of the cosmic Christ in all world religions.
14. From dualism (either/or) to dialectic (both/and).
15. From sentimentalism to a passionate embrace of awe at our existence.
16. From a flight from the world to a commitment to social and personal transformation.
17. From Eurocentrism to a celebration of the wisdom of ancient and primordial peoples' spiritualities of micro/macrocosm.
18. From worship as words—read, preached, and sung—to worship as a nonelitist celebration of our shared existence.
19. From Divinity in the sky to Divinity of Mother Earth crucified.[11]

I do not see how any Christian believer or theologian can take lightly the demands made on our inherited faith that are inherent in our passing from a "modern" era to a postmodern one.

While there are "flaky" and unpredictable individuals within the New Age movement, no one can deny that the issues named by Bednarowski, Sheldrake, and Griffin—a theologian, a scientist, and a philosopher, respectively—are of pressing concern to us all. And to the survival of God's creation. We are learning today a new view of sin and redemption when we make ourselves vulnerable to the agenda of planetary suffering and healing. And as far as kooks go, anyone who has hung around a church rectory knows how many oddballs turn up to drink at our ecclesial water fountains. New Age has no monopoly on kooks.

New Age: Strengths and Weaknesses

Having attempted a summary look at the phenomenon of New Age, its meaning, and its reasons for existing, I would like now to offer a critique of it, first by judging its positive contributions and then by naming its weaknesses.

Some of the strengths of New Age we have already alluded to. It takes mysticism and the quest for the experience of the Divine seriously; it does not settle for religion as a mere sociological phenomenon or morality alone: it insists that we have a right to mystical experience as well. Thomas Aquinas, who has not been respected as the mystic that he was, argued that the experience of God should not be exclusively for the old or the few. Does this make Aquinas New Age? Or does it put some New Agers in good company? Another strength of New Age is its listening to today's science and insisting on our need for a *cosmology* to live our lives in. Anthropocentrism has ruled our civilization long enough, and it is deeply involved in the failures of our culture, especially those of ecological injustice and adultism. (It is, after all, the young and their children who are inheriting the depleted beauty and health of this once glorious planet. It is also they who are in the deepest despair over issues of lack of good employment and the economic elitism that education is more and more falling prey to.) In this regard New Age is dealing with sin and redemption—as I suggested above—in ways that carry us beyond the sexual neurosis and guilt that occupy much ecclesiastical literature on sin—as if "sins of the flesh" were more serious in a culture than "sins of the spirit." In fact, sins of the flesh make for more titillating news, but, as Aquinas states explicitly, sins of the spirit are far more dangerous—despair, acedia, fear, for example. But have the churches instructed us in this truth or taught remedies to the sins of despair, acedia, and fear?

New Age is also to be commended for its explorations into body consciousness. Just the return of massage as a meditation experience and a form of deep communication between persons is a gift that Esalean and its many New Age offshoots have brought to the West which has been rendered so dualistically asunder by the fear of body and the compulsion that controls matter that has come from the Augustinian/Cartesian/Newtonian European worldview.[12] Implications for those working in the health fields are incalculable when we open up to understanding the body again as a vehicle of the sacred, a source of revelation, and a self-organizing system of bioenergetic healing. The interest in the New Age movement in rituals and in spiritual practices of the primal peoples of the earth can also prove to be a valuable contribution to our culture and its religious traditions. While there is a danger in syncretism or a mentality of spiritual "shopping" and "consumerism," there is an even greater danger in the kind of isolation that breeds self-righteousness and a mentality of "only we are saved." To guard against superficial mingling of faith traditions, we require in our time a movement of "deep ecumenism." By this I mean the coming together of the wisdom or mystical traditions of all the world's religions (focused on the maternal as well as the paternal), which will take place more in the shared praxis of prayer than in theological position papers. The poet Rainer Maria Rilke charges us to go out and do "heart-work." It is this heart-work that must be called forth from all our traditions today, because the earth is in such jeopardy. Mysticism is about heart-work.

On the weakness side, New Age has to become more and more vigilant about the following issues. First, as I touched on earlier, it can easily fall into an "all-light" view of reality. This is bad physics as well as bad psychology and bad theology and bad politics. It feeds the status quo and offers legitimization to the privileged at the expense of the less privileged. (Some New Agers say that victims of apartheid, for example, *chose to be born black in South Africa in this century!*)

Darkness is everywhere in the universe, in our psyches and life experiences and in the Godhead itself. The latter the mystical tradition calls the "apophatic Divinity," what Eckehart calls the "superessential darkness" of the Godhead. The darkness of our psyches is named in the mystic phrase the "dark night of the soul." We all undergo such dark nights personally, and today collectively as well. Indeed, I would propose that our entire species is involved in a great "dark night of the soul" in our time. It is necessary to enter into the darkness and not cover it up with excessive light energies. This is where the fact of and archetype of the crucifixion of Jesus can play a truly redemptive role. The Good Friday experience cannot be avoided or there will be no Easter awakening of any depth. The Via Negativa precedes the Via Creativa and Via Transformitiva in the spiritual journey of the Four Paths that the Creation Spiritual tradition names and invites us to (the first path, that of the Via Positiva, being the path of awe, wonder, and delight). The tradition of the cross in Christianity is a powerful reminder of the omnipresence of suffering in this universe. A cosmic Christ who has no wounds is not only not Christian—it ignores the truth of the lives of all prophets and all beings. A true cosmic Christ has wounds as well as light to announce.

New Age can be notoriously indifferent to the suffering of others and to issues of injustice—so much that I have referred to it at times as a "fundamentalism of the rich," for it flirts with the notion that "we are saved and you aren't." And the "we" is often those who can afford thousand-dollar-per-day weekend seminars with exclusively light-oriented gurus. There is a danger in all mysticism—because the unleashed mystic is so powerful an energy force—of its becoming self-centered. New Agers often are self-centered. What they need to learn is that consciousness without conscience is no way to be human or to usher in a new era.

Conscience (prophecy) and consciousness (mysticism) are meant to serve each other. A kind of attitude of arrogance and righteousness can take over if one has no awareness of the suffering of others and no sociopolitical-economic consciousness of how injustice comes about and maintains itself. Here the teachings of the prophets of the Hebrew Bible, who are always biased in favor of the poor, can render New Age more honest. The "spiritual practice" of New Agers attending workshops with persons of their own class and race exclusively is an indication of the one-sidedness of a movement that does not explore the collective shadow.

The ignoring of justice also lays the God-seeker open to trivializing the spiritual journey. Preoccupation with "past lives," the turning of one's conscience over to "channelers," and the quest for the perfect crystal or guru can all take over one's consciousness when one's conscience is ignored.

Another weakness to New Age is being so "new" that it ignores all tradition, as if salvation will come from our own efforts alone, or as if all the efforts of our ancestors were futile and banal. Spirituality is more evolutionary than that—we carry our religious genes in our genetic code, and our religious ancestors and elders want to be present when we pray and celebrate, to lend us their energy. Whether you call these elders our ancestors or the communion of saints is not the point so much as the basic humility born of an awareness that our culture is not necessarily "an error outlived," as Carl Jung put it. We should explore the great mystics and efforts at mysticism of our ancestors in order to ground our quest for mysticism today. It is this sense of grounding that one does not always feel in groups of New Agers, where air energy is often more in evidence than earth energy and where the danger of cult looms because historical awareness and appreciation for tradition are ignored. Again, there are remnants of the Newtonian and individualistic era which New Agers decry in theory but sometimes succumb to in practice and which suggests that "I am saved" but our ancestors weren't and those trying to connect to them still are not.

Much of this rejection of our ancestors comes, I believe, as I indicated above, from New Agers' not dealing fully with their wounded child, and especially the wounded religious child. But deal with it they, indeed all of us, must or it will return to haunt us in equally deadening ways. Salvation is not the salvation of an individual. (Though all mysticism is deeply personal, healthy mysticism is never private or individualistic.) Salvation is of the whole body of our species and beyond. Again, one can sense the wisdom here of a truly incarnational spirituality which leads to prophetic justice and healing, one that heals and celebrates with all God's children and not just some.

These, then, are some strengths and weaknesses that I observe in the New Age movement of our time. The human race always falls into sin when it settles for dualisms (either/or) instead of a both/and consciousness, and the New Age is no exception. While its eschatological emphasis is to be commended, for example, still with eschatology there ought to be apocalyptic awareness as well. The fact is that New Age and the end of a former age come together: creativity *and* destruction happen together, light *and* dark, future *and* past occur together. While some persons are called to leave our institutions and begin new ones and some are called to begin the new within the old structures, nevertheless we cannot turn our back on the reality of our species's need for some structure and institutionalization. We will not change civilization without a concerted effort to bring along our institutions, kicking and screaming if necessary, into the new millennium. This is part of one's commitment to incarnation, to matter, to the body, to the political and economic realities of life. It, along with suffering, is part of our being grounded.

Spirituality for a New Era:
Lessons for Churches from New Age

Many of the contributions I have named from New Age are important to assisting the churches and to educating them to make deeper rapport with their better selves. It might even be appropriate to speak of the establishment churches and seminaries' confessing their sins, or at the least admitting their faults, in order to let go of ways that kill the Spirit if they desire to become places where the

Spirit can be encountered by young and old alike. I would include the following lessons among those which churches can learn from the New Age movement:

Rediscover eschatology. The sense of a future and of the hope that a vision for the future brings with it is something that many feel blessed by in the New Age movement. Often our religious institutions are so busy looking to the past—whether at the "original sin" or at the historical Jesus who was killed 1,950 years ago or at what our dead theologians taught—that the message is very clearly conveyed that religion is exclusively about the past. As Carl Jung put it, "We are still looking back to the pentecostal events in a dazed way instead of looking forward to the goal the Spirit is leading us to."[13] And again, Jung warns us: "Life has also a tomorrow, and today is understood only when we can add to our knowledge of what was yesterday the beginnings of tomorrow."[14] Western Christianity often appears more committed to the past than to the future; often more keen on wallowing in its old age than in being an instrument of promise for a new age. Such a commitment to the past can well constitute a sin called "nostalgia," a living in a *projection* of the past that probably never really existed in the first place and that is in no way livable today anyway. The past—or better, our memories of it—can be idolatrous. A faith that lacks an eschatology and something hopeful to offer about the future is a dead faith useful for nothing but offering a tired legitimation to the status quo.[15]

Cease lack of mysticism. Go to your mystical heritage and start mining it. Return to the spirit of your founder—not only to Jesus, but also the prophetic voices of a Luther or Hildegard or Francis or Aquinas or Wesley or Calvin—and put questions to them about mysticism and spirituality. (A Presbyterian minister who was a student at the Institute of Culture and Creation Spirituality a few years ago did a study on Calvin's mysticism and found things he had never been shown in the seminary. So much education depends on the questions we ask and the issues we are seeking after.) Start redeeming the right hemisphere of the brain and cease committing idolatry toward the left hemisphere just because a now-discredited Cartesian worldview taught us and our seminaries to do so.[16]

We will never recover mysticism without letting go of theism (the idea that God is "out there"—an idea that gave birth to atheism) and rediscovering panentheism (the experience of God in us and all things in God).

Cease anthropocentrism. A good example of anthropocentrism is an ideology of original sin, which is corrosive to the spiritual process to the extent that it has us thinking that life begins with human sin instead of with creation and its amazing eighteen-billion-year drama which was, for our species, certainly a drama filled with blessing. An original blessing. Even our bodies boast an eighteen-billion-year history, all their elements having been birthed in a supernova explosion five and a half billion years ago! Anthropocentrism bores people. Teach celebration and body awareness through teaching the new creation story from science and the amazing truths of our holy bodies. Hire scientists to teach on seminary faculties. Teach massage as a spiritual practice and with it the rediscovery of the blessing that all creation is, including ourselves. All art involves our interaction with matter and is therefore nonanthropocentric when undergone in art-as-meditation.

Move beyond the quest for the historical Jesus to the quest for the cosmic Christ. In this tradition of cosmic wisdom will be found the basis for a sacred cosmology and a renewed worship and education, a renewed deep ecumenism and respect for the artist and native spiritualities as well as a revitalized Christology and a living mysticism. To rediscover the cosmic Christ is not to ignore the historical Jesus but only to cease Jesusolatry. (Fundamentalists commit this heresy in the heart and many liberal theologians do it in their heads.) A healthy Christology balances the historical Jesus with the cosmic Christ. The first task of cosmic wisdom is not to redeem people from sin but to reveal the mysteries of God, says Thomas Aquinas. The second task is to produce creation as an artist makes art, and the third task is to restore creation, and the fourth task is to bring creation to its full completion. A theology of the incarnation that ignores this sense of cosmic wisdom and concentrates only on redemption ideologies is not only boring but bereft of spiritual depth.

After studying the cosmic Christ texts of the New Testament, one finds it apparent that the theological traditions of rationalism and pietism ignored the cosmic Christ. Yet this vision lies deep in the church's heart and memory.

Cease left-brain-itis. Become mystics and teachers of mysticism. Just as consciousness without conscience is a one-sided way to be spiritual, so too is conscience without consciousness. Much of the modern era taught us to develop a conscience while rendering us oblivious of consciousness or mysticism. A dreary kind of Kantian, duty-oriented existence is what follows when awe or mysticism is so repressed. The response to such duty-oriented dreariness is often to reject consciousness altogether.

I believe that churches have considerable work to do in order to recover their mystical tradition and to teach it. Father Bede Griffiths, the Benedictine monk who has been running an ecumenical ashram in India since 1955, has argued that Christianity must recover and nurture its mystical tradition or go out of business—it has nothing to offer otherwise. I like the seriousness with which Father Griffiths takes the issue of the return of mysticism to the church. The churches have to learn that religion is not just about morality; and certainly it is not just about endorsing the cultural status quo with sacralized legitimations.

Religion could begin its renewal by retraining all its clergy and seminary professors. Whether as five-day workshops or semester courses, creation spirituality programs are available that can awaken the right brain, even of professors. There, the ways to educating the heart by way of art as meditation practices and ritual-making are available, as well as the new science that makes for an enlivened cosmology and nature mysticism. Recovering the right hemisphere of our brains is a matter of *psychic justice*. If we have two hemispheres to our brains and utilize only one, then we are unbalanced, and that is the essence of injustice. From psychic injustice, social injustice often springs and nurtures itself.

Another concrete step is to redo seminary education so that our young spiritual leaders-to-be will know their own mysticism in light of our traditions, including that of the historical Jesus who was a mystic and prophet; and in light of the cosmic Christ teachings in Wisdom literature and in the theologies of the New Testament. Deep ecumenism is *not* about spiritual shopping or shoplifting. It requires that one journey down one's own well or spiritual tradition. It requires heart-work *before* the encounter with other mystical practices. If we cannot offer that heart-work to one another out of our own traditions, then we ought to, as Bede Griffiths puts it, fold up shop and go out of business.

Rediscover our doctrines in light of a creation spirituality tradition. In many ways, what the churches are being asked to do is to take more seriously their claim to believe in the three articles of faith, identified by Martin Luther as (1) creation, (2) redemption, and (3) sanctification (or what Eastern Christianity calls divinization). So much of Western Christianity has been so exclusively occupied with the second article of faith—that of redemption—for so long that we have ignored both the mystical aspect of creation, its revelatory power, and its ethical, prophetic demands. The third article of faith, how we are divinized by the experience of the Divine, has also been roundly neglected. At the heart of this good news is the truth of our being artists like God. The churches, then, must pay more attention to the first and third articles of faith. In doing so, we will also be renewing the doctrine of a *trinitarian* Divinity—one that is Creator and Spirit as well as Redeemer/Teacher. God as Creator requires a rediscovery of the sacredness of creation; and God as Spirit requires a rediscovery of the work of the Spirit in our lives.

Renew forms of worship. Currently our forms of worship in the West are far too intellectual and wordy; rare is the church or synagogue where circle dances that can assist us to name our cosmic belief system (we live in a curved universe, we are told) can be played out. Liturgical dancers cannot do this for us. All persons should participate in the circle dances (the center of the circle is a sacred place for the physically disabled), thereby recovering the mutual grace of delight and childlikeness that comes with rediscovering one has a place in the universe.

Lead the way in renewal of education. To renew education is a spiritual issue, both because our minds are God's awesome gifts to us and to neglect them is to insult the Creator; and also because it is through their minds and creativity that the poor can liberate themselves and we can reinvent work for all and justice for the oppressed. And because bad education or education that is not available to all, including the poor (indeed, especially the poor!), is a sin against the Creator of the human mind, the God of justice. The churches can and ought to consciously and deliberately reject the Cartesian biases of academia in their seminary systems and to substitute for them a mystical/prophetic model of education. Such a model would educate both head *and* heart, mind *and* body, left hemisphere *and* right hemisphere of the brain, mind *as well as* feelings. Such a model has been tested and tried for over fifteen years in the Institute of Culture and Creation Spirituality and is available for imitation or adaptation. It works, and the key to it is the body—our hearts, after all, are located in our bodies. Since artwork is heart-work, art as meditation becomes the basic prayer form of this spiritual tradition.[17]

Essential, too, is to teach our mystics. Rare is the mainline seminary that teaches Meister Eckehart, Hildegard of Bingen, or Julian of Norwich, for example, as theologians—much less as mystics. Yet they are not only theologians of the first order but mystics/prophets as well. Liberation theologies from the Southern Hemisphere are a necessary part of any curriculum, of course, but so too must we in the Northern Hemisphere start taking responsibility for our own liberation, for our context is very different from that of the Southern. As I have written elsewhere, I believe that a rediscovery of the creation-centered spiritual tradition may well constitute the work of liberating so-called first-world peoples today—and the primary liberation we need is from addictions.[18] Mysticism is the mirror image of addiction: it is our way out of addiction. Spirituality is about praxis, and Northerners need to get out of our head-centered and institutionally oriented religiosity and into the praxis of the spiritual. The mystical tradition in general, and the creation spiritual tradition in particular, can assist us in that task. It is a scandal that seminaries put their students through clinical pastoral education, as they have been doing for two or three decades, but offer no accredited work in "laboratories" of mystical practices. We train the psyche but not the spirit.

Make a commitment to deep ecumenism. Surely all religions of the world have been imbued with the Holy Spirit and offer something of the power and revelation of the Divine—a fact that the Second Vatican Council recognized in its fine document on nonchristian religions, *Nostra aetate*. We need to call on other traditions for this wisdom, not in some eclectic, cafeterialike way, but out of the strength and stance we derive from having made a journey ourselves through our own spiritual practice derived from our own spiritual heritage. It is when people travel into their own well that we journey to a shared underground river of the living waters of wisdom. Then we can drink mutually from the same waters. But there is no getting to these waters without some journeying along a spiritual path.

At this moment when the world is opening up to becoming a global village, though one with a great variety of histories and traditions, so it is a time for honoring the varieties of wisdom all around us. It is a time for North-South interaction and of East-West interaction at the level of "deep ecumenism." Westerners cannot engage in this creative moment in the history of our species without having done some of their own heart-work as well.

But deep ecumenism is not just being satisfied with the religions or religious forms we have inherited from the past. The earth and its Maker may well be asking a larger thing of us in this coming millennium, and that is the birthing of religious forms that name the best of the past along with forms that we may never have seen previously as a species. For the situation is truly *new* on this planet as regards the hopes and fears about its demise and about those systems that make human life not only possible but wonderful.

Rediscover the premodern era. I have no doubt that the one period in Western history that can shed light on the 1990s is what we may call the renaissance of the twelfth and early thirteenth centuries. This renaissance, like the one we are undergoing today, was successful because it was a grass-roots movement emerging from women, freed serfs, and the young. A rediscovery of the goddess gave it its spiritual and creative impetus, one that resulted in commune movements, the birth of the universities, the growth of cities, the invention of cathedrals (the throne where the goddess sits in the center of the universe, city, and soul), such as Chartres Cathedral and five hundred other cosmic temples built in a one-hundred-twenty-five-year period, dedicated to Mary, the goddess in Christianity who defended the poor. It gave us Hildegard of Bingen, Francis of Assisi, Thomas Aquinas, Mechtild of Magdeburg, Meister Eckehart. In short, it gave us the fullest flowering of creation mysticism that the West has ever seen.

It is so important that those from a Protestant heritage throw off the lie that has taught them that Christianity runs from Luther back to Augustine and then to Paul. The Middle Ages belong to Protestants as well as Catholics. This is very important news as we move out of the modern era, for it gives us grounding in a premodern era that was both creative and prophetic, and this under the inspiration of a biblically renewed Christianity.[19] It allows us to "go back" and get a perspective on our time in light of our inherited past.

Conclusion

One might ask: Is the New Age movement itself the bearer of a spirituality for a New Era? I would answer, No, it is not. For it cannot carry the weight of all that is needed to change, nor can any one religion or any one discipline—we need science, mysticism, and art working together to birth the new cosmology. New Age cannot, for example, bring along our institutions such as our churches and academia—though it can help considerably in their renewal, especially by awakening certain individuals within them. Nevertheless, New Age is an important movement along the way of the in-depth transformational path that our species is necessarily embarked on in these latter days of the present millennium. Moving from a machine paradigm of the universe to an organic one is no small shift of consciousness. It calls for a deep shift in the way we see the world and respond to it. We ought not to trivialize the immense spiritual and moral issues of our day, either, by succumbing to a silly privatized and ungrounded version of the New Age on the one hand, nor by sterile, rigid flights to a stale religious orthodoxy and defensiveness on the other. Let us open up minds, hearts, and traditions to the Spirit once again. The survival of the planet depends on this.

There will be aberrations and mistakes as we make our way, groping in the dark. Paradigm shifts do not come easily and without pain and doubt. But the greatest danger is not from the errors we make in our trial and error—trial and error are, after all, at the heart of every effort at creativity. The greatest danger looms in our refusal to make the shift at all. This refusal can be a personal one or a collective one. Any group that refuses to undergo the shift, and thus to respond to the signs of our times and the work of the Spirit calling us to a New Pentecost, will render itself obsolete—morally and spiritually at first, and financially eventually. For without a vision of the New, the youth will be offered no spiritual adventure, and they will grow old very fast. When that happens, a species dies.

Notes

1. THE CRY OF THE DESPERATE:
CHRISTIANITY'S OFFER OF A NEW AGE

1. See Gerald May, *Addiction and Grace* (San Francisco: Harper & Row, 1988), for an extended discussion on addiction and the search for God.

2. Andrew Weil, *The Natural Mind* (Boston: Houghton Mifflin Co., 1972).

3. See Marilyn Ferguson, *The Aquarian Conspiracy: Personal and Social Transformation in the 1980s* (Los Angeles: Jeremy P. Tarcher, 1980).

4. See, e.g., Constance E. Cumbey, *The Hidden Dangers of the Rainbow* (Lafayette, La.: Huntington House, 1983).

5. I am aware that many people who are drawn to the New Age movement do not seek it out of desperation.

6. See Morton Kelsey, *Companions on the Inner Way: The Art of Spiritual Guidance* (New York: Crossroad, 1983), particularly pp. 81–126, for a discussion of the various ways God breaks into our lives. Among these ways are dreams, healing, meditations, love, art, the Eucharist, and mental disturbance.

7. I deal with the problem of isolation in more depth in my book *Beyond Depression: A Practical Guide for Healing Despair* (Rockport, Mass.: Element Books, 1992).

8. Douglas Dawe, *Jesus: The Death and Resurrection of God* (Atlanta: John Knox Press, 1985).

9. Ibid., pp. 78–79.

10. Walter Wink, *Naming the Powers* (Philadelphia: Fortress Press, 1984); *Unmasking the Powers* (Philadelphia: Fortress Press, 1986); *Engaging the Powers* (Minneapolis: Fortress Press, 1992).

11. See Ted Peters, *The Cosmic Self* (San Francisco: HarperCollins, 1991), particularly pp. 53–91 and 133–167.

2. IN ANY AGE:
CAN WE HEAR GOD?

1. Jane Wagner, *The Search for Signs of Intelligent Life in the Universe* (New York: Harper & Row, 1986), p. 162.

2. Benjamin Hoff, *The Tao of Pooh* (New York: Penguin Books, 1982), p. 77.

3. C. S. Forrester, *The General* (New York: Bantam Books, 1936).

4. Susan B. Thistlethwaite, "On the Trinity," *Interpretation* 45, no. 2 (April 1991): 159–171.

5. Starhawk, *Dreaming the Dark: Magic, Sex, and Politics* (Boston: Beacon Press, 1988), p. 9.

6. Jurgen Habermas, "Does Philosophy Still Have a Purpose?" in *Philosophical-Political Profiles* (Cambridge, Mass.: MIT Press, 1983).

7. Bertrand Russell, *Marriage and Morals* (New York: Bantam Books, 1963), p. 83.

8. Harold Kushner, *When All You Ever Wanted Isn't Enough* (New York: Penguin Books, 1990).

9. Christine Downing, *The Goddess: Mythological Images of the Feminine* (New York: Crossroad, 1981), p. 146.

10. Robert Bellah, *Habits of the Heart* (Berkeley, Calif.: University of California Press, 1985).

11. John Donne, "The Anatomie of the World, the First Anniversary," in *The Complete Poetry and Selected Prose of John Donne,* ed. Charles M. Coffin (New York: Modern Library, 1952), p. 191.

12. Joseph Campbell, *The Hero with a Thousand Faces* (Princeton, N.J.: Princeton University Press, 1968).

13. Habermas, "Does Philosophy Still Have a Purpose?" p. 18.

14. Walter Capps, "The Quest for Transcendence," *Word and World* 7, no. 1 (Spring 1987): 125–130.

15. M. C. Hammer, *Please Hammer Don't Hurt 'Em* (Capitol Records, Inc., 1990).

16. Matthew Fox, *The Coming of the Cosmic Christ: The Healing of Mother Earth and the Birth of a Global Renaissance* (San Francisco: Harper & Row, 1988), p. 236.

17. Anne M. Clifford, "Creation," in *Systematic Theology: Roman Catholic Perspectives* (Minneapolis: Augsburg Fortress, 1991), pp. 244–245. Clifford cites both Jürgen Moltmann, *God in Creation: A New Theology of Creation and the Spirit of God* (San Francisco: Harper & Row, 1985), p. 21; and Sallie McFague, *Models of God: Theology for an Ecological, Nuclear Age* (Philadelphia: Fortress Press, 1987), p. 110.

18. David Buttrick, *Homiletics* (Philadelphia: Fortress Press, 1987).

19. *Foundations for a Communication Strategy for the Evangelical Lutheran Church in America* (Chicago; Evangelical Lutheran Church in America, March 1989), p. 8.

20. I am indebted to James P. Petersen, ELCA Associate Director for Communication, Region 2, for developing this concept in its relationship to contemporary culture, from materials provided by David Leuke, in *Evangelical Style and Lutheran Substance* (St. Louis: Concordia Publishing House, 1988). The concept is also used by Dr. Carl George in workshops for the Fuller Institute, Pasadena, California.

21. Hannah Arendt, *The Human Condition* (Chicago: University of Chicago Press, 1958) and *On Violence* (New York: Harcourt Brace Jovanovich, 1970).

22. Bellah, *Habits of the Heart.*

3. THE FORMER AGE AND THE NEW AGE:
THE PERENNIAL QUEST FOR THE SPIRITUAL LIFE

1. I have examined thirty-three different ways in which human beings experience the nonphysical world in *Companions on the Inner Way* (New York: Crossroad, 1983).

2. The quotation is from a French literary critic, Hippolyte Taine, writing a history of English literature translated into English in 1872.

3. I am deeply indebted to Huston Smith for his profound description of world religions in his book *The Religions of Man* (San Francisco: Harper & Row, 1965). It is a must for anyone who would seek to understand the perennial religious quest. A new and totally revised edition of this book is available under the title *World Religions.*

4. The opening words of the Buddhist text (*Dammahada*) are quoted in Smith's *The Religions of Man,* p. 121.

5. Bruce Abrams, "Value of Other Human Relationships," *Cleveland Plain Dealer* 1, no. 17 (23 April 1990): 12.

6. In my book *God, Dreams and Revelations* (Minneapolis: Augsburg Fortress, 1991), I have shown how central dreams and visions were in the early church's theory of revelation.

7. Gary Moore, ed., *What Survives? Contemporary Explorations of Life After Death* (Los Angeles: Jeremy P. Tarcher, 1990).

8. In my book *Afterlife: The Other Side of Dying* (New York: Crossroad, 1982), I have shown the nature of the kingdom of heaven and its reasonableness for modern people.

9. In my book *Caring: How Can We Love One Another* (Ramsey, N.J.: Paulist Press, 1982), I offer suggestions on how we can be more caring.

10. I have presented a practical program for adult education in my book *Can Christians Be Educated?* (Birmingham, Ala.: Religious Education Press, 1979).

4. THE NEW AGE:
HISTORICAL AND METAPHYSICAL FOUNDATIONS

1. See C. F. M. Joan, *Decadence* (London: Faber & Faber, 1948); E. A. Burtt, *In Search of Philosophical Understanding* (New York: New American Library of World Literature, 1965); E. F. Schumaker, *A Guide for the Perplexed* (New York: Harper & Row, 1978); Huston Smith, *The Forgotten Truth* (New York: Harper & Row, 1976); Richard Weaver, *Ideals Have Consequences* (Chicago: University of Chicago Press, 1948); Gerald Heard, *The Five Ages of Man* (New York: Julian Press, 1963); R. Buckminster Fuller, *Operating Manual for Spaceship Earth* (New York: Simon & Schuster, 1969).

2. Marilyn Ferguson, *The Aquarian Conspiracy: Personal and Social Transformation in the 1980s* (Los Angeles: Jeremy P. Tarcher, 1980).

3. Karl Jaspers, *Man in the Modern Age* (London: Routledge & Kegan Paul, 1951); F. S. C. Northrop, *The Logic of the Sciences and Humanities* (New York: Macmillan Co., 1947); Viktor Frankl, *Man's Search for Meaning* (Boston: Beacon Press, 1962); J. Bronowski, *Science and Human Values* (New York: Harper & Row, 1990); Paul Davies, *Superforce, God and the New Physics* (New York: Simon & Schuster, 1984); Daniel Bell, *The Coming of the Post-Industrial Society* (New York: Basic Books, 1973).

4. Glenn A. Olds, *The Christian Corrective* (Nashville: Board of Education of the Methodist Church, National Methodist Student Movement, 1951).

5. Erich Fromm, *The Anatomy of Human Destructiveness* (New York: Holt, Rinehart & Winston, 1973); M. Scott Peck, *People of the Lie* (New York: Simon & Schuster, 1983); Michael Harrington, *The Politics at God's Funeral* (New York: Penguin Books, 1985).

6. See recent concerns with religious views of *Creation, Peace, and Justice* (Seoul Conference, 1990), and the imaginative leadership of the

Cathedral of St. John the Divine, New York City, under the prophetic leadership of Dean James Morton, cochair of the Global Forum.

7. Manly Hall, *Secret Teachings of All Ages* (Los Angeles: Philosophical Research Society, 1950).

8. See the early *Perennial Philosophy*, by Aldous Huxley (New York: Harper & Brothers, 1945); and Lawrence Hyde, *Isis and Osiris* (New York: E. P. Dutton & Co., 1948), and *Nameless Faith* (London: Rider & Co., 1949).

9. Hall, *Secret Teachings*.

10. Note especially this influence in the writings of K. Wilbur, William Thompson, and Huston Smith.

11. Meredith A. Puryear, *Healing Through Meditation and Prayer* (Virginia Beach, Va.: A.R.E. Press, 1978); D. Chernin and G. Manteuffel, *Health: A Holistic Approach* (Los Angeles: Theos Publishing House, 1984); L. E. Sullivan, *Healing and Restoring* (New York: Macmillan Publishing Co., 1989); B. L. Shlemon, *Healing Prayer* (Notre Dame, Ind.: Ave Maria Press, 1975).

12. Note the special inventory and studies in M. Ferguson, early publications of mind/matter, and the thoughtful publications of the Institute of Noetic Sciences.

13. See especially the influence of the early works of Alan Watts; introductions to the West of Sri Aurobindo's works, and the remarkable ashram and New Age community, Aurouille, in Pondicherry, India; the popularization of Shirley MacLaine and transcendental meditation and their educational impact on the campuses of America and Europe.

14. See the literature and handbook practices of the rash of "communes," often with their resident gurus, noticeably inspired by Ram Dass, Yogi Bashan, and others.

15. See, of course, the highly publicized excesses of the total community of Antelope, Oregon, and the legal entanglements and dissolution of that sect and setting.

16. Note the early invitation for Dewey to visit China and his influence in shaping the teacher training in the China of the 1920s and '30s.

17. See the influence in the early work of Henry Wieman, Bernard Eugene Meland, and others at the University of Chicago, and more recent formulations in process philosophy and theology.

18. See the Suggested Readings on these thinkers.

19. Note especially the constructive role played by the Institute of Noetic Sciences and its journal and publications over the years since its founding in the early 1970s.

20. See Hans Selye, *From Dream to Discovery: On Being a Scientist* (New York: McGraw-Hill Book Co., 1964); Martin Buber, *I and Thou* (New York: Charles Scribner's Sons, 1970); Abraham Heschel, *Man Is Not*

Alone (New York: Farrar, Straus & Young, 1951); E. Laszlo, *Introduction to Systems Philosophy* (New York: Gordon & Breach Science Pubs., 1972); R. B. Fuller, *Synergetics* (New York: Macmillan Publishing Co., 1977).

21. A wide range of popular culture, books, and movies have addressed this theme.

22. See the provocative *State of the World* annual reports by Lester Brown, the documentaries by the Better World Society, and the research reports from the Population Institute at Brown University.

23. Ibid.

24. Barbara Ward and Rene Dubos, *Only One Earth* (New York: W. W. Norton & Co., 1972).

25. Unpublished lecture, Palmer Lectureship, 1985, Alaska Pacific University, appearing in her new book, *Metaphors of Interrelatedness* (Albany, N.Y.: State University of New York Press, 1992).

26. Sandra M. Schneiders, *Women and the Word* (Mahwah, N.J.: Paulist Press, 1986), and *The Gender of God in the New Testament* (Mahwah, N.J.: Paulist Press, 1986).

27. See the telling conferences and publications of the John C. Fetzer Foundation, Kalamazoo, Mich.; Chernin and Manteuffel, *Health: A Holistic Approach;* P. C. Reisser et al., *The Holistic Healers* (Downers Grove, Ill: Intervarsity Press, 1987); Tracy Deliman and John S. Smolowe, eds., *Holistic Medicine* (Reston, Va.: Reston Publishing Co., 1982).

28. Note the striking conference on this theme sponsored by the Institute of Noetic Sciences in Washington, D.C., in 1988, and the Fetzer Foundation's global conference on "Healing the Whole Person and the Whole World" in 1988.

20. See the widely influential Course in Miracles publications and study groups, now worldwide, in a new spirituality based on transformative thought and meditation.

30. See especially the work of Thomas Berry, *Befriending the Earth* (Mystic, Conn.: Twenty-Third Publishers, 1991).

31. See Viktor Frankl's early work, *Man's Search for Meaning;* Seyyed Hossier Nasp, *Man and Nature: The Spiritual Crisis of Modern Man* (Vershire, Vt.: Mandala Books, 1990); and R. Hartman, *The Structure of Value* (Carbondale, Ill.: Southern Illinois University Press, 1967).

5. THE NEW AGE:
THE MOVEMENT TOWARD THE DIVINE

1. The items that follow are taken from the contents listing of William Bloom and John Button, *The Seeker's Guide: A New Age Resource Book* (London: Aquarian Press, 1992).

2. John Kirkpatrick Sale, *Human Scale* (New York: Coward, McCann & Geoghegan, 1980).

3. Arthur Hastings, *With the Tongues of Men and Angels* (Fort Worth, Tex.: Holt, Rinehart & Winston, 1991), p. 202.

4. Thomas Berry, *Befriending the Earth* (Mystic, Conn.: Twenty-Third Publishers, 1991), p. 21.

6. THE NEW AGE:
THE MOVEMENT TOWARD SELF-DISCOVERY

1. José Argüelles, "Future Memory," *Magical Blend* no. 15 (1987): 57.

2. Ibid.

3. See the entry on Crowley in *Encyclopedia of Occultism and Parapsychology,* vol. 1, ed. Leslie Shepard (Detroit: Gale Research, 1978). Crowley's lifestyle included the publication of pornographic poetry and the routine use of mind-altering drugs.

4. Spangler's major writings include *Emergence: The Rebirth of the Sacred* (New York: Dell, 1984); *Explorations: Emerging Aspects of the New Culture* (Forres, Scotland: Findhorn Publications, 1980); *Revelation: The Birth of a New Age* (San Francisco: Rainbow Bridge, 1976); *Towards a Planetary Vision* (Forres, Scotland: Findhorn Foundation, 1977).

5. Benjamin Creme, *Messages from Maitreya the Christ,* vol. 1 (London: The Tara Center, 1980), p. 206.

6. A summary of the Maitreya affair can be found in J. Gordon Melton, "Benjamin Creme," *New Age Encyclopedia* (New York: Gale Research, 1990).

7. Marilyn Ferguson, *The Aquarian Conspiracy: Personal and Social Transformation in the 1980s* (Los Angeles: Jeremy P. Tarcher, 1980), p. 3.

8. Dixie Hummer Toelkes, "Shattered Dreams and Transformations," *Choices and Connections '88–'89,* ed. Susan Jean Gifford (Boulder, Colo.: Human Potential Resources, 1987), p. 57.

9. Sandra T. Adair, "Tips for Winning at Win/Win," *Choices and Connections '88–'89,* p. 157.

7. THE NEW AGE:
THE MOVEMENT TOWARD THE WORLD

1. Thomas Berry, *The Dream of the Earth* (San Francisco: Sierra Club Books, 1988), pp. 47–48.

2. Brendan Lehane, *The Quest of Three Abbots* (London: John Murray, 1968), pp. 41–50.

3. For a fine overview of the spirit and influence of Celtic Christianity,

see Christopher Bamford, *Ecology and Holiness: The Heritage of Celtic Christianity* (Great Barrington, Mass.: Lindisfarne Press, 1982), p. 12.

4. Of the many excellent books critiquing contemporary cultural trends and the New Age by William Irwin Thompson, I recommend *At the Edge of History* and *Passages About Earth*, republished in 1990 as a joint volume by Lindisfarne Press, and *The Reimagination of the World* (Santa Fe, N. Mex.: Bear & Co., 1991) coauthored with David Spangler.

5. Matthew Fox, *Creation Spirituality* (San Francisco: HarperCollins, 1991), pp. 16–17.

6. David Spangler has authored several books and study papers interpreting a New Age spirituality. See *Emergence: The Rebirth of the Sacred* (New York: Delta/Merloyd Lawrence, 1984), and *The New Age* (Issaquah, Wash.: Morningtown Press, 1988).

7. Jean Houston, *The Search for the Beloved* (Los Angeles: Jeremy P. Tarcher, 1987), p. 17.

8. Mary Allen Schmiel, "The Finest Music in the World: Exploring Celtic Spiritual Legacies," in *Western Spirituality: Historical Roots, Ecumenical Routes*, ed. Matthew Fox (Notre Dame, Ind.: Fides/Claretian, 1979), p. 185.

9. Fr. Daniel Martin, "Celtic Spirituality," unpublished paper, 1987, quoting from Eriugena's *Periphyseon: On the Division of Nature* (Indianapolis: Bobbs-Merrill, 1976), vol. 3, p. 678. For an extensive treatment of the philosophy of Eriugena, see Benedict Fitzpatrick, *Ireland and the Foundations of Europe* (London: Funk and Wagnalls, 1927), pp. 176–228.

10. Hildegard of Bingen, with commentary by Matthew Fox, *Illuminations* (Santa Fe, N. Mex.: Bear & Co., 1985), p. 93.

11. Matthew Fox, *Meditations with Meister Eckhart* (Santa Fe, N. Mex.: Bear & Co., 1983), p. 14.

12. Joanna Macy, "The Greening of the Self," *Dharma Gaia: A Harvest of Essays in Buddhism and Ecology*, ed. Alan Hunt Badiner (Berkeley, Calif.: Parallax Press, 1990), p. 55.

13. W. H. Auden, "For the Time Being: A Christmas Oratorio," in *The Collected Poetry* (New York: Random House, 1945), p. 466.

14. Joseph Campbell with Bill Moyers, *The Power of Myth* (New York: Doubleday, 1988), p. xv.

8. NEW AGE SPIRITUALITY:
A POSITIVE CONTRIBUTION

1. Robert Walsh, "Asian Psychotherapies," in *Current Psychotherapies*, 4th ed., ed. Raymond J. Corsini and Danny Wedding (Itasca, Ill.: F. E. Peacock Publishers, 1989), p. 551.

2. Ibid., p. 550.

3. Marsha Sinetar, *Ordinary People as Monks and Mystics: Lifestyles for Self-Discovery* (Mahwah, N.J.: Paulist Press, 1986), p. 53.

4. Ibid., pp. 60–68.

5. J. Gordon Melton, Jerome Clarke, and Aidan A. Kelly, *New Age Almanac* (New York: Visible Ink Press, 1991), p. 363.

6. Dr. Jack Porter presents this example in his course on psychopathology at West Chester University, Pennsylvania.

7. Norman Cousins, *Anatomy of an Illness as Perceived by the Patient* (New York: W. W. Norton & Co, 1979), pp. 35–38.

8. Ibid., pp. 39–44.

9. Ibid., pp. 120–121.

10. Ibid., pp. 44–45, 120–122.

11. Jane E. Brody, "Laying On Hands Gains New Respect," *New York Times*, March 26, 1988.

12. Elizabeth Keller and Virginia M. Bzdek, "Effects of Therapeutic Touch on Tension Headache Pain," *Nursing Research* 35, no. 2 (1986), 101–105.

13. Ibid., pp. 102–103.

14. Dolores Krieger, "Therapeutic Touch: The Imprimatur of Nursing," *American Journal of Nursing* 75, no. 5 (1975), 784–787.

15. Ibid., p. 786.

16. Ibid., p. 707.

17. John C. Masters et al., *Behavioral Therapy: Techniques and Empirical Findings* (San Diego: Harcourt Brace Jovanovich, 1987), p. 496.

18. Ibid., p. 496.

19. Ibid., pp. 496–497.

20. Ibid.

21. Ibid., p. 499.

22. Melton, Clarke, and Kelly, *New Age Almanac*, pp. 417–418.

23. Ibid., pp. 418–420.

24. Ibid., p. 420.

25. J. E. Lovelock, *Gaia: A New Look at Life on Earth* (Oxford: Oxford University Press, 1979), p. 6.

26. Ibid., p. 7.

27. Ibid., p. 6.

28. Ibid., p. 10.

29. Ibid., p. 9.

30. Peter Russell, *The Global Brain: Speculations on the Evolutionary Leap to Planetary Consciousness* (Los Angeles: Jeremy P. Tarcher, 1983), pp. 21–27.

31. Ibid., pp. 27–31.

32. Ibid., pp. 221–228.

33. Michael E. Kraft, "Environmental Values for the 21st Century," Presentation at Conference of Council of Independent Colleges, Chicago, 1991.

34. Richard J. Myers, "An Activist's Perspective: The Inner Nature of the Environmental Crisis," *Quadrant: The Journal of Contemporary Jungian Thought* 23, no. 2 (1990): 44–45.

35. Ibid., pp. 46.

36. Ibid., pp. 51.

37. Ibid., pp. 44.

38. Ibid., pp. 45–50.

39. Ibid., p. 50.

10. SPIRITUALITY FOR A NEW ERA

1. Mary Farrell Bednarowski, "Literature of the New Age: A Review of Representative Sources," *Religious Studies Review* 17, no. 3 (July 1991): 209.

2. These and all other citations in this article from Aquinas can be found in my book *Sheer Joy: Conversations with Thomas Aquinas on Creation Spirituality* (San Francisco: HarperCollins, 1992).

3. See my *Breakthrough: Meister Eckhart's Creation Spirituality in New Translation* (New York: Doubleday, 1991), passim.

4. Rupert Sheldrake, *The Rebirth of Nature: The Greening of Science and God* (New York: Bantam Books, 1991), p. 171.

5. Ibid., p. 207.

6. Ibid., p. 209.

7. Of course, Sheldrake is not the only scientist speaking out in this manner. Consider Brian Swimme, *The Universe Is a Green Dragon* (Santa Fe, N. Mex.: Bear & Co., 1985); Erich Jantsch, *The Self-Organizing Universe* (Elmsford, N.Y.: Pergamon Press, 1980); Thomas Berry, *The Dream of the Earth* (San Francisco: Sierra Club Books, 1988), among others.

8. On the relationship between the dialectic of mysticism and prophecy, see my *On Becoming a Musical, Mystical Bear: Spirituality American Style* (Paramus, N.J.: Paulist/Newman Press, 1973) as well as my *Original Blessing* (Santa Fe, N. Mex.: Bear & Co., 1983).

9. See my *A Spirituality Named Compassion* (San Francisco: Harper-Collins, 1990).

10. David Griffin, ed., *Sacred Interconnections: Postmodern Spirituality, Political Economy, and Art* (Albany, N.Y.: State University of New York Press, 1990), p. 3.

11. Matthew Fox, "A Mystical Cosmology: Toward a Postmodern Spirituality," in Griffin, *Sacred Interconnections*, pp. 29ff.

12. See the issue of the journal *Creation Spirituality* dedicated to the theme of "The Body as Sacred," May/June, 1991.

13. Carl Jung, *Letters*, vol. 2. Ed. Gerhard Adler and Aniela Jaffe. Bollingen Series 95 (Ann Arbor, Mich.: Books on Demand, n.d.), p. 436.

14. Carl Jung, *Two Essays on Analytical Psychology.* 2d ed. Vol. 7 of *Collected Works*, ed. Gerhard Adler et al. Trans. R. F. C. Hull. Bollingen Series 20, no. 7 (Princeton, N.J.: Princeton University Press, 1966), p. 46.

15. I have written about the negative senex archetype and its influence on our spiritualities in my *The Coming of the Cosmic Christ* (San Francisco: Harper & Row, 1988), pp. 180–198.

16. I have written at some length about redeeming worship in ibid., pp. 211–227, and have been engaged practically in the same effort, most recently in Asheville, North Carolina, in October 1991, where several hundred people gathered for a week to explore new (and ancient) forms of worship.

17. The classic work on art as meditation is M. C. Richards, *Centering in Pottery, Poetry, and the Person* (Middletown, Conn.: Wesleyan University Press, 1989).

18. See my *Creation Spirituality: Liberating Gifts for the Peoples of the Earth* (San Francisco: HarperCollins, 1991).

19. For more on the twelfth-century renaissance and the goddess see, for example, Henry Adams, *Mont-Saint-Michel and Chartres* (Garden City, N.Y.: Doubleday & Co., 1959), and William Anderson, *Green Man: The Archetype of Our Oneness with the Earth* (San Francisco: HarperCollins, 1990). On the biblical renewal that inspired this renaissance, see M. D. Chenu, *Nature, Man, and Society in the Twelfth Century* (Chicago: University of Chicago Press, 1968).

Suggested Readings

1. THE CRY OF THE DESPERATE:
CHRISTIANITY'S OFFER OF A NEW AGE

Basil, Robert, ed. *Not Necessarily the New Age: Critical Essays.* Buffalo, N.Y.: Prometheus Books, 1988.

Canale, Andrew. *Understanding the Human Jesus.* Ramsey, N.J.: Paulist Press, 1985.

———, *Beyond Depression. A Practical Guide for Healing Despair.* Rockport, Mass.: Element Books, 1992.

Ferguson, Marilyn. *The Aquarian Conspiracy: Personal and Social Transformation in the 1980s.* Los Angeles: Jeremy P. Tarcher, 1980.

May, Gerald. *Addiction and Grace.* San Francisco: Harper & Row, 1988.

Moore, John, and Douglas Gillette. *King, Warrior, Magician, Lover.* San Francisco: Harper & Row, 1990.

Peters, Ted. *The Cosmic Self.* San Francisco: HarperCollins, 1991.

Spangler, David. *The New Age.* Issaquah, Wash.: Morningtown Press, 1988.

3. THE FORMER AGE AND THE NEW AGE:
THE PERENNIAL QUEST FOR THE SPIRITUAL LIFE

Badinger, Allan Hunt, ed. *Dharma Gaia: A Harvest of Essays in Buddhism and Ecology.* Berkeley, Calif.: Parallax Press, 1990.

Kelsey, Morton. *Companions on the Inner Way: The Art of Spiritual Guidance.* New York: Crossroad, 1983.

————. *Reaching: The Journey to Fulfillment*. San Francisco: Harper-Collins, 1989.

————. *Through Defeat to Victory*. Rockport, Mass.: Element Books, 1991.

————. *Psychology, Medicine and Christian Healing*. San Francisco: Harper & Row, 1988.

————. *God, Dreams and Revelation*. Minneapolis: Augsburg Fortress, 1991.

Smith, Huston. *World Religions*. San Francisco: HarperCollins, 1991.

Wilbur, Ken. *No Boundary: Eastern and Western Approaches to Personal Growth*. Boston: Shambhala Publications, 1979.

4. THE NEW AGE:
HISTORICAL AND METAPHYSICAL FOUNDATIONS

Bell, Daniel. *The Coming of the Post-Industrial Society*. New York: Basic Books, 1973.

Capra, Fritjof. *The Tao of Physics*. New York: Bantam Books, 1976.

Eliade, Mircea. *The Quest: History and Meaning in Religion*. Chicago: University of Chicago Press, 1969.

————. *The Sacred and the Profane: The Nature of Religion*. New York: Harcourt, Brace & Co., 1959.

Frankl, Viktor. *Man's Search for Meaning*. New York: Washington Square Press, 1965.

Fuller, R. Buckminster. *Operating Manual for Spaceship Earth*. New York: Simon & Schuster, 1969.

Smith, Huston. *The Forgotten Truth*. New York: Harper & Row, 1976.

Teilhard de Chardin, Pierre. *The Phenomenon of Man*. London: William Collins Sons & Co., 1955.

5. THE NEW AGE:
THE MOVEMENT TOWARD THE DIVINE

Berry, Thomas, and Brian Swimme. *The Universe Story*. San Francisco: HarperCollins, 1992.

Bloom, William, and John Button. *The Seeker's Guide*. London: Aquarian Press, 1992.

Hastings, Arthur. *With the Tongues of Men and Angels*. Fort Worth, Tex.: Holt, Rinehart & Winston, 1991.

Lash, John. *The Seeker's Handbook*. New York: Harmony Books, 1991.

Spangler, David. *Emergence: The Rebirth of the Sacred*. New York: Doubleday, 1989.

————. *Manifestation: The Inner Art*. New York: Bantam Books, 1992.

————. *A Pilgrim in Aquarius.* Moray, Scotland: Findhorn Press, 1993.

Spangler, David, and William Irwin Thompson. *Reimagination of the World.* Santa Fe, N. Mex.: Bear & Co., 1991.

6. THE NEW AGE:
THE MOVEMENT TOWARD SELF-DISCOVERY

Chaisson, Eric. *The Life Era: Cosmic Selection and Conscious Evolution.* New York: Atlantic Monthly Press, 1987.

Creme, Benjamin. *Transmission: A Meditation for the New Age.* North Hollywood, Calif.: Tara Center, 1989.

FM-2030. *Are You a Transhuman?* New York: Warner Books, 1989.

Lemesurier, Peter. *This New Age Business.* Moray, Scotland: The Findhorn Press, 1990.

Melton, J. Gordon, Jerome Clark, and Aidan Kelly. *The New Age Encyclopedia.* Detroit: Gale Research, 1990.

Russell, Peter. *The Global Brain: Speculations on the Evolutionary Leap to Planetary Consciousness.* Los Angeles: Jeremy P. Tarcher, 1983.

Spangler, David. *The New Age and Beyond.* Issaquah, Wash.: Morningtown Press, 1989.

8. NEW AGE SPIRITUALITY:
A POSITIVE CONTRIBUTION

Cousins, Norman. *Anatomy of an Illness as Perceived by the Patient.* New York: W. W. Norton & Co., 1979.

Hay, Louise L. *You Can Heal Your Life.* Santa Monica, Calif.: Hay House, 1984.

Laurie, Sanders G., and Melvin J. Tucker. *Centering: A Guide to Inner Growth.* Rochester, Vt.: Destiny Books, 1983.

Lipnack, Jessica, and Jeffrey Stamps. *The Networking Book: People Connecting with People.* New York: Routledge & Kegan Paul, 1986.

Lovelock, J. E. *Gaia: A New Look at Life on Earth.* Oxford: Oxford University Press, 1979.

Melton, J. Gordon, Jerome Clarke, and Aidan A. Kelly. *New Age Almanac.* New York: Visible Ink Press, 1991.

Roman, Sanaya. *Spiritual Growth: Being Your Higher Self.* Tiburon, Calif.: H. J. Kramer, 1989.

Russell, Peter. *The Global Brain: Speculations on the Evolutionary Leap to Planetary Consciousness.* Los Angeles: Jeremy P. Tarcher, 1983.

Sinetar, Marsha. *Ordinary People as Monks and Mystics.* Mahwah, N.J.: Paulist Press, 1986.

9. NEW AGE SPIRITUALITY:
A CRITICAL APPRAISAL

Drummond, Richard. *A Life of Jesus the Christ.* San Francisco: Harper & Row, 1989. In a volume the publishers describe as New Age, the author, a respected Presbyterian theologian and historian of religions, suggests how one might view Jesus and his redemptive work in a framework that includes reincarnation.

Jung, C. G. "The Spiritual Problem of Modern Man," in *Modern Man in Search of a Soul.* New York: Harcourt, Brace & Co., 1933. See also his essay "Psychological Aspects of the Mother Archetype," most easily obtained in the small Modern Library volume edited by V. de Lazlo, *The Basic Writings of C. G. Jung.* New York: Random House, 1959.

Melton, J. G., and R. L. Moore. *The Cult Experience.* New York: Pilgrim Press, 1982. While more about cults than about the New Age as such, the authors (a church historian and a psychologist of religion) outline well the contributions of the anthropologist Victor Turner to understanding new and old rituals and groupings, and offer an implicit challenge to churches.

Miller, Elliott. *A Crash Course on the New Age Movement.* Grand Rapids: Baker Book House, 1989. The author, a converted New Ager, provides one of the more sane, though still dogmatic, views of the New Age from the perspective of conservative Christians.

Peck, M. Scott. *People of the Lie.* New York: Simon & Schuster, 1983. Opens up issues of personal, social, and transpersonal evil, though from a psychiatric more than a theological perspective. Also useful are his book on community-making, *The Different Drum* (New York: Simon & Schuster, 1987), and his earlier work on a disciplined life, *The Road Less Traveled* (New York: Simon & Schuster, 1978).

Rollins, Wayne G. *Jung and the Bible.* Atlanta: John Knox Press, 1983. Exhibits how an able New Testament scholar with a sound grasp of Jung understands the particularity of the Christian heritage.

Santmire, H. Paul. *The Travail of Nature.* Philadelphia: Fortress Press, 1985. The author carefully traces how Christians have thought about nature, in a chewy book.

10. SPIRITUALITY FOR A NEW ERA

Bednarowski, Mary Farrell. "Literature of the New Age: A Review of Representative Sources," *Religious Studies Review*, July 1991.

Fox, Matthew. *Breakthrough: Meister Eckhart's Creation Spirituality in New Translation.* New York: Doubleday, 1991.

————. *Creation Spirituality: Liberating Gifts for the Peoples of the Earth*. San Francisco: HarperCollins, 1991.

————. *Original Blessing: A Primer in Creation Spirituality*. Santa Fe, N. Mex.: Bear & Co., 1983.

————. *Sheer Joy: Conversations with Thomas Aquinas on Creation Spirituality*. San Francisco: HarperCollins, 1992.

————. *A Spirituality Named Compassion*. San Francisco: HarperCollins, 1990.

Griffin, David, ed. *Sacred Interconnections*. Albany, N.Y.: State University of New York Press, 1990.

————. *The Reenchantment of Science: Postmodern Proposals*. Albany, N.Y.: State University of New York Press, 1988.

Sheldrake, Rupert. *The Rebirth of Nature: The Greening of Science and God*. New York: Bantam Books, 1991.

Swimme, Brian. *The Universe Is a Green Dragon*. Santa Fe, N. Mex.: Bear & Co., 1985.

1995